Vol. CIV

No. 2

Bible Expositor and Illuminator

SPRING QUARTER

March, April, May 2022

Editor in Chief: Kenneth Sponsler

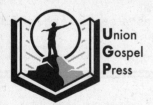

Union Gospel Press

Edited and published quarterly by
**THE INCORPORATED TRUSTEES OF THE
GOSPEL WORKER SOCIETY
UNION GOSPEL PRESS DIVISION**
Rev. W. B. Musselman, Founder
Price: $7.00 per quarter*
$28.00 per year*
*shipping and handling extra
ISBN 978-1-64495-214-6

LOOKING AHEAD

This quarter we are going to take the opportunity to study the written correspondence between the church's greatest theologian and one of its most troubled congregations. There is no such thing as a perfect church, so there is always room for growth. Therefore, the lessons in this series will challenge you as you consider how Paul's rebukes and counsel to the Corinthian church could apply to your own church life.

The quarter is divided into two units, the first of which will cover selected passages from I Corinthians. In lesson 1, Paul rebukes the church for allowing itself to be divided over leadership. Lesson 2 shows that the message of the cross of Jesus Christ is the central component of the ministry of the church and the hope of the believer.

In lesson 3, we will see that all work in the church is built upon the foundation of Jesus Christ. Lesson 4 warns of the danger of sexual immorality and shows that the church is the temple of the Holy Spirit. The focus of lesson 5 is showing compassion to other people when exercising our liberty in Christ. Lesson 6 goes further into this idea as Paul rebukes the Corinthians for gorging themselves at the community meal of the Lord's Supper. In lesson 7, we turn our attention to Easter as we read Paul's incredible defense of the gospel and the resurrection of Jesus Christ.

In Unit II, we turn to II Corinthians as Paul's correspondence to this church continues. In lesson 8, we see that God is the God of all comfort. Lesson 9 shows us that the new covenant of love that was given by Christ is superior to the old covenant of law. Lesson 10 discusses the future hope that we all have coming in heaven and gives a glimpse of the glory that awaits.

Lesson 11 teaches us that we are ambassadors for Christ and that there is no greater purpose in life than that. Our motivation to be Christ's ambassador comes from God's great love for us. Lesson 12 deals with spiritual warfare and explains how the weapons of Christians are different from the weapons of the world. Lesson 13 closes the unit and the quarter with a study of Paul's heavenly vision and the purpose behind the thorn in his flesh.

This quarter will give us much food for thought as we see how a church full of sinners should be living out the message of the gospel.

—*Robert Ferguson, Jr.*

Not Conformed but Transformed

Arnold Studebaker

Christians are different. They are not the same as they used to be before they met Jesus, and they are not the same as the nonbelievers around them. Like Christians today, new believers in Paul's day throughout the Roman Empire faced a steep learning curve as they began to walk with Jesus.

What makes Christians different? In Romans 12:2, Paul says, "Be not conformed to this world: but be ye transformed by the renewing of your mind, that ye may prove what is that good, and acceptable, and perfect, will of God."

We see in this verse that a new mind is essential to the difference. Christians think differently; they have different attitudes and different values. Paul describes the pagans of the Roman world this way: "And even as they did not like to retain God in their knowledge, God gave them over to a reprobate mind, to do those things which are not convenient" (Rom. 1:28). Today we understand "not convenient" as referring to things that ought never to be done.

The Christian knows God and seeks His will. Paul assures the believers, "We have the mind of Christ" (I Cor. 2:16). The unbeliever, though, disregards God and pursues his own worldly pleasure. Lacking a godly foundation, the unbeliever's thinking becomes wicked and debased.

Christians have the mind of Christ because of the presence of the Holy Spirit dwelling within. As Paul says of the church in I Corinthians 3:16, "Know ye not that ye are the temple of God, and that the Spirit of God dwelleth in you?" Promised to every sinner who repents and trusts Jesus as Lord and Saviour (cf. Acts 2:38), the Holy Spirit empowers Christians to be different.

Because Christians think differently, they talk differently and behave differently from unbelievers. In his letters, the apostle Paul taught Christians specific examples of the differences. His teachings are still instructive.

For instance, in Galatians 5:22-23, Paul enumerates the fruit of the Spirit, namely: "love, joy, peace, longsuffering, gentleness, goodness, faith, meekness, temperance." God's Holy Spirit within the believer produces these attributes in the believer's life.

Paul contrasts the fruit of the Spirit with the works of the flesh manifested by unbelievers. In Galatians 5:19-21 he mentions examples, including adultery, idolatry, hatred, witchcraft, strife, murder, and drunkenness.

The stark contrast between the fruit of the Spirit and the works of the flesh illuminates the difference between Christians and unbelievers. Says Paul, "And they that are Christ's have crucified the flesh with the affections and lusts. If we live in the Spirit, let us also walk in the Spirit" (vss. 24-25).

Paul is sometimes very pointed in his instruction. In Ephesians 4 he says, "Put off . . . the old man, which is corrupt according to the deceitful lusts; and be renewed in the spirit of your mind; and . . . put on the new man, which after God is created in righteousness and true holiness. Wherefore, putting away lying, speak every man truth with his neighbor. . . . Let him that stole steal no more: but rather let him labour, working

(Editorials continued on page 186)

Scripture Lesson Text

I COR. 1:1 Paul, called *to be* an apostle of Jesus Christ through the will of God, and Sosthenes *our* brother,

2 Unto the church of God which is at Corinth, to them that are sanctified in Christ Jesus, called *to be* saints, with all that in every place call upon the name of Jesus Christ our Lord, both theirs and ours:

3 Grace *be* unto you, and peace, from God our Father, and *from* the Lord Jesus Christ.

4 I thank my God always on your behalf, for the grace of God which is given you by Jesus Christ;

5 That in every thing ye are enriched by him, in all utterance, and *in* all knowledge;

6 Even as the testimony of Christ was confirmed in you:

7 So that ye come behind in no gift; waiting for the coming of our Lord Jesus Christ:

8 Who shall also confirm you unto the end, *that ye may be* blameless in the day of our Lord Jesus Christ.

9 God *is* faithful, by whom ye were called unto the fellowship of his Son Jesus Christ our Lord.

10 Now I beseech you, brethren by the name of our Lord Jesus Christ, that ye all speak the same thing, and *that* there be no divisions among you; but *that* ye be perfectly joined together in the same mind and in the same judgment.

11 For it hath been declared unto me of you, my brethren, by them *which are of the house* of Chloe, that there are contentions among you.

12 Now this I say, that every one of you saith, I am of Paul; and I of Apollos; and I of Cephas; and I of Christ.

13 Is Christ divided? was Paul crucified for you? or were ye baptized in the name of Paul?

14 I thank God that I baptized none of you, but Crispus and Gaius;

15 Lest any should say that I had baptized in mine own name.

16 And I baptized also the household of Stephanas: besides, I know not whether I baptized any other.

NOTES

4

Divisions in Corinth

Lesson Text: I Corinthians 1:1-16

Related Scriptures: I Corinthians 10:31-33; I Corinthians 12:1-31

TIME: A.D. 55   PLACE: from Ephesus

GOLDEN TEXT—"Now I beseech you, brethren, by the name of our Lord Jesus Christ, that ye all speak the same thing, and that there be no divisions among you; but that ye be perfectly joined together in the same mind and in the same judgment" (I Corinthians 1:10).

Introduction

One of the gravest dangers facing any church is division. Too many churches have been destroyed by divisive factions who pridefully struggle for control and power. The Corinthian church, the focus of our study this quarter, had several divisions that threatened its health and existence. It seems that many of the people had favorite church leaders, which caused them to divide into various camps.

Church divisions are usually over lesser matters. Most true believers are not divided over the fundamental aspects of our faith.

Sadly, things often get messy on matters of preference: styles of music, the number of services, and even the color of the carpet. This week's lesson teaches us that such tension in the church is unbiblical and should be avoided at all costs. Our focus must be on proclaiming the gospel to the lost and on worshipping the Lord. Love is the essential ingredient.

LESSON OUTLINE

I. GRATITUDE FOR THE
   CHURCH—I COR. 1:1-6

II. GRACE IN THE CHURCH—
    I Cor. 1:7-9

III. HARMONY IN THE CHURCH—
     I Cor. 1:10-16

Exposition: Verse by Verse

GRATITUDE FOR THE CHURCH

I COR. 1:1 Paul, called to be an apostle of Jesus Christ through the will of God, and Sosthenes our brother,

2 Unto the church of God which is at Corinth, to them that are sanctified in Christ Jesus, called to be saints, with all that in every place call upon the name of Jesus Christ our Lord, both theirs and ours:

3 Grace be unto you, and peace,

from God our Father, and from the Lord Jesus Christ.

4 I thank my God always on your behalf, for the grace of God which is given you by Jesus Christ;

5 That in every thing ye are enriched by him, in all utterance, and in all knowledge;

6 Even as the testimony of Christ was confirmed in you:

Authority in Christ (I Cor. 1:1).

As he did in many of his letters, Paul identifies himself as the author at the outset of the epistle. There is no reason to question this, as this letter has been ascribed to Paul throughout the entire two-thousand-year history of the church. In addition, the theology and writing style clearly align with the rest of Paul's epistles.

{Paul asserts his divine calling as an apostle right away,}**Q1** and his God-given authority in that role is a persistent theme of this letter. He did not appoint himself to be an apostle for Christ. In fact, he was a persecutor of the church before he ever became an apostle (cf. Acts 7:58; 8:1-3; 9:1-5). He was called to be an apostle by the will of God. He did not seek the appointment for himself, nor was he selected by a church committee. He was selected by Christ Himself (cf. II Tim. 1:11).

The general definition of an apostle is "one who is sent." But when Paul calls himself an apostle, he means more than that. Apostles in the first-century church had a unique calling and were specially equipped to preach the gospel, often accompanied by signs and wonders. {More important was the fact that Paul's apostolic authority enabled him to write the very words of Scripture, which meant his messages had authority from God.}**Q2**

Sosthenes is listed as a companion of Paul at the time he penned this letter. Little is known of him. The ruler of the synagogue in Corinth was named Sosthenes (Acts 18:17), and many scholars believe these men were one and the same.

Saints in Christ (I Cor. 1:2-3).

The recipients of the letter, as stated by Paul, were the saints in Corinth. These were people who were being sanctified in Christ Jesus. {To be sanctified means to be made holy, set apart from evil, and devoted to God.}**Q3** Every Christian is in the process of being sanctified by the Holy Spirit. We are set apart for Christ once we are saved; then the Holy Spirit sanctifies us through the finished work of Christ. We cannot sanctify ourselves, just as we cannot save ourselves.

{A saint is one who is called to be holy; therefore, all believers are saints.}**Q4** We are all linked together with everyone who calls on the name of Jesus, which means there must be unity among believers. Fittingly, Paul addresses the Corinthians as saints to prepare them for his rebuke by reminding them of their calling to holiness and unity in Christ.

As is typical in Paul's letters, he opens this epistle with a prayer for grace and peace for his audience. Grace and peace are like holy partners. Without God's grace, we could never attain the peace that only comes through Christ. It is also through this grace that we can find peace in all our circumstances. We cannot survive without the grace and peace of God.

Gratitude in Christ (I Cor. 1:4).

As we will see throughout this quarter, the Corinthian church was far from perfect. Corinth was a city where immorality ran rampant, and the cultural immorality penetrated the church as well.

Nevertheless, although Paul often had stern rebukes for this church, he never treated them as anything less than brothers and sisters in the Lord (cf Acts 18:8-10). He desired to bring them to obedience in Christ and strengthen their fellowship with the Lord. He was grateful that God had poured out His grace on them through Jesus Christ.

Enriched in Christ (I Cor. 1:5-6). Paul wanted the Corinthians to be enriched in Christ in every way, including in their speech and knowledge. Paul focused on these two things because they were both highly revered in Corinth and had possibly become an area of pride for the church members. He wanted them to understand that they were gifted in these areas only because of God's grace, not their own abilities.

The testimony about Christ was made clear to the Corinthians through the preaching of Paul when he came to that city. They received the gospel message by faith in Christ, and they now needed to learn to grow in their faith and rely on Christ for all things.

GRACE IN THE CHURCH

7 So that ye come behind in no gift; waiting for the coming of our Lord Jesus Christ:

8 Who shall also confirm you unto the end, that ye may be blameless in the day of our Lord Jesus Christ.

9 God is faithful, by whom ye were called unto the fellowship of his Son Jesus Christ our Lord.

Gifted by grace (I Cor. 1:7). The purpose of spiritual gifts is to edify the church as a whole. Spiritual gifts are never given so a person can use them for personal gain or benefit. We all benefit when each believer uses his or her gift in a way that brings glory to God and blessing to the church. We cannot earn these gifts, nor can we choose which ones we receive. The Holy Spirit grants them according to His purposes (cf. 12:11).

When we use our gifts according to God's purposes, we are enriched by the Holy Spirit (vs. 5). We need not fear that we are ill-equipped; God will give us whatever we need to fulfill His will.

We must use our spiritual gifts faithfully and selflessly until Christ returns. As we serve the Lord in this present day, we eagerly await His return. The return of Christ could happen at any time, and we should always work with this in mind. Until He returns, however, we must rely on the presence and power of the Holy Spirit to work in and through us as we faithfully obey the will of God.

Righteous by grace (I Cor. 1:8-9). Many Christians make the mistake of trying to produce godliness on their own. There is simply no way we are ever going to produce good works of our own volition. We often find ourselves doing what we know we should not do and not doing what we know we should do (cf. Rom. 7:18-19).

We do not have the ability to do God's will on our own. We need the Holy Spirit living in us and working through us to produce holiness in our lives. The good news is that God promises to do exactly that for us. We are not given the task of producing our own godliness.

{We will never be able to stand before God blameless on any merit we achieve. We must rely on God to sustain us.}Q5 We are never going to be good enough (or good at all, for that matter) by attaining a level of greatness or purity in our own strength or morality. If you find yourself trying really hard to be obedient only to fall flat on your face time and time again, take heart. You can (and must) trust God to hold you up and sustain you.

God promises to sustain us and make us guiltless until the time when Christ returns. Before God, we are all guilty. We have sinned and fallen short of His glory (Rom. 3:23). Nothing we do can change that fact. But if you have repented and trusted in Christ's sacrifice, He has erased your sin and has given you His righteousness. You can now stand before God with no guilt. When God forgives your sin, He erases all record of it, and He will never charge you with it again.

We do not have to worry about the staying power of God's grace; He is faithful to do what He said He would do. God cannot lie (Num. 23:19; Titus 1:2; Heb. 6:18), so we can have full confidence in everything in His Word. He has called us into the fellowship of Jesus Christ and will equip us to stay there. It is His faithfulness, not ours, on which His promises stand.

HARMONY IN THE CHURCH

10 Now I beseech you, brethren, by the name of our Lord Jesus Christ, that ye all speak the same thing, and that there be no divisions among you; but that ye be perfectly joined together in the same mind and in the same judgment.

11 For it hath been declared unto me of you, my brethren, by them which are of the house of Chloe, that there are contentions among you.

12 Now this I say, that every one of you saith, I am of Paul; and I of Apollos; and I of Cephas; and I of Christ.

13 Is Christ divided? was Paul crucified for you? or were ye baptized in the name of Paul?

14 I thank God that I baptized none of you, but Crispus and Gaius;

15 Lest any should say that I had baptized in mine own name.

16 And I baptized also the household of Stephanas: besides, I know not whether I baptized any other.

Quarreling in the church (I Cor. 1:10-11). {Paul now turns his attention to the first major issue that he deals with in this letter: divisions.}Q6 He makes an appeal by the name of Jesus Christ to each person in the Corinthian church to be united in Christ. The church is not an individual effort, nor is it merely a collection of like-minded people striving for a common goal. {That may describe some social clubs or community groups, but the church is unique because it is the body of Jesus Christ on earth and represents Him to the world.}Q7

In order to prevent divisions from taking root, Paul tells the church to "be perfectly joined together in the same mind and in the same judgment" (vs. 10). This does not discount the fact that the church is made up of many different personalities, nor does it mean that we will agree on every little point.

Paul's words are telling us that we are to take on the mind of Christ and to think of others more highly than we think of ourselves (cf. Phil. 2:3-5). Every person in the church must judge according to Scripture. We must aim to bring glory to God with all of our decisions, not only in the decisions themselves, but also in the way we treat one another while we deliberate. We can put on the mind of Christ only if we walk in the love of Christ.

When Paul talks about divisions, he is referring to anything that would cause a split in the church. Divisions can tear a church apart, and we must guard at all costs against anything that would divide us. We should always discuss any differences of opinion in a mature and godly way, keeping our focus on Jesus to keep us humble. It is vital to be of the same mind and same judgment in decisions. None of us are going to get our way all the time, and we must resolve to put our pride aside and work for the good of the church.

The report of division came from a group within the Corinthian church led by a woman named Chloe. This group had reported to Paul that there was a lot of conflict in the church and sought his help to rectify the problem. {Yet even while addressing this, Paul refers to the people as his brothers, showing that we are still family even when we strongly disagree with one another.}Q8 We should follow this pattern in our own conflicts by lacing our words with grace.

Favoritism in the church (I Cor. 1:12-13). Divisions often occur when people become devoted to their favorite preacher or leader and ignore other godly teachers. When this happens, people become more focused on the messenger instead of the message. {In Corinth, different factions followed Paul, Apollos, and Peter.}^Q9 They were devoted to their favorites, although none of these men encouraged such a following. Paul reminds us that preachers are merely messengers and are not to receive praise that belongs to God alone.

The way to avoid such division is for every church member to follow Christ in a cooperative effort. We are, of course, to love our leaders and those God has called to oversee us. However, we should never show favoritism. Christ is not divided, and the church that follows Him should not be, either. It was Christ who was crucified for us, and we are baptized in the name of Jesus, not in the name of Paul or anyone else. We should be united together in harmony as we serve the Lord together.

True perspective on baptism (I Cor. 1:14-16). Picking up on his final question in verse 13, Paul goes so far as to express his thanks that he did not baptize anyone in the Corinthian church except two men, Crispus and Gaius. While on the surface this may sound like a very unusual statement for a minister to make, Paul had a very important reason for it. He wanted to communicate the intensity of his dislike for the favoritism of the Corinthians. {Though baptism in itself is commanded by Jesus and is a good and joyous ordinance, Paul was thankful that he himself had not baptized many people in Corinth, for it meant no segment of the membership had cause to cling to him above other leaders in the church.}^Q10

Paul cringed at the idea of someone in the church bragging that he was baptized by Paul or, worse yet, that he was baptized in the name of Paul. The apostles had made it clear that we are to be baptized in the name of Jesus (Acts 2:38), and Jesus specified that it is to be done in the name of the Father, Son, and Holy Spirit (Matt. 28:19). The notion that anyone could be baptized in the name of a mere human being is ridiculous and dishonors Christ, our true Saviour.

As a last aside, Paul notes that he did baptize the household of Stephanas but could think of no one else. There was no need for correction on minor details from anyone who remembered otherwise. Paul's main point stood firm. The believers in Corinth should look to Jesus alone as their Leader and unite in giving all honor to Him.

—*Robert Ferguson, Jr.*

QUESTIONS

1. What does Paul assert at the outset of this letter?

2. What was so important about Paul's claim to apostleship?

3. What does it mean to be sanctified?

4. What is a saint?

5. Why must we rely on God to sustain us and make us blameless instead of trying to sustain ourselves?

6. What was the major issue in Corinth that Paul dealt with first in this letter?

7. How is the church different from a social club or community group?

8. What does Paul's choice to call the Corinthians "brothers" in verse 11 show us about disagreements in the church?

9. What was the cause of division in the Corinthian church?

10. Why was Paul glad that he had not baptized many in Corinth?

—*Robert Ferguson, Jr.*

Preparing to Teach the Lesson

In our first lesson for this quarter, Paul's first concern for the church at Corinth is their lack of unity. Reliable sources had apparently informed him that the believers there had become divided into factions. Paul found their disunity extremely disappointing, since it failed to properly reflect a unified devotion and service to Christ alone. Their divisions were based on earthly loyalties to mere human leaders, and they cast shame upon the reputation of Christ and His church.

Paul desired that they be united in their doctrine and their spiritual fellowship as a testimony to the unity of Christ Himself. There are not many christs, but only one!

TODAY'S AIM

Facts: to realize that all Christians are called to unity in Christ through the Holy Spirit.

Principle: to understand the biblical basis of Christian unity.

Application: to strive for unity in Christ through the Holy Spirit with other true believers, no matter what their church disagreements might be.

INTRODUCING THE LESSON

Today's lesson is about divisions and unity within the church as the body of Christ. Paul was earnestly concerned about the divisions in the church at Corinth.

Ask your class to share any personal stories they might have about becoming estranged from people they were once close to. What were the reasons for their estrangement? Have they since reconciled with that person? If not, why not?

If we allow estrangements and divisions between ourselves and others who are close to us, how can we ever hope to make progress in healing the discord within our churches, within our denominations, or between denominations? Promoting unity within the body of Christ must begin with reconciling our estranged individual relationships with those who are closest to us.

DEVELOPING THE LESSON

1. Greetings and blessings (I Cor. 1:1-9). Although Paul's greeting follows the common form of first-century letters, the content of his greeting is uniquely Christian. First identifying himself as an apostle of Jesus Christ, he qualifies his apostleship as being "through the will of God." By this he means that he was sovereignly chosen to that office. It was never his personal ambition to obtain the position of apostle. God made him one.

Paul next introduces Sosthenes as his brother in the faith as well as the co-author of this letter. This was most likely the same Sosthenes who had been a ruler in the synagogue at Corinth. He was beaten by the Greeks there during an insurrection by the Jews against Paul's teachings (cf. Acts 18:12-17). Apparently, he had since been converted and now accompanied Paul on his missionary travels.

In verse 2, Paul pointedly reminds the Corinthians that they have been sanctified along with all Christians everywhere who call on the name of the Lord Jesus Christ, who is Lord of both those in Corinth and those with Paul.

After pronouncing both grace and peace upon them, Paul speaks of his thankfulness for the Corinthian believers and prays that God will endow them with the blessings they need to be faithful in their testimony of the gospel. In verse 7, Paul touches on the subject of spiritual gifts, noting that his readers did not lack any. Gifts will become a major topic in the later chapters of this epistle.

2. Divisions and contentions (I Cor. 1:10-13). Paul here begins the main body of his epistle. He pleads with the Corinthians to be united in their testimony, to be "in the same mind and in the same judgment." In other words, to avoid all hint of divisions among themselves.

Paul had apparently been informed by messengers from Corinth about the factions that had formed among them. Portions of the church there had begun dividing into cliques focused around human leaders such as Apollos, Peter, and even Paul himself.

Paul's rebuke is vehement. He interrogates them with a series of intense, and apparently sarcastic, questions (vs. 13). "Is Christ divided?" This may have been asking essentially, Are there many christs, or only one? The apostle continues: Was Paul crucified for them? Were they baptized in his name? The believers should be feeling ashamed of their divisions—not bragging about them!

3. Concerns over baptism (I Cor. 1:14-16). The divisions among the Corinthians prompted Paul to express thanks that he himself had not unwittingly contributed to these divisive allegiances by baptizing a large number of them while he was there.

Paul wanted the Corinthians to understand that it did not matter which particular leader baptized an individual believer. No matter who performs the baptism, the believer's exclusive allegiance is to Christ alone, not to the person who baptized him or her.

ILLUSTRATING THE LESSON

Following after human leaders as our chief loyalty divides Christians. Believers should be united in fellowship based only upon Jesus Christ and the truth of His gospel.

ALL BELIEVERS ARE ONE IN CHRIST!

Repent! United in Jesus Christ Repent!

Divided

Following mere men   Following mere men

CONCLUDING THE LESSON

Today's Christians should humbly thank God and pray for one another rather than boastfully compare church facilities, church attendance, how much money their church has, or even how theologically sophisticated their members are.

God is not pleased by such worldly priorities. We should not compete over earthly measures of success but join together in pure, spiritual service to Christ.

If a fellowship is few in number or impoverished or less schooled in doctrine, it should spur others to loving concern and generous help to build them up as they have need.

As Paul writes elsewhere, our motivation should be "for the perfecting of the saints, for the work of the ministry, for the edifying of the body of Christ: till we all come in the unity of the faith, and of the knowledge of the Son of God, unto a perfect man, unto the measure of the stature of the fulness of Christ" (Eph. 4:12-13).

ANTICIPATING THE NEXT LESSON

Next week's lesson focuses on true spiritual wisdom, which comes from God alone.

—*John Lody.*

PRACTICAL POINTS

1. Christian workers know the value of their fellow workers in ministry (I Cor. 1:1-2).
2. Grace and peace for Christian service are only available through faith in Christ (vs. 3).
3. Gifted workers and ministries must be purposeful about giving thanks to God (vss. 4-6).
4. Rely on God's strength daily for a life that is pleasing to Him (vss. 7-9).
5. The Holy Spirit unites people with different backgrounds, interests, and opinions as one body advancing God's kingdom (vs. 10).
6. Some within the church are contentious and divisive, but in the name of Christian unity we should rebuke those who seek to cause divisions (vss. 11-16).

—Cheryl Y. Powell.

RESEARCH AND DISCUSSION

1. When addressing conflicts between believers, how can it help to remind involved parties of our unity in Christ?
2. What is the relationship between "grace" and "peace"?
3. Why do you think Paul repeatedly refers to Jesus in the first 10 verses of I Corinthians? Discuss.
4. Discuss both the risks and benefits to the kingdom of God of so many Christian denominations operating in our world today.

—Cheryl Y. Powell.

ILLUSTRATED HIGH POINTS

That ye come behind in no gift (I Cor. 1:7)

Canadian Adrian Pearce had cherished the present for forty-eight years, yet he had never opened it. Bringing it out year after year, he placed it under his Christmas tree, then he packed it away for another year.

The gift was given to him by a high school girlfriend. The giver was located and given the honor of unwrapping the present. Finally, a small book entitled "Love Is" saw the light of day!

It is not enough to know that we have been given gifts by God and to remind ourselves periodically that we are thus blessed. Let us seek out the giver Himself to open the gifts, use us, and reveal His love to the world. And let us not wait forty-eight years to ask Him to do it!

Ye be perfectly joined together (vs. 10)

In the 1700's, the first puzzles were made to teach children geography. Maps were pasted onto wood and cut into pieces. By the 1900s, the industry introduced puzzles for adults. These were hard. The pieces did not interlock and there was no guide picture on the box. In the 1950s and 60s, the Stave Puzzle Company introduced another innovation: they used only original one-of-a-kind, artwork. The paintings were made specifically to be cut into a puzzle.

A puzzle can illustrate truths about God's kingdom. We are each a small piece. When fit together, we show God's full picture. However, properly fitting together can be a challenge. The church's original standard we are striving to replicate is Jesus Himself, the perfect Son of God.

—Therese Greenberg.

Golden Text Illuminated

"Now I beseech you, brethren, by the name of our Lord Jesus Christ, that ye all speak the same thing, and that there be no divisions among you; but that ye be perfectly joined together in the same mind and in the same judgment" (I Corinthians 1:10).

Paul opens his first letter to the Corinthian church in his customary way, with greetings, thanksgiving, and encouragement. He calls the members "saints," and also warmly expresses his gratitude for the faithfulness of God, who has blessed the church.

In verse 10, however, Paul signals a serious change in his tone with the little word "now." *Vine's Expository Dictionary of New Testament Words* (Nelson) also translates it as "but" or "even so." Paul will spend the rest of the letter addressing problems that threaten to undermine the church from within.

Paul beseeches the divided congregation, which he founded on his second missionary journey, to unite. "Beseech" is a strong verb that means "to admonish" or "to plead earnestly." In fact, the Bible uses a form of this word to describe the ministry of the Holy Spirit, who calls us to Himself, through conviction of sin, to give us comfort and counsel (cf. John 14:26).

Paul further strengthens this admonition by invoking the name of Jesus Christ. Here he appeals to a far higher authority than even his own authority as an apostle; he calls upon the "name which is above every name" (Phil. 2:9). This is the Lord himself, the Head of the church, who prayed that all His followers be one in Him as He is one with the Father. In fact, this unity is the key to convincing the world that God has really sent Jesus (John 17:21).

Sadly, the church at Corinth was a shameful picture of disunity. They had split into factions, each following a particular human teacher. Some claimed loyalty to Paul; others to Cephas (the Aramaic name for Peter); and still others to Apollos, "an eloquent man, and mighty in the scriptures" (Acts 18:24), who hailed from Alexandria, Egypt. Another faction claimed exclusive loyalty to Christ.

Now Paul fires off three related commands in rapid sequence. He tells the Corinthians to "speak the same thing," cease their divisions, and be "perfectly joined together in the same mind and in the same judgment."

When Paul tells the church "to speak the same thing," he instructs them to declare the Word of God, and not to advocate their own opinions. Later in the letter, he warns them "not to think of men above that which is written" (I Cor. 4:6). To elevate mere men beyond what the Scriptures advise encourages false doctrine and promotes prideful, worldly wisdom.

Finally, Paul tells them to have the "same mind" and the "same judgment." He is not suggesting that the church has to agree on everything, but they must agree on the *essential* thing—that Christ alone is the power and wisdom of God (I Cor. 1:24)! Their deep schisms would be healed if they fully trusted in Christ alone. For the sake of unity, they should no longer aggressively compete over which human teacher they preferred, but adopt the humble mind of Christ Himself (cf. Phil. 2:2-8).

—*Mark Winter.*

Heart of the Lesson

As Paul traveled through Greece on his second missionary journey, he established the Corinthian church and ministered there for a year and a half. Years later, he wrote a letter with an important message: God's matchless glory and abounding grace demand a radical break from sin. The Corinthians had shifted their focus from Christ's values to their culture's values, from holiness and humility to worldliness and pride. The church that Paul had built on the foundation of grace, instructed in pure doctrine, and nurtured in love was in danger of breaking apart under the weight of cliques and sinful lifestyles.

1. Paul's greeting (I Cor. 1:1-3). Pride had slipped into the Corinthian church and threatened its unity and godly influence. Paul, therefore, began his letter by establishing his authority as Christ's apostle. He reminded his readers that they were saints, recipients of Christ's righteousness, and set apart by God in order to display His glory.

In this letter, Paul taught the Corinthians that God's calling and grace had formed the foundation of their unity. The Corinthian church was made up of both Jews and Gentiles, who usually did not get along. As believers, however, their faith in Jesus had bonded them together as members of God's family. Peace and love, not rivalry or factions, should have characterized their church.

2. God's gifts (I Cor. 1:4-9). Grace is the greatest gift anyone can receive from God. Unmerited, undeserved, unending favor from God is what believers receive the moment they place their faith in Jesus. Through Christ, believers have been reconciled to God the Father and placed in His family.

In this section, Paul reminded the Corinthian believers about the far-reaching effects of God's grace, including access to His throne through prayer and knowledge of His will in Scripture. At the moment of salvation, the Corinthian Christians had received every spiritual resource they needed to honor God. The Corinthian believers had received Jesus' righteousness and the promise that they would one day stand before Him faultless and part of His family forever (cf. Jude 1:24-25).

3. The church's division (I Cor. 1:10-16). If the greatest gift Christians can receive is God's grace, then the greatest affront to God is to ignore His grace. The grace that had broken down the barrier between the Corinthians and God had also leveled the dividing walls among the Corinthian believers. Unfortunately, the Corinthians had picked up the bricks of pride and jealousy and started to rebuild thick walls of division in their church. So Paul pleaded with them to remember their unity in Christ.

When Paul planted the Corinthian church, several gifted leaders helped him. The Jewish couple Priscilla and Aquila assisted Paul in Corinth until they departed for Ephesus (cf. Acts 18:18-19). After Paul left Corinth, Apollos, an eloquent teacher, ministered to the Corinthians. Unfortunately, instead of viewing Paul and Apollos as servants of Christ, many Corinthian believers began to divide and make following them, not following Christ in unity, their chief aim.

Paul rebuked the Corinthians for their schisms and reminded them that though he may have baptized a few of them, that act by no means made him their god. No Christian leader should be given the allegiance that belongs to Jesus alone.

—*Malia E. Rodriguez.*

World Missions

While visiting family, I attended the church of my youth, the place where I had given my life to Jesus at fourteen. News of a split in the church had reached me, but I was unprepared for the gloom that rested on the service and the sadness I felt as I searched the faces of people I loved, godly people who had shared their knowledge of the Bible with me and supported me with prayer.

The division began when the pastor's daughter married the son of a deacon. The pastor was not happy, and he expressed disdain for everyone who had attended the wedding. His family problems overflowed into the church and caused the people to take sides. I left that service deeply saddened.

Paul, in writing to the Corinthians, felt a similar heartache. Word had come to him that there were contentions among the believers at Corinth (I Cor. 1:11). Some followed the teachings of Paul, others Apollos, and still others Peter. They argued over who should be followed.

Appalled by discord amongst these believers, Paul asked two thoughtful questions: "Is Christ divided? Was Paul crucified for you?" (vs. 13). These questions were intended to shift the focus from their differences and put it where it belongs—on the One who redeemed them.

Church arguments can be caused by many things—money, power, pride, worship style, cultural differences, and so on. Matthew Henry makes the point that divisions in the church are "a very melancholy evidence of the corruption and depravity of human nature" (*Matthew Henry's Commentary,* Hendrickson). Notwithstanding our sinful inclinations, we are called to glorify God in everything we do, including and especially in our associations with other believers. Our love for one another must transcend our personal differences because it identifies us as Jesus' disciples (John 13:35).

Some disagreements are necessary. Concerning these, Charles Colson writes, "Holding the church to its historic faith, both in its practices and institutions, is a necessary corrective. . . . But shouldn't this be done in love and with understanding, showing grace instead of rancor?" (*Being the Body,* Thomas Nelson).

Paul gives us a golden rule regarding disputes in the church: "Not seeking my own profit, but the profit of many, that they may be saved" (I Cor. 10:33).

As we offer ourselves to God daily as a living sacrifice (Rom. 12:1), He leads us to love His people. He accomplishes this by placing an endless supply of His love in our hearts (5:5).

Believers are to be "perfectly joined together in the same mind" (I Cor. 1:10). This means having the mind of Christ, who "took upon him the form of a servant" (Phil. 2:7). Paul pleaded for unity in the church. But he did not appeal to them to live in peace for his own benefit; he made his plea in the name of our Lord Jesus Christ (I Cor. 1:10), the highest authority.

Our love for one another pleases God. It is compared to "precious ointment" (Ps. 133:1-2) that was poured upon the head of Aaron. We must do all we can, in whatever ministry God has given us, to promote peace and avoid divisions.

Missionaries, whether persecuted or at peace, must always exhibit kindly affection for one another (Rom. 12:10).

—Rose McCormick Brandon.

The Jewish Aspect

During the first century, the city of Corinth was one of the most important cities in Greece due to its seaport location. It was the leading commercial city in southern Greece and had an international and cosmopolitan way of life. The city's population included Romans, Greeks, Jews, and sea travelers from throughout the world. Corinth was known for its rampant sexual immorality as well as idolatry and religions of all kinds. As a result of the city's great commerce, there were people of great wealth as well as many who were squalidly poor.

The church at Corinth reflected the city's demographics, with a significant disparity between the rich and the poor. The socioeconomic division was part of the friction and divisiveness within the church. In addition, the church was divided into factions based on various teachers. "This seems to be a list of the factions (i.e., Paul's group, Apollos' group, Peter's group, Jesus' group). Much has been made of the characteristics of the leaders (i.e., Paul = freedom party, which included Gentiles by faith alone; Apollos = philosophical party; Cephas = Jewish traditionalist or legalistic party, cf. 2 Cor. 11:18-33); Christ = those of special rank, calling, giftedness, or spirituality (cf. possibly 2 Cor. 12:1)" (www.freebiblecommentary.org).

Paul began his ministry at Corinth in the synagogue. However, he soon sought another meeting place due to opposition by the Jews. A large portion of the church in Corinth consisted of Gentile converts who were, however, familiar with Jewish teachings. There were some Jews in the church as well.

Paul's letters often included greetings that were in accord with both Greek and Jewish customs. He reproved the Corinthian church for their divisions and exhorted them, by the name of the Lord Jesus Christ, to be of one mind. In ancient Judaism, a name represented one's character and authority. "Paul will often (more than 17 times in the letter) refer to Jesus as the Lord Jesus Christ; it is well to recall what the title means. . . . designating not only master and boss, but also the Lord revealed in the Old Testament (known as Yahweh or Jehovah)" (enduringword.com).

The Corinthians called on the name of the Lord (I Cor. 1:2). And Abraham had called on the name of the Lord (Gen. 12:8; 13:4), as did Isaac (26:25), Elijah (I Kgs. 18:24), and David (I Chr. 21:26).

In calling the church at Corinth to unity, Paul reminded them that "God is faithful, by whom ye were called unto the fellowship of his Son Jesus Christ our Lord" (I Cor. 1:9). God's faithfulness and dependability was a common theme in the Hebrew Scriptures (Deut. 7:9, Ps. 36:5, Isa. 49:7). Paul said that they should not have divisions and that there should be no schism in the body. "The ancient Greek word for divisions is 'schismata.' Although we derive our English word 'schism' from this Greek word, it does not really mean a 'party' or a 'faction', it properly means 'tear or rend.' Paul's plea is that they stop ripping each other apart, tearing up the body of Christ" (enduringword.com).

Paul used the body as a metaphor elsewhere in his letter to the church at Corinth. "For as the body is one, and hath many members, and all the members of that one body, being many, are one body: so also is Christ" (I Cor. 12:12). He stated that the contentions and quarreling among them was akin to dividing Christ. He implored them to be joined together in the same mind and judgment.

—Deborah Markowitz Solan.

Guiding the Superintendent

Corinth, We Have a Problem! Paul was troubled by what he had heard from some of the people in the church in this city (I Cor. 1:11). He gets to the task quickly and encourages the church to change. First Corinthians will deal with some of the key problems that have developed in the church since he left. He begins by dealing with dissension that threatens to divide the young church.

The first problem that Paul addresses is a self-centered attitude that focuses on what separates them, not on what they have in common—that they are a church. In the original language, the word for "church" means "to be called out" (vss. 2, 9). Paul reminds the Corinthian believers what it means to be a church or called-out ones.

DEVOTIONAL OUTLINE

1. Called to be holy (I Cor. 1:1-9). Paul begins his letter on a positive note, reminding the church that they had been called by God; this position they had in God despite their faults and failures. They were all called to be sanctified; called to be saints. The idea behind this is that they were called to be set apart for God's service. A saint is a Christian, one who is very much alive and very much struggling to live a God-pleasing life. God's calling for all saints is a gracious gift that has "enriched" them with all spiritual gifts. The idea of enrichment means that the saints are very wealthy in spiritual gifts (cf. chapters 12-14).

A major facet of being called to holiness is the divine promise that we will be kept until the day of the Lord's return. Believers are all called, set apart, enriched, and kept. All this is no excuse for unholy living; it is, rather, the very basis for continued growth in our relationship with God and others.

2. Called to fellowship (I Cor. 1:10-16). The apostle points out that not only were the Corinthian believers called to salvation but they were also called to fellowship in God's Son, Christ Jesus. This fellowship does not depend on their own efforts, but on Christ's faithfulness.

This leads Paul to his first discussion of the problems in the church. Instead of fellowshipping together in one mind, the Corinthians were dividing up into various cliques, focused around their favorite preachers. Each clique claimed superiority for their preacher over the others. Paul encouraged them to focus on what they all shared in common— their relationship with Christ—not the things that might divide them.

Paul fires off three key questions, "Is Christ divided?, was Paul crucified for you? or were ye baptized into the name of Paul?" (vs. 13). Paul went on to focus on the third question.

In a hostile pagan city like Corinth, to undergo Christian baptism was an especially clear sign that one was a follower of Christ, and it opened one up to much persecution from the unsaved majority of the city. But Paul did not come to Corinth to start his own religious club. He himself did not baptize many believers there. He was not minimizing the value of baptism; he was just concerned that the people he baptized might exalt him instead of Christ!

CHILDREN'S CORNER

Many children think that being a Christian comes about by doing good things. This lesson should emphasize that being a follower of Jesus is a matter of being called into a relationship, first with Jesus Himself (vss. 1-8), and then also with fellow believers (vss. 9-16).

—Martin R. Dahlquist.

SCRIPTURE LESSON TEXT

I COR. 1:17 For Christ sent me not to baptize, but to preach the gospel: not with wisdom of words, lest the cross of Christ should be made of none effect.

18 For the preaching of the cross is to them that perish foolishness; but unto us which are saved it is the power of God.

19 For it is written, I will destroy the wisdom of the wise, and will bring to nothing the understanding of the prudent.

20 Where *is* the wise? where *is* the scribe? where *is* the disputer of this world? hath not God made foolish the wisdom of this world?

21 For after that in the wisdom of God the world by wisdom knew not God, it pleased God by the foolishness of preaching to save them that believe.

22 For the Jews require a sign, and the Greeks seek after wisdom:

23 But we preach Christ crucified, unto the Jews a stumblingblock, and unto the Greeks foolishness;

24 But unto them which are called, both Jews and Greeks, Christ the power of God, and the wisdom of God.

25 Because the foolishness of God is wiser than men; and the weakness of God is stronger than men.

26 For ye see your calling, brethren, how that not many wise men after the flesh, not many mighty, not many noble, *are called:*

27 But God hath chosen the foolish things of the world to confound the wise; and God hath chosen the weak things of the world to confound the things which are mighty;

28 And base things of the world, and things which are despised, hath God chosen, *yea,* and things which are not, to bring to nought things that are:

29 That no flesh should glory in his presence.

30 But of him are ye in Christ Jesus, who of God is made unto us wisdom, and righteousness, and sanctification, and redemption:

31 That, according as it is written, He that glorieth, let him glory in the Lord.

NOTES

True Wisdom

Lesson Text: I Corinthians 1:17-31

Related Scriptures: I Corinthians 2:1-16; Jeremiah 9:23-24;
Romans 1:18-32; 11:33-36

TIME: A.D. 55   PLACE: from Ephesus

GOLDEN TEXT—"But God hath chosen the foolish things of the world to confound the wise; and God hath chosen the weak things of the world to confound the things which are mighty" (I Corinthians 1:27).

Introduction

Division is a great enemy of any church, whether at the individual level, the local level, or the denominational level. If we are to avoid division and strive for unity, then there must be a uniting element that draws all Christians together. The question is, what is that one thing that unites us? What is it that allows a Christian who is visiting a congregation for the first time to walk in and commune with a group of people he does not even know?

According to Paul, the unifying element is the cross of Jesus Christ. The cross is where we all met Jesus at the moment of faith and repentance. The cross is where Christ satisfied the debt of sin we owed God by paying our just penalty. The cross is where Jesus took our sins on His body and purchased our redemption (I Pet. 2:24). No matter which church you belong to or which denomination you are in, the cross is where your spiritual life began.

LESSON OUTLINE

I. POWER FROM GOD—
I COR. 1:17-25

II. CALLING FROM GOD—
I Cor. 1:26-29

III. BOASTING IN GOD—
I Cor. 1:30-31

Exposition: Verse by Verse

POWER FROM GOD

I COR. 1:17 For Christ sent me not to baptize, but to preach the gospel: not with wisdom of words, lest the cross of Christ should be made of none effect.

18 For the preaching of the cross is to them that perish foolishness; but unto us which are saved it is the power of God.

19 For it is written, I will destroy the wisdom of the wise, and will

bring to nothing the understanding of the prudent.

20 Where is the wise? where is the scribe? where is the disputer of this world? hath not God made foolish the wisdom of this world?

21 For after that in the wisdom of God the world by wisdom knew not God, it pleased God by the foolishness of preaching to save them that believe.

22 For the Jews require a sign, and the Greeks seek after wisdom:

23 But we preach Christ crucified, unto the Jews a stumblingblock, and unto the Greeks foolishness;

24 But unto them which are called, both Jews and Greeks, Christ the power of God, and the wisdom of God.

25 Because the foolishness of God is wiser than men; and the weakness of God is stronger than men.

The cross and baptism (I Cor. 1:17). Last week's lesson ended with what may seem like an unusual statement: Paul wrote that he was glad that he had not baptized many of the Corinthians (vss. 14-16). In verse 17, he goes on to explain his reasoning—that baptism was not the focus of his ministry, but rather preaching the gospel.

Before we go any further, it is necessary to state emphatically that Paul is not disparaging or deemphasizing the importance of baptism. He is not saying that baptism was not a concern of his ministry. Paul's teaching in other passages clearly shows that he held water baptism in high regard (cf. Rom. 6:1-4; Col. 2:11-12).

{Paul's point is not that baptism is unimportant but that the message of the gospel takes precedence over it.}Q1 There is no saving power in baptism, but people do come to faith through the gospel. An unbeliever who gets baptized is still unsaved. Baptism is an act that *follows* salva-

tion, not one that *produces* salvation. {The emphasis of Paul's ministry was to bring the gospel to the lost and bring them to faith and repentance (cf. Acts 17:30-31; Rom. 10:9; II Cor. 7:10).}Q2

Paul was also not concerned with giving a polished presentation of the gospel. He did not want to display a flashy oratory skill (though he surely had such skill as an ex-Pharisee) because he did not want to detract from the plain facts of the gospel message, which is packed with the power to save. High speech would have certainly impressed the Corinthians, who were steeped in Greek culture and philosophy. But Paul recognized that in this environment, the power and glory of the gospel would be detracted from if he tried to steal glory for himself through persuasive or fancy speech.

{The power of the gospel rests in Jesus' completed redeeming work, the cross of Christ (cf. John 19:30).}Q3 Paul did not want the Corinthians' focus to be on his speaking ability, but on God's glory in the cross.

The cross despised (I Cor. 1:18-19). The interests of the world are diametrically opposed to the interests of God. Genuine love does not give a person his harmful desires; it provides for his deepest needs. Christ met the world's deepest need in the cross, but on their own, the lost do not understand their need for redemption.

{Because of this, the world rejects the message of the cross and considers it to be foolish.}Q4 In the world's eyes, if a hero dies, he at least goes down fighting. It is honorable, if not glamorous, for the hero to go out in a blaze of glory.

But to the world, Christ was just a Jewish man, maybe a prophet, who had no power or pride at all. He allowed Himself to be accused without defending Himself and crucified without putting up a fight. If He did not have the power to defend Himself, how could He have the power to rise from the grave?

Jesus is the epitome of meekness. Meekness, of course, does not necessarily imply weakness; the strongest people in the world can exhibit that quality. But it cannot be denied that Jesus allowed Himself to appear weak in the eyes of His enemies. He let them have their way with Him and did not do all He could have to counter the impression of His defenselessness. Why?

Jesus could have destroyed His enemies and annihilated those who crucified Him. He could have led a parade through the streets of Jerusalem and gained a national following for Himself. That would certainly have been impressive by the world's standards! But if He had gone that route, we would still be dead in our sins. We needed Jesus to die on the cross, bearing our sins for us and taking our punishment and sentence of death.

{While the world considers the message of the cross to be foolish, believers understand it to be the power of God.}[Q5] In the apparent weakness of the cross, the power of God for our salvation played out and was made manifest. It is by the power of Jesus' cross that God destroys worldly wisdom.

The cross and the world's foolishness (I Cor. 1:20-21). After establishing that the cross of Christ is the power of God for the Christian, Paul then turns his attention to the wise, the scribes, and the great debaters in Corinth. Like a gunslinger in the Old West, he boldly calls them out to expose their weakness in the face of the power of God.

God did not consult with those whom the world considers wise when it came to the plan of salvation. God does not need, nor does He want, the counsel of man on anything. We have nothing to contribute to the mind of God.

There is no one who is wise enough to debate with God, and it is better to be called a fool for God by the world than to be called a fool for the world by God. A wise person knows that anything apart from God is foolish, so he does not engage in worldly pursuits.

The cross and the world's expectations (I Cor. 1:22-24). The contrast between the world's thinking and God's thinking is astonishing. Man is impressed by things with high entertainment value. As a society, we spend billions of dollars on various forms of amusement.

{For the Jews of Paul's day, the most impressive thing was miraculous signs from God.}[Q6] Jesus' opponents were constantly looking for a sign from Him that would prove to them that He was sent from God (cf. Matt. 12:38-42; 16:4; John 6:30). And out of mercy and compassion, Jesus gave them many signs. The Gospels contain many miracles, all of which served as signs that Jesus is the Son of God. Sadly, no matter what they saw, the Jewish authorities of Jesus' day were never satisfied.

{The Greeks were more impressed by worldly wisdom than they were by signs.}[Q7] Not concerned with visible demonstrations of power, Greek culture was fascinated by philosophers and orators who could provide knowledge to the masses. The Greeks were very much in love with knowledge and human reasoning.

In spite of both Jewish and Greek rejection of the message of the cross of Christ, Paul reaffirms that he and those with him were committed to preaching the gospel. Human opinion, whether hostile or affirming, should have nothing to do with what Christians proclaim. Truth is truth regardless of how it is perceived by others.

As far as the Jews were concerned, the cross was a stumbling block. The Greek word for this is *skandalon*, from which we get the word "scandal." {To the Jews, there was something scandalous about the cross of Christ. They were offended by it.}[Q8] What they perceived as an instrument of torture and death was used by God as an instrument of deliverance and salvation.

{The Greeks, on the other hand, considered the preaching of the cross to be foolish. They did not understand it, nor did they care to.}[Q9] They had absolutely no interest in listening to such nonsense, as they were much too wise to accept such a counterintuitive message. They failed to see the power in a message that, to them, looked like a failure. The foolishness of the crucifixion made them unable to even consider the further proclamation of Christ's resurrection.

Paul states that for believers, the cross is neither scandalous nor foolishness, but the power and wisdom of God. The cross is a tremendous sign of God's sovereignty, power, and love. It is also emblematic of God's wisdom. The wisdom of the world mocked Jesus by telling Him to save Himself from the cross, but the wisdom of God demanded that He stay put and surrender His life in order to redeem sinners from their penalty. Believers understand that it can hardly be considered a failure, as Jesus was raised from the dead three days after He died, and He is alive forevermore.

The difference between first-century Jews, Greeks, and Christians is quite clear. Jews were in love with signs, Greeks were in love with wisdom, but Christians are in love with Jesus.

The cross and its greatness (I Cor. 1:25). There is no comparison between the wisdom and strength of God and the wisdom and strength of the world. Paul states that the foolishness of God is greater than the wisdom of men and the weakness of God is stronger than the power of men.

Of course, there is no actual foolishness or weakness in God. God is omnipotent (all-powerful) and omniscient (all-knowing). Paul is speaking comparatively here, showing that nothing humans can do is worthy of comparison next to God. Men may consider God to be weak and foolish, but they prove their own foolishness and weakness when they oppose Him.

CALLING FROM GOD

26 For ye see your calling, brethren, how that not many wise men after the flesh, not many mighty, not many noble, are called:

27 But God hath chosen the foolish things of the world to confound the wise; and God hath chosen the weak things of the world to confound the things which are mighty;

28 And base things of the world, and things which are despised, hath God chosen, yea, and things which are not, to bring to nought things that are:

29 That no flesh should glory in his presence.

Called by God (I Cor. 1:26-27). Paul calls on the Corinthians to consider themselves in light of God's calling. Not many of them were considered wise, strong, or noble by the world's standards. God is not out recruiting the cream of the crop and leaving everyone else out in the cold. He is looking for people who will by His grace bring glory to His name. The Lord specializes in using people the world would pass over because this displays His glory and power.

God chooses the things the world considers foolish and uses them to display the foolishness of the world. The Lord can use anyone who has come to faith in Him. He is not limited by our weaknesses. By faith, Christ is our strength, which means we can do everything God calls us to do (cf. Phil. 4:13).

Exalted by God (I Cor. 1:28-29). Many of the Corinthian believers were not considered intelligent or strong by the elitists of their day. They were not great scholars, philosophers, or speakers. God saw value, however, in people whom the world had rejected. He chose the ones the world despised and used them for His mighty purposes. While history has forgotten the names of those faithful Corinthian Christians, heaven never will. They are still enjoying the eternal life that God gave them.

God can take someone who is considered nothing by society and use that person to glorify Himself. He has taken some of us off the trash heap of our world and given us powerful and impressive assignments as His ambassadors. Sometimes He uses us to do things that the world considers productive or great, leaving them befuddled and making it difficult to deny His power and glory. But believers know that we cannot brag about our accomplishments. We were helpless and hopeless without God.

BOASTING IN GOD

30 But of him are ye in Christ Jesus, who of God is made unto us wisdom, and righteousness, and sanctification, and redemption:

31 That, according as it is written, He that glorieth, let him glory in the Lord.

Identity in Christ (I Cor. 1:30). The key to our success as Christians is our new identity in Christ. And even that identity is not something we achieved. It is because of God that we are saved, as we could not come to God on our own. We had to be drawn by Him (cf. John 6:44).

Our salvation is completely the work of God. It is the grace of God that saves and keeps us. We are saved by faith (Eph. 2:8), live by faith (Hab. 2:4), and walk by faith (II Cor. 5:7). Everything that is worth having is found in Christ, as Jesus has become our wisdom by opening our eyes to His true worth. We no longer rely on worldly pleasures or power. We trust in Christ for everything.

Jesus is also our righteousness, sanctification, and redemption. We

have no righteousness on our own, but Jesus gave us His righteousness so that we could be accepted by God (cf. II Cor. 5:21). He then sanctified us, or set us apart, for His service and promised to make us holy.

Boasting in Christ (I Cor. 1:31). The picture Paul has painted of the Christian is a person who was despised by the world and considered to be of little value. But God chose each believer, even in our desperate condition, and made His power evident in our lives.

{Boasting does not have to be a bad thing—as long as we are boasting about the Lord.}[Q10] Paul refers to Jeremiah 9:23-24 as scriptural support that we must never seek our own glory, but only the glory of the Lord. Only in Christ do we have anything of eternal value.

—*Robert Ferguson, Jr.*

QUESTIONS

1. What was Paul's main point about baptism?
2. What was Paul's emphasis in his ministry?
3. What was the power of Paul's message?
4. How does the world perceive the message of the cross of Christ?
5. How do Christians view the cross of Christ?
6. What were the Jews most impressed by?
7. What were the Greeks most impressed by?
8. How did the Jews receive Paul's message?
9. How did the Greeks receive Paul's message?
10. When is boasting a good thing for a Christian?

—*Robert Ferguson, Jr.*

Preparing to Teach the Lesson

What do most unbelievers think about when they see pastors or other Christians portrayed in the mass media? What tends to be their honest reaction to the gospel we preach?

Even if they do not come out and say so, they probably see it as mere foolishness. They see people pushing God on others and raving about someone who supposedly rose from the dead thousands of years ago.

Our modern secular society has been conditioned to value only knowledge that has been certified as scientific and materially practical in the here and now. Anything outside these categories is looked upon, at best, as harmless make-believe. At worst, it is portrayed as dangerous fanaticism.

The great tragedy for people who follow this thinking is that what they perceive as foolish make-believe is their only hope of salvation and eternal life. God sovereignly arranged for this blindness, since "it pleased God by the foolishness of preaching to save them that believe" (I Cor. 1:21). Only by the power of the Holy Spirit can this kind of blindness be removed and the light of salvation shine into darkened hearts.

TODAY'S AIM

Facts: to note the sharp contrast between God's wisdom and the purported sophistication of the world.

Principle: to understand that God's wisdom in the gospel is foolishness in the eyes of the world but that worldly wisdom is powerless to save anyone.

Application: to devote ourselves to the godly wisdom of the saving gospel rather than become obsessed with gaining mere worldly sophistication, which leads to pride and can save no one.

INTRODUCING THE LESSON

Our lesson this week concerns the contrast between the sophistication that is valued so highly by secular culture and the wisdom of God in the gospel, which alone has the power to save those who believe it.

DEVELOPING THE LESSON

1. Foolishness and the power of God (I Cor. 1:17-24). Paul here begins one of the most powerful passages to be found in the New Testament. In order to properly understand the essence of the gospel and its saving purpose, we must understand the apostle's arguments here.

Paul did not use florid, erudite language when he preached the gospel. He refrained from such pretentiousness for fear that it would make his preaching devoid of saving power. That is something for pastors to consider the next time they try to make their sermons impressively eloquent!

Why would overly sophisticated words and arguments harm the effectiveness of Paul's gospel message? Because the gospel is *supposed* to seem foolish to those who are wise according to the world.

But why does God insist on using such foolishness as the means of His salvation? Because in its arrogant wisdom, the world denies God's existence, His creatorship, His sovereignty, and thereby His absolute right to be glorified and worshipped by His creation (I Cor. 1:21; cf. Rom. 1:18-25). Since the world sees itself as too wise to acknowledge Him, God determined, in His justice, to use what the world calls nonsense to accomplish His salvation.

Like a two-edged sword, the gospel is intended to cut in both directions: on the one hand, it condemns those who scoff at its apparent foolishness; on the other hand, it saves those who embrace it with simple trust and devotion as the Word of God for their salvation.

2. No boasting allowed (I Cor. 1:25-31). Paul now begins to demonstrate God's preference for using weak and foolish things for His purposes. He has always done so throughout the history of His redemptive plan.

As we see with Noah, God ignored the mighty and the sophisticated of the world and focused His purposes on those who are little esteemed by it.

After Noah, He called Abraham, Isaac, Jacob, and Joseph. Then He called a humble shepherd, Moses, from his desert flocks to deliver a nation of slaves. In this, God demonstrated His supreme authority, even over the most powerful empire on earth at the time—Egypt.

And so this same principle continued down to the day of Christ's birth in a stable at Bethlehem. Jesus Himself was despised and rejected by the world (cf. Isa. 53:2-3; John 1:10-11). And God continues to prefer to use the weak, foolish, and despised, even down to our present day.

Why does God do this? The answer is as obvious as God's own glory: to abolish all possibility of human boasting. As Paul puts it, "That no flesh should glory in his presence" (I Cor. 1:29).

God's use of foolish things negates any claim someone might make that he saved himself. No one can take credit for being wise enough to believe that something as seemingly foolish as the gospel could ever save them. Such faith is obviously a miracle—it only comes as the sovereign gift of Almighty God.

ILLUSTRATING THE LESSON

Christians should devote themselves to God's wisdom in Christ and the gospel rather than the wisdom of worldly sophistication.

GOD'S WISDOM, NOT THE WORLD'S

WORLDLY WISDOM — Pride, Boasting, Sophistication, Material Success

GODLY WISDOM — Humility, Devotion, Service, Compassion

CONCLUDING THE LESSON

The wisdom of this world cannot save anyone from God's righteous wrath and judgment against sin. But we also need to keep in mind that since we all live in this sin-cursed world, the pursuit of secular knowledge can be useful in some ways. We all need such knowledge to function in the world and to some extent it reveals the wonder and beauty of what God has created. We must understand the world in order to communicate effectively with it. But we depend on God's power, not our ability to win arguments.

There is indeed a stark contrast between the saving wisdom found in the gospel of Jesus Christ and the secular knowledge and sophistication valued by human society generally. Worldly wisdom focuses on material success and earthly concerns, and it tends to engender pride, arrogance, and rivalry. The gospel focuses on spiritual, heavenly concerns—especially the salvation of sinners and service to others.

ANTICIPATING THE NEXT LESSON

Next week's lesson focuses on Jesus Christ as the only trustworthy foundation for our lives.

—*John Lody.*

PRACTICAL POINTS

1. Wise teachers study and prepare, but they understand that true power is in the saving gospel—not in the human knowledge and skills they acquire (I Cor. 1:17).
2. The world values human wisdom and information, but only the gospel of Christ will save (vss. 18-19).
3. God chooses the things that the world considers foolish to accomplish His purposes (vss. 20-21).
4. Philosophies and prejudices keep many from trusting in the saving gospel of Christ (vss. 22-23).
5. The gospel is so simple that a child can receive it, while geniuses often cannot understand it (vss. 24-28).
6. Christians should boast in Christ alone (vss. 29-31).

—Cheryl Y. Powell.

RESEARCH AND DISCUSSION

1. What is the true purpose of baptism?
2. Is Paul teaching against Christians pursuing advanced secular education or wisdom? Why or why not?
3. What elements of the gospel might be most difficult to receive for those who boast high levels of worldly intelligence and wisdom?
4. In what ways can it be more difficult for believers to share their faith in this "information age" than at other times in history?

—Cheryl Y. Powell.

ILLUSTRATED HIGH POINTS

Not with wisdom of words (I Cor. 1:17)

Words, words, words—the world is full of them! Twenty-four-hour news/editorial stations, lifestyle advisers, and motivational coaches are ubiquitous in today's empowerment-hungry society.

There are even motivational speakers to motivate motivational speakers. They offer such advice as, "Ask a few positive questions with good chances of 'yes' answers, such as 'everybody feeling good?'" Or, "Ask them to stand up, stretch, and welcome a few people they haven't yet met."

Sadly, after all these "empowering" words and "encouragements," not one of the enthusiastic, expectant listeners are any closer to God.

The foolishness of God is wiser than men (vs. 25)

Here are a few things that so-called experts were wrong about:

"A rocket will never leave Earth's atmosphere."—*New York Times*, 1936.

"When the Paris Exhibition closes, electric light will close with it and no more will be heard of it."—Oxford professor Erasmus Wilson, 1878.

"If excessive smoking actually plays a role in the production of lung cancer, it seems to be a minor one."—W. C. Heuper, National Cancer Institute, 1954.

"Rail travel at high speed is not possible because passengers, unable to breathe, would die of asphyxia."—Dr. Dionysius Lardner, 1830.

In a world obsessed with statistics, studies, and celebrated experts, only the Word of God can be relied upon completely! "I will destroy the wisdom of the wise, and will bring to nothing the understanding of the prudent." (I Cor. 1:19).

—Therese Greenberg.

Golden Text Illuminated

"But God hath chosen the foolish things of the world to confound the wise; and God hath chosen the weak things of the world to confound the things which are mighty" (I Corinthians 1:27).

The Corinthian church had become haughty and contentious. In the words of Paul, they were "puffed up" (I Cor. 4:18)—literally, "inflated." Today we might say such people are arrogant, conceited, or have a "swollen head."

Some in the church believed they were superior because they spoke in tongues; others abhorred and scorned those who ate meat sacrificed to idols. The well-to-do members were getting drunk at the love feasts, which included the Lord's Supper, and leaving little food for the poorer members of the church. The church had also broken into cliques, convinced that their particular religious leader was better than the rest.

The apostle reminded the Corinthians that not many of them were wealthy, influential, or wise by worldly standards. This was not something to be ashamed of, since God masterfully uses people who are rejected by the world. In verse 27, Paul twice reminds the Corinthians that God chooses weak and foolish things to confound the wise and mighty of this world.

Paul goes on to powerfully use the example of the cross, which ran counter to the thinking of both Jew and Gentile. The Greek philosophers taught a dualistic worldview: matter was evil, and spirit was good. Plato likened the human experience to a charioteer guiding two winged horses. The horse that represents the immortal soul is clean and white, yearning to rise to celestial heights. The other horse, symbolizing the human body with all its unholy desires, is a dark, deaf, lumbering beast that attempts to drag the soul to the realm of evil, the earth. The philosophers sometimes described the body as a prison for the soul, hindering it from rising to the eternal realms of beauty and wisdom. Therefore, the Greeks scoffed at the idea of a deity who would descend in human form to suffer and die, since flesh was inherently corrupt.

To the Jew, the proclamation of the cross was a stumbling block, something scandalous and deeply offensive. The Jews were expecting a political messiah. They expected a great military leader and deliverer who would slay their oppressors and rule Israel in righteousness (cf. Isa. 11:1-5). According to Maimonides, a medieval Jewish scholar, the messiah would specifically return all the exiled Jews to Israel and rebuild the temple, which had been destroyed by the Romans in A.D. 70. However, the messiah would not be God incarnate but simply an inspired leader, as the rabbis taught that Yahweh would never take on human flesh. To the Jew, the thought of a crucified saviour was repugnant.

Paul wisely begins his letter to the Corinthians by reminding them that they cannot earn their salvation; it is only by accepting God's "foolish" ways that they can be redeemed and heal divisions. He emphasizes the point in I Corinthians 3:19 by inverting it, referring to the wisdom of the world as foolishness in the sight of God (cf. Isa. 29:14).

—*Mark Winter.*

Heart of the Lesson

Divisions, cliques, and factions. These words define the world we live in, but they should never describe the church. As Paul continued teaching the Corinthian church about unity, he explained the one event that should unify believers—the Cross.

1. The call of God (I Cor. 1:17). The call of God in our lives changes our purpose, perspective, and destiny. God had a special calling for Paul's life. When Jesus appeared to him on the Damascus road, He gave him a new purpose and a new name. Saul, which means "asked for" became Paul, which means "humble" or "small." Saul, the pride-filled, rising star among the Pharisees, met Jesus and became the humble apostle of grace (cf. Acts 20:24).

Based on Paul's background as a Pharisee, steeped in legalistic righteousness, God had given him a unique perspective on grace. As a Pharisee who trained under the respected teacher Gamaliel (cf. Acts 22:3), Paul was equipped with an in-depth knowledge of the Old Testament in order to show how Jesus fulfilled a multitude of prophecies. Even though Paul had the education and knowledge to impress his audience, he committed himself to preach the simple gospel message, armed only with the wisdom and power of God.

2. The wisdom of God (I Cor. 1:18-25). Paul's conversion signified a clear break with his past and inaugurated a completely new way of thinking. Even though as believers we find our worth and identity in Christ, we often continue to seek out wealth, fame, worth, and significance in the wrong places. Paul called that foolishness.

Wisdom, on the other hand, treasures God's revelation and considers worldly significance nothing compared to knowing Him. The cross was the culmination of thousands of years of revelation and demonstrated the power of our Triune God to defeat sin. Our response to the cross shows whether we believe God (wisdom) or reject Him (foolishness).

In this section, Paul quoted Isaiah 29:14, in which God condemned the Israelites' reliance on human wisdom. Like the Israelites in Isaiah's day, who refused to obey God and admit that they needed forgiveness, Paul worried that the pride-prone Corinthians had forgotten the wisdom of the cross.

In Paul's day, many Jews refused to believe Jesus was the Messiah because He did not match their expectations of a powerful leader who would destroy the Roman Empire. Many of the Gentiles, who believed they could find ultimate wisdom and enlightenment through human reason, rejected the cross because it seemed to defy human logic and required humility. For those who do receive the gospel, it demonstrates God-given wisdom and power that leads to eternal life.

3. The glory of God (I Cor. 1:26-31). No one can be saved through intellect or morality. Paul reminded the Corinthians that God had not saved them because of their intelligence or nobility. God often chooses the weak, unknown, and uneducated to demonstrate His wisdom, power, and glory. God's goal is to make His glory known to all people.

As believers who had been saved by grace through faith, the Corinthians had no reason to boast about their salvation (vs. 29). Faith is a gift from God (cf. Eph. 2:8), who replaces our sin with Christ's righteousness (cf. II Cor. 5:21) so that with our thoughts and actions we will point others to God's glory.

—Malia E. Rodriguez.

World Missions

In 1895, Canadian missionaries Jonathan and Rosalind Goforth were at the point of total exhaustion, overwhelmed by the need to evangelize while building a mission station at Changte, Hunan province, China. They found the people eager for the gospel, but they and fellow missionaries struggled to keep up a rigorous preaching schedule while constructing their living quarters.

They prayed for a Chinese assistant evangelist. In their memoir, *Miracle Lives of China* (Wipf & Stock), Rosalind and Jonathan Goforth wrote, "It seemed like asking for rain from a clear sky . . . we had not even one convert in the Changte district."

On the day they prayed, Wang Fu-Lin, urged by the Spirit, left his home and started for the new mission station. Once a hopeless opium-addicted derelict, a couple of years earlier he had surrendered to Christ and been discipled by Jonathan.

When Wang arrived at the mission gate he looked like a beggar—his clothes were stiff with dirt, his socks and shoes torn, and his hat patched. But he had come to preach.

At first, other missionaries at the station were unwilling to let Wang preach or even to allow him to be the gatekeeper. But knowing that Wang possessed good speaking skills, and believing that God had sent him, Jonathan Goforth gave him clean clothes and scheduled him to preach.

It soon became evident that Wang was an answer to prayer. He preached continually until his death. It was said of him that he could lay out facts one after the other in logical order until all the listeners' arguments against Christ were answered. He wove his personal story into God's great story of redemption and concluded that if God could save him, there was hope for all.

Human wisdom is repulsed by the untidy and unlikely. Its bias is toward the strong, the rich, the good-looking, and the educated. By contrast, God chooses the weak, the base, and the despised because His power shines through all such human limitations.

In the selection of leaders, we cannot discount the supernatural power of God that comes upon ordinary people and chooses them for extraordinary work. This was the case with Wang Fu-Lin. Through his preaching, many were led to trust in Jesus as their Lord and Saviour.

Paul pointed out that the church is made up of "not many wise men after the flesh, not many mighty, not many noble are called: But God hath chosen the foolish things of the world to confound the wise" (I Cor. 1:26-27).

Paul knew what it was like to be an unlikely candidate for ministry. After preaching in Damascus, he arrived in Jerusalem and tried to have fellowship with the disciples. But they rebuffed him out of fear and considered him an imposter. Then along came Barnabas, who used his influence and reputation to introduce Paul to the disciples. When they heard his story, they believed he was God-sent (Acts 9:22-28).

Devotional writer Selwyn Hughes called divine wisdom the "most glorious of all qualities" (*Wisdom for Living*, CWR), and it is found only in Jesus (I Cor. 1:30).

Human wisdom saw Wang Fu-Lin as only a beggar. But godly wisdom saw that beggar as an answer to prayer. The best thing about true wisdom is that we can ask God for it and He will freely give it to us (Jas. 1:5).

—Rose McCormick Brandon.

The Jewish Aspect

In ancient Judaism, the study of Torah (the first five books of the Hebrew Bible) was considered to be the highest ideal for Jewish men, outweighing all other commandments. Torah study was important so that children could be taught to observe all of God's commandments (Deut. 11:19). In addition, "According to Rabbinic Judaism, the study is ideally done for the purpose of the mitzvah ("commandment") of Torah itself" (www.wikipedia.org).

Since the time of Moses, the Jewish study of Torah has included reading, writing, memorizing, discussing, and debating its meaning and application. The emphasis on the study of Scripture led to a high value on Jewish education as well as education in general. Modern Judaism places education as a top priority. Jews are better educated than any other major religious group in the world, with an average of 13.4 years of schooling (www.pewforum.org).

Three books of the Hebrew Scriptures (Proverbs, Job, and Ecclesiastes) are known as wisdom literature, and they recognize God as the source of all wisdom. "My son, forget not my law; but let thine heart keep my commandments" (Prov. 3:1). Despite the emphasis on knowledge and wisdom, the Hebrew Scriptures are filled with accounts of the Israelites' lack of wisdom and understanding and their disobedience to God, refusing to walk in His ways. Jeremiah, known as the weeping prophet, warned of God's coming judgment based on their refusal to keep His commandments. He admonished them not to glory in their own wisdom, might, or riches (Jer. 9:23). "The Prophet no doubt has a regard to what has gone before. He saw, as I have often said, that he addressed the deaf; for the Jews were so swollen with false confidence, that the word of God was regarded worthless by them" (www.studylight.org).

Paul rebuked the church at Corinth for relying upon *sophia*—human wisdom—which considered the preaching of the cross and the substitutionary death of the Messiah as foolishness, nonsense, and folly. Paul reminded them of the words of the prophet Isaiah, who said, "Therefore, behold, I will proceed to do a marvellous work among this people, even a marvellous work and a wonder: for the wisdom of their wise men shall perish, and the understanding of their prudent men shall be hid" (Isa. 29:14). God's wisdom, Paul said, is entirely different from the wisdom of man. Paul also reminded the Corinthians of Solomon's instruction about God's wisdom: "O ye simple, understand wisdom: and, ye fools, be of an understanding heart" (Prov. 8:5). He said that the foolishness of God is wiser than men.

We should remember Abraham and the Israelite people, who were called by God, not because of their worldly wisdom or noble birth. "The Lord of hosts hath purposed it, to stain the pride of all glory, and to bring into contempt all the honourable of the earth" (Isa. 23:9). Those who glory should glory in the Lord (Jer. 9:24; Isa. 55:8-9); the weakness of God is stronger than the strength of men. Our faith should be in the power of God.

Speaking to the Romans about the wisdom of God and the foolishness of man (cf. Rom. 1:22; 11:33-36), Paul reminded them of man's fleeting existence and foolishness in contrast to the Lord's eternal power and wisdom (cf. Isa. 40:1-31).

—*Deborah Markowitz Solan.*

Guiding the Superintendent

God's ways are not man's ways. No better example of this can be found than in how Paul describes how God saved the Corinthian believers.

The Greek culture of Paul's day boasted in its wisdom. Corinth was no exception. To this day, in fact, people still consider ancient Greece as the cradle of human wisdom and philosophy. As a result of this atmosphere, the believers at Corinth were prone to exalting human wisdom and thus dividing the church. To counter this thinking, Paul reminded them that they had not trusted in human wisdom to be saved. Now they were in danger of trusting in human wisdom instead of the gospel.

DEVOTIONAL OUTLINE

1. The issue (I Cor. 1:17-19). Paul was unapologetic about the gospel he preached and which the Corinthian believers had received. Because of its great power, there was no reason for Paul to use human eloquence or wisdom in his preaching. The gospel, which the world considers foolishness, is in reality God's wisdom for man's salvation. God's ways are not man's ways!

Paul cited Isaiah 29:14 to establish His message. The people of Isaiah's day were acting the same way as those in Corinth. They had turned to human wisdom rather than to God.

2. Who is saved? (I Cor. 1:20-25). Those who were considered wise by worldly standards had rejected the gospel as foolishness, but those who were humble in their thinking had been saved by it. In this way, God had confounded human wisdom, making it foolishness. Paul's preaching style reinforced this idea. He did not preach in a manner that pandered to either the Jews' or the Gentiles' thinking. The message of the cross is intellectually unacceptable to both Jews and Gentiles. But to those who are saved by it, the gospel is both the power and the wisdom of God.

3. How are they saved? (I Cor. 1:26-28). The believers at Corinth were not saved by following human wisdom. Rather, it was God who called and chose them through the preaching of the gospel. Most of them were not wise, influential, or noble by worldly standards. But they were saved, while the wise, the influential, and the noble remained in their sins and under God's righteous wrath.

Paul surveys the whole history of God's redemption, and he points out that God has always chosen to use foolish things to confound the wise, weak things to confound the mighty, and lowly and despised things that the world considers to be worthless to bring to nothing those things that the world considers to be most valuable.

4. Why are they saved? (I Cor. 1:29-31). Paul was not denigrating the believers in Corinth; he was merely demonstrating to them that they had no reason to boast before God. Paul paraphrased Jeremiah 9:24 to show that God's redemptive plan is designed to negate all human boasting and to maximize His own glory. Salvation is all of God!

CHILDREN'S CORNER

Children are continually bombarded with human wisdom that attempts to conceal man's true lost condition. Children do not need to be ashamed of the gospel. The gospel is essential to God's plan for salvation. To accept the gospel is not foolishness; it is to receive true, divine wisdom for salvation.

—*Martin R. Dahlquist.*

Scripture Lesson Text

I COR. 3:10 According to the grace of God which is given unto me, as a wise masterbuilder, I have laid the foundation, and another buildeth thereon. But let every man take heed how he buildeth thereupon.

11 For other foundation can no man lay than that is laid, which is Jesus Christ.

12 Now if any man build upon this foundation gold, silver, precious stones, wood, hay, stubble;

13 Every man's work shall be made manifest: for the day shall declare it, because it shall be revealed by fire; and the fire shall try every man's work of what sort it is.

14 If any man's work abide which he hath built thereupon, he shall receive a reward.

15 If any man's work shall be burned, he shall suffer loss: but he himself shall be saved; yet so as by fire.

16 Know ye not that ye are the temple of God, and *that* the Spirit of God dwelleth in you?

17 If any man defile the temple of God, him shall God destroy; for the temple of God is holy, which *temple* ye are.

18 Let no man deceive himself. If any man among you seemeth to be wise in this world, let him become a fool, that he may be wise.

19 For the wisdom of this world is foolishness with God. For it is written, He taketh the wise in their own craftiness.

20 And again, The Lord knoweth the thoughts of the wise, that they are vain.

21 Therefore let no man glory in men. For all things are yours;

22 Whether Paul, or Apollos, or Cephas, or the world, or life, or death, or things present, or things to come; all are yours;

23 And ye are Christ's; and Christ *is* God's.

NOTES

Christ—Our Only Foundation

Lesson Text: I Corinthians 3:10-23

Related Scriptures: I Corinthians 3:1-9; Ephesians 2:19-22

TIME: A.D. 55   PLACE: from Ephesus

GOLDEN TEXT—"For other foundation can no man lay than that is laid, which is Jesus Christ" (I Corinthians 3:11).

Introduction

Every builder understands the importance of laying a good foundation prior to building a structure. The most beautiful, ornate house in the world is destined for destruction if the foundation is not solid. It may not be the most exciting aspect of a construction project, but it is arguably the most important. If the foundation is faulty, then the entire structure is bound to collapse. There are no shortcuts to this part of the building project, and the builders must pay close attention to it.

The church, likewise, must also be built on a firm foundation. Our theology, doctrine, and practice must be rooted in something sure that is not going to shift, bend, or break every time a storm rears its ugly head. The church is not limited to a physical structure such as a house of worship but comprises all genuine believers in Jesus. Therefore, it is our lives that must be built on a sure foundation.

LESSON OUTLINE

I. THE FOUNDATION OF THE CHURCH—I COR. 3:10-15

II. THE TEMPLE OF GOD— I Cor. 3:16-17

III. THE STRENGTH OF WISDOM—I Cor. 3:18-23

Exposition: Verse by Verse

THE FOUNDATION OF THE CHURCH

I COR. 3:10 According to the grace of God which is given unto me, as a wise masterbuilder, I have laid the foundation, and another buildeth thereon. But let every man take heed how he buildeth thereupon.

11 For other foundation can no man lay than that is laid, which is Jesus Christ.

12 Now if any man build upon this foundation gold, silver, precious stones, wood, hay, stubble;

13 Every man's work shall be

made manifest: for the day shall declare it, because it shall be revealed by fire; and the fire shall try every man's work of what sort it is.

14 If any man's work abide which he hath built thereupon, he shall receive a reward.

15 If any man's work shall be burned, he shall suffer loss: but he himself shall be saved; yet so as by fire.

The foundation for the church (I Cor. 3:10-11). {The purpose of this week's lesson is to show that the foundation of the church is Jesus Christ. Everything we believe and live according to begins and ends with Him.}[Q1] When the winds of trials and tribulations blow against us, we know we can stand firm because our foundation is strong and immovable. It should bring us great joy to know that our lives are built on the foundation of Christ.

The work of the church is definitely not a one-person effort. God has not designed anyone to be able to do everything. A "super Christian" does not exist. Everyone has a purpose and a place of importance in the church, but no one can do everything necessary for the church to be healthy. We need all believers to do what God has called them to do in order for the church to function at its full capacity.

Paul had just stated that we are God's fellow laborers and God's building (vs. 9). Using the building analogy, Paul goes on to explain that his role as a church leader was to lay the foundation. He did that when he proclaimed Christ to them and taught the essential truths about Him. Others such as Apollos, who was a powerful preacher of God's Word (cf. Acts 18:24-28), came behind him and built on the foundation that Paul had already laid. Paul is careful to note that this was all done by the grace of God, and each worker must take care to faithfully work for the Lord.

Paul was not in Corinth to make a name for himself. At one time, he was a rapidly advancing young Pharisee with strong ambitions (cf. Gal. 1:13-14), but those days were behind him once he became a follower of Jesus. When Paul arrived in Corinth, his sole purpose there was to plant a church, or lay the foundation, in a city devoted to polytheism, the worship of multiple deities. Paul was there to proclaim the name of Jesus to a city steeped in paganism.

{When construction on a building begins, only one foundation is laid. There is no need for multiple foundations, and the mere thought of this is foolish.}[Q2] The entire structure is built on one foundation, and the foundation Paul is speaking of is Jesus Christ. We as Christians have no other foundation than Christ, and He is the one the church is built on.

The foundation for good works (I Cor. 3:12-13). Now that the foundation has been laid, it is time to build on it. Christ our Foundation has given His life on the cross and has been raised from the dead. These facts are essential to all Christian doctrine and practice. The foundation can only be laid one time, and there is only one. All of our current and future work is to be conducted on the finished work of Jesus and His resurrection.

The strength and beauty of any structure depends on the quality of building materials. There is only one foundation, but many materials are used in construction. Some materials are better than others, and some will therefore stand the test of time better than others. Paul uses some examples of imperishable and perishable materials to show us the need for diligence in Christian works. {His examples of imperishable materials are gold, silver, and precious stones.}[Q3] These items are costly and call for skill and patience in their use.

{Perishable materials are cheaper and generally require less care. Paul uses wood, hay, and straw as examples.}Q4 How sad it is to have such a beautiful foundation only to use shoddy materials to build on it.

Each person must carefully choose what kind of building materials he is going to use to build on the foundation, for his work will be evaluated. This is not a matter of competing with other builders to see who did the best, but rather to determine the level of our faithfulness and love for the Lord.

Some Christians work diligently and use imperishable materials. They serve in faith, wholeheartedly seeking to do His will in all things. When our lives reflect Jesus and our hearts seek to honor Him, God will treasure our works (cf. Jas. 1:27). Others are cheap and lazy and use perishable materials. They serve grudgingly, out of compulsion, and not from faith. If we trust in Jesus just enough to put our faith in Him but still hold back areas of our lives, we will not have much to be rewarded for.

Our devotion to Christ will be revealed by the types of materials we used to build our lives on the foundation He laid. In the end, each person's work will be evaluated, and nothing will be hidden. {"The day" refers to the day when the fire of judgment will be applied to each of our works.}Q5 This will not be the final Day of Judgment in store for unbelievers, but a thorough assessment of believers' works in this life. Gold, silver, and precious stones will survive the fire, but the wood, hay, and straw will be consumed, leaving the builder with nothing to show for the work he has done.

The foundation for rewards (I Cor. 3:14-15). {Those whose work survives the fire of judgment will be rewarded for their service.}Q6 One thing is for sure: our foundation is eternal and is unaffected by fire. Our work, however, is subject to the fire and open to judgment. Those who take the time to use imperishable materials will receive a re-ward. They took time to serve God with all their hearts, regardless of the trials and persecutions that resulted from it.

Those who use perishable materials are immature, stagnant believers who serve themselves and not Christ. They have faith in Him and are saved, but they show little devotion to Him in their daily lives. {Those who use perishable materials will be saved "so as by fire" because of their faith in Jesus, but they will have little to no reward for their service.}Q7

Those who trust in Christ are spared from God's judgment, but God will evaluate our service for Him. Salvation comes by grace through faith, not by works (cf. Eph. 2:8-9). Salvation is based on faith in Christ's work, while rewards depend on how well we follow the Spirit's leading in living our lives for Christ. It is imperative that we never become confused about this.

THE TEMPLE OF GOD

16 Know ye not that ye are the temple of God, and that the Spirit of God dwelleth in you?

17 If any man defile the temple of God, him shall God destroy; for the temple of God is holy, which temple ye are.

God's new temple (I Cor. 3:16). The temple still stood in Jerusalem when Paul wrote I Corinthians in A.D. 55 and was not destroyed until A.D. 70, fifteen years later. It was still the most impressive physical structure in Israel and very important to the worship life of God's chosen people. It had always been the place where God's presence resided on earth.

The nature of the temple changed, however, after the death and resurrection of Jesus. On the Day of Pentecost, the Holy Spirit filled the believers who were gathered in the upper room. This was a fulfillment of Christ's promise to send the Holy Spirit to His followers (John 16:7; Acts 1:8). {Because the Holy Spirit lives inside each believer, the New Testament temple is not a building, but the living church.}[Q8]

God's precious temple (I Cor. 3:17). The temple was where the presence of God resided in the Old Testament. In the New Testament era, which we still live in today, the Spirit of God no longer resides in a building. The Spirit of God resides in those who believe in Jesus Christ, and they together are the church.

Paul issues a stern warning to anyone who would bring harm to God's temple. Those who do so will be destroyed by God. God's temple, which is His people, is sacred to Him. No matter what happens in this life, justice is sure.

THE STRENGTH OF WISDOM

18 Let no man deceive himself. If any man among you seemeth to be wise in this world, let him become a fool, that he may be wise.

19 For the wisdom of this world is foolishness with God. For it is written, He taketh the wise in their own craftiness.

20 And again, The Lord knoweth the thoughts of the wise, that they are vain.

21 Therefore let no man glory in men. For all things are yours;

22 Whether Paul, or Apollos, or Cephas, or the world, or life, or death, or things present, or things to come; all are yours;

23 And ye are Christ's; and Christ is God's.

False wisdom (I Cor. 3:18). No one likes to think of himself as foolish or ignorant. We tend to view ourselves as reasonably intelligent people with relevant opinions. Many even like to be innovative in their thoughts, feeling they have come upon new information or have a new way to look at old ideas. And God made us to be creative, so this is not necessarily bad.

{When people think more highly of their own opinions than they do of God's Word, however, they are deceived into moving away from biblical truth,}[Q9] which is deemed old-fashioned and irrelevant by the world at large. It would be much better to actually become a fool in order to find true wisdom.

Paul warns us sternly not to deceive ourselves. It is wrong and dangerous to think that we can replace God with the opinions and theories of man. In a day and age when people allow the media to do their thinking for them through talking points instead of serious, civil debate, we are falling prey to false worldviews without even filtering our sources through Scripture.

Many are deceived by theories formulated by atheist scientists and philosophers. Universities are training people in philosophies that are more and more opposed to the teachings of Scripture. Politicians are running on platforms that are demonic (promoting same-sex marriage and abortion just to name two examples), and then people vote for them and put them in places of power where they write laws that promote sin. That is why Paul warns us not to be fooled by what the world calls wisdom.

Foolishness in God's eyes (I Cor. 3:19-20). There needs to be a recommitment to teaching, believing, and obeying what Scripture has always taught. Keep in mind that the world will mock those who stand on Scripture because the Word of God is foolishness to the world. It makes no sense to them. However, the wisdom of the world is foolishness to God, so no matter what you believe, someone is going to consider you a fool. The question is, Who do you want to be called a fool by—the world or God?

While the world thinks that faith in God is silly and pointless and that science has replaced God in our thoughts and actions, it is important to remember that no one can fool God. Scientists, philosophers, liberal theologians, and government leaders have come and gone, but God's Word remains, and it alone has stood the test of time. Paul states very clearly that the wisdom of the world is foolishness to God.

Paul quotes two Old Testament texts to support his contention that God reigns supreme over the thoughts and opinions of man. First, God catches the worldly-wise in their craftiness (Job 5:13). The Lord exposes their wicked schemes and will bring judgment on those who rebel against His Word. Second, God knows that the wisdom of the world is vain, or empty (Ps. 94:11).

The source of true wisdom (I Cor. 3:21-23). {Since God considers the wisdom of the world to be foolish, it is a terrible idea to boast in men before God.}Q10 After all, if the world's thinking is foolishness, then what reason is there to boast in it?

This points back to Paul's previous command not to boast in the presence of the Lord, and that if we do boast, to boast in the Lord (1:29-31). This is also why the church should not divide over their favorite leaders or preachers. Neither Paul, Apollos, Peter, nor anyone else held a special key to truth that the others did not. We should all be preaching the same truth, built upon the same foundation: that it is Jesus Christ who delivers people from their bondage to sin.

There is only one gospel, but many who proclaim it. We receive Christ because we trust in Him to forgive us of our sins, give us His righteousness, and lead us to follow Him. This can only be done because of the power of the cross and the indwelling presence of the Holy Spirit in our lives (cf. 1:18, 24).

Our salvation is not dependent on who proclaimed the gospel to us. I do not even remember the name of the evangelist who preached the sermon the night that I got saved as a ten-year-old boy at church camp. It was a sermon based on fear tactics, but that is not why I went forward to accept Christ. I went because the Holy Spirit convicted me of my sin and convinced me of my need for Jesus Christ.

The teachings I had heard all my life from my parents, my pastor, and my Sunday school teachers rang true at that moment. The same Jesus I had heard about at home and at church was present with me that night at camp. No one gets credit for that except the Lord, and I am so thankful that He accepted me long before I accepted Him. Thank you, Jesus!

Since our salvation is not dependent on who taught us the gospel, we should never boast in men. Of all the people I have led to the Lord, none of them accepted Christ because of me.

—Robert Ferguson, Jr.

QUESTIONS

1. According to Paul, on what foundation is everything built?
2. How many foundations are there, and is there room for competition?
3. What are gold, silver, and precious stones examples of?
4. What are wood, hay, and straw examples of?
5. What will be applied to each person's work?
6. What will happen to those whose works survive God's judgment?
7. What will happen to those who used perishable materials?
8. What is the New Testament temple of God?
9. How do people deceive themselves in their own wisdom?
10. Why is it a terrible idea to boast in men before God?

—Robert Ferguson, Jr.

Preparing to Teach the Lesson

Throughout I Corinthians 2 and 3, the apostle Paul has been admonishing the Corinthian believers about being divided in their loyalties by primarily following human leaders and teachers. He has warned them about being seduced by sophisticated words of worldly wisdom, which have no power to save anyone.

Because they have allowed themselves to be charmed away from their unity in Christ by such empty words, Paul's conclusion is that this indicates they must still be woefully immature and carnally oriented rather than yielded to the guidance of the Holy Spirit as they should be by now. He laments the fact that although he has many deep truths to share with them from the riches of Christ's spiritual treasury, they themselves are unfit to receive them in their current childish state.

Beginning in verse 10 of chapter 3, Paul sets about re-laying their spiritual foundation in preparation for rebuilding them into mature servants of Christ. He desires to see them become equipped to minister to others in a manner that will glorify Christ alone, rather than be continually pulled astray by divided loyalties.

TODAY'S AIM

Facts: to be reminded that Christ is the believer's only foundation.

Principle: to understand what it means to have no other foundation than Christ.

Application: to make sure we faithfully build only upon Christ's foundation, realizing that the church is God's holy temple. We must not rely on vain human wisdom but rather employ all the good things that God has provided for our ministry to glorify His holy name.

INTRODUCING THE LESSON

In today's lesson, Paul expounds on what it means to live with Christ as our only foundation. As we serve the Lord, we are building His church, which is a holy temple of God. As we build, we dare not build with anything but our best efforts and resources, for we are building to the glory of God Himself.

DEVELOPING THE LESSON

1. No other foundation (I Cor. 3:10-15). Paul begins by identifying himself as "a wise masterbuilder," who has laid the foundation. He is speaking metaphorically about the foundational doctrines that he taught when he first established the church at Corinth. Paul was indeed the consummately wise master builder of the church's doctrinal foundation. His epistle to the Romans is the definitive vindication of this claim. Specifically, this foundation is identified with the doctrine of salvation by grace through faith in Jesus Christ, excluding any works of the law. Jesus Christ, as truthfully and accurately proclaimed by the apostles and in Scripture, can be our only foundation.

Paul mentions "gold, silver, precious stones" (vs. 12). These elements are metaphors for true teaching that is in line with Paul's foundational doctrine. "Wood, hay, stubble" are metaphors for erroneous teachings that are in conflict with the truth of that foundation.

The trial by fire that Paul speaks of primarily refers to the judgment on every believer's work when we stand before the Lord (cf. 5:10). God does send judgments in this life. A stunning example in Paul's time can be seen in the impending destruction of Jerusalem and its temple in A.D. 70. But this judgment ultimately redounded to the benefit of God's people; the sacrificial system was abolished, tangibly vindicating Paul's contention that the old covenant has been superseded by the gospel of Christ. The church, the body of Christ, is now God's temple.

2. God's temple (I Cor. 3:16-17). Paul's building metaphor must be followed in the context of the early chapters of this letter. It therefore applies especially to the issue of those who took over teaching the Corinthians after Paul had established the foundation. The focus of this passage is most definitely on the church and not on individual believers.

Nevertheless, these two verses are often mistakenly interpreted as applying to the individual physical bodies of believers and to issues such as healthy diet, exercise, and avoiding harmful substances. It has even been taken as prohibiting suicide. Those issues are certainly addressed in Scripture, but this is not one of those places. Individual believers are indeed indwelled by the Holy Spirit, but what is being addressed here is the church as a whole.

As the body of Christ, the church is God's holy temple, indwelt corporately by the Holy Spirit. Those who defile this temple are, first and foremost, false teachers, including the Judaizers of Paul's time. It is they whom God will surely destroy.

3. Vain wisdom (I Cor. 3:18-20). Here Paul reiterates his warning against the know-it-alls who were seeking to lead the Corinthians astray from the pure doctrinal foundation that he had established there. He strenuously recommends that all such know-it-alls become fools so that they may acquire true, godly wisdom. He quotes Job 5:13 and Psalm 94:11 to prove that such worldly-wise men offer only vain words that are powerless to save anyone.

4. Heirs of all (I Cor. 3:21-23). Paul's conclusion is that the Corinthians must fully rid themselves of their infatuation with valuing various human teachers above all else, since all the things that matter are already theirs as heirs of God in Christ.

Paul's list of the blessings of their divine inheritance includes their teachers, the whole world, life, death, and all that is now or ever shall be in the future. Why, then, should they be vainly divided over the words of a few mere men?

ILLUSTRATING THE LESSON

The illustration depicts Christ as the church's only foundation.

NO OTHER FOUNDATION: CHRIST

CONCLUDING THE LESSON

Our riches in Christ are so much more than what any mere man using the sophisticated reasoning of the world can offer us. We must keep our spiritual vision firmly fixed on Christ as the only foundation for our inheritance in heaven. Indeed, since Christ has all authority in heaven and earth (cf. Matt. 28:18), He is the Lord of all. Only through Jesus do we stand on solid ground; all else is just quicksand.

ANTICIPATING THE NEXT LESSON

Next week's lesson focuses on what it means to be members of Christ's body, the church.

—*John Lody.*

PRACTICAL POINTS

1. Jesus Christ is the only foundation for all we teach and do (I Cor. 3:10-11).
2. Our churches, our homes, and our lives must be built on Jesus Christ alone to last (vss. 12-15).
3. God protects the church from those who would defile it, for it is His holy temple (vss. 16-17).
4. Faithfulness to God's Word seems foolish to those who do not believe (vss. 18-20).
5. Believers may honor leaders for their service, but worship belongs to God alone (vss. 21-22).
6. Unity in God's kingdom is only possible through Christ (vs. 23).
—Cheryl Y. Powell.

RESEARCH AND DISCUSSION

1. What happens when the church is built on a foundation other than Christ? What are some of those other foundations? What steps can be taken to avoid such errors?
2. What rewards might a believer who is faithful in service to Christ expect to receive? Discuss.
3. What external and internal factors threaten the unity of churches? Why is it so important to protect unity in our churches? What could you do to strengthen the unity of your local church?
4. Why might it be tempting for believers to glory or boast in human leaders? Discuss.
—Cheryl Y. Powell.

ILLUSTRATED HIGH POINTS

I have laid the foundation (I Cor. 3:10)

Paul emphasizes the importance of laying a proper foundation before building to greater heights. Let us look at three steps to laying a firm foundation.

The first step is to dig deep. There are three main things we need to dig into: the Word of God (cf. I Pet. 2:2; Acts 17:11), prayer (cf. I Thess. 5:17), and heart-searching repentance from sin (cf. II Chr. 7:14).

The next step is to pour footings. These are concrete pillars that hold the weight of a building. For believers there are basic doctrines on which the Christian faith stands (cf. Titus 1:9).

Finally, every pillar must be treated with an impenetrable sealant. Our seal is the Holy Spirit (cf. II Cor. 1:22).

Foundation . . . which is Jesus Christ (vs. 11)

After a fire brings down a house, the homeowner is required to have his foundation inspected by a structural engineer before rebuilding. There are multiple methods used. The first is a visual assessment. Are there any scorch marks, cracks, or leanings? Next comes the audible test. A sounding hammer is struck against the foundation as the inspector listens for the high-frequency ring of healthy concrete.

Jesus, praise God, is the firmest foundation. His work is invulnerable to both the storms of life and the fires of judgment. He withstands it all. He provides purity and strength in any and all adversities that we experience.

With Christ as our foundation, we will withstand the fires of judgment, but let us build upon this worthy foundation a high-quality structure of gold, silver, and precious stones (vss. 12-14).
—Therese Greenberg.

Golden Text Illuminated

"For other foundation can no man lay than that is laid, which is Jesus Christ" (I Corinthians 3:11).

The Corinthian church was building a shoddy edifice. Embroiled in debates and divisions, exalting themselves above one another, and casting a blind eye to sin, they were raising a shaky structure of wood, hay, and straw (cf. I Cor. 3:12), worthless materials that would eventually be consumed in the fire of divine judgment.

Paul reminded the church that a true foundation already existed. Preaching what had been revealed to him by God, Paul proved himself to be a wise builder, who had laid a solid basis upon which others could successfully build. That foundation was none other than Jesus Christ.

Isaiah prophesied in the eighth century B.C. that this divine Cornerstone would be laid by Yahweh Himself (Isa. 28:16). This stone was tried, meaning that it was proven to be strong and dependable. The one who trusts in this stone will always be secure, never needing to consider any alternative to trust in.

The psalmist also foresaw this divine foundation when he wrote, "The stone which the builders refused is become the head stone of the corner" (Ps. 118:22). Centuries later, Peter quoted this Scripture when he stood accused before the Jewish religious leaders (cf. Acts 4:11). He boldly declared that the risen Christ had empowered him to heal, thus acknowledging the very Cornerstone whom these leaders had rejected.

In ancient construction, the cornerstone was the largest and strongest in a foundation. It was always set first and carefully positioned, since it would de-termine the integrity of the entire structure. If the cornerstone was placed incorrectly, all the other stones would be out of alignment; if it was weak, the adjoining walls would collapse. Writing around A.D. 93, the Jewish historian Josephus described the foundation of Solomon's Temple: "The King laid the foundations of the temple very deep in the ground, and the materials were strong stones, and such as would resist the force of time." As impressive as these stones were, they could not compare to Christ, the Cornerstone of the church (cf. Eph. 2:19-23).

In the parable of the husbandmen, or tenant farmers, Jesus applies the cornerstone imagery to himself. He tells the story of a vineyard owner who tries to collect his share of the harvest from his tenant farmers. Shockingly, all the owner's messengers are beaten and driven away. Finally, the vineyard owner sends his son, thinking that the laborers would surely respect him, but instead they murder him. The enraged father destroys the farmers and rents his vineyard to others. Jesus told this parable to warn that those who reject Him as the Cornerstone would be smashed by it and ground into dust.

The Corinthians had not rejected Christ outright, but they were building carelessly, ignoring Christ as the foundation that had been laid for them. They were raising their church on a foundation of sin, not on the foundation of the "apostles and prophets, Jesus Christ himself being the chief corner stone" (Eph. 2:20). As a result, if they did not repent, their church was doomed to fail.

—*Mark Winter.*

Heart of the Lesson

If a building is going to weather the devastating force of a natural disaster, it must have a strong foundation. Likewise, in order for the church, which is God's building, to withstand the destructive attacks of Satan, it must be built on the unbreakable foundation of Jesus.

1. Solid foundation (I Cor. 3:10-11). God is the architect and designer of the church, but He uses and equips trustworthy Christians to help build His church.

In the first century, God called and equipped the apostle Paul to help lay a solid foundation for His church. Paul traveled to Corinth and shared with them the gospel of Jesus. As a master builder empowered by the Holy Spirit, Paul built the Corinthian church on the foundation of Christ's death for their sins and His resurrection from the dead.

After Paul left Corinth, Apollos and Peter continued the construction of the Corinthian church by continuing the teaching that salvation comes only by faith in Jesus.

2. Strong building materials (I Cor. 3:12-17). Paul described two kinds of builders in the church: wise and foolish. Those who build with gold, silver, and precious stones are the ministers who teach good doctrine and the pure gospel of Christ. Ministers who build with wood, hay, and straw neglect the gospel and concentrate on distractions and divisiveness.

On the future day of judgment, Jesus will return not to determine a believer's salvation but to judge the quality of each Christian's work (cf. II Cor. 5:10). Just as fire burns up wood, hay, and straw, the fire of Christ's judgment will burn away impure motivations and un-biblical thoughts and actions. Believers who build with gold, silver, and precious stones, whose actions are motivated by love for God and a desire to please Him, will receive eternal rewards.

Next, Paul reminded the Corinthians that they were not only builders but also the actual stones that comprise God's temple—the place where the Holy Spirit dwells. God is holy, and His dwelling place must be holy. Anyone who defiles the church by teaching a different gospel or unsound doctrine, or by living a life dominated by sin, will receive judgment from God Himself (cf. Matt. 18:6-7).

3. Sensible builder (I Cor. 3:18-23). Jesus is the leader and the foundation of the church (cf. Eph. 1:22-23). His death and resurrection replaces division with unity, hatred with love, and pride with humility. Some of the leaders in the Corinthian church, however, were still motivated by pride and foolishness. They were self-deceived, unable to distinguish God's wisdom from worldly foolishness. Paul's letter was intended as a wake-up call to help them return to the humility and wisdom of the cross.

Paul quoted from Job 5:13 and Psalm 94:11, both of which show that God is omniscient. He knows the thoughts of every person. Paul warned the boastful, divisive ministers in Corinth that God would judge them for leading others astray. In their foolishness, they were actually assisting Satan's efforts to destroy the church.

At the foot of the cross, all believers have equally important, God-given roles in the church. Because of the cross, believers belong to Christ as members of God's family and exist to bring Him glory.

—*Malia E. Rodriguez.*

World Missions

Two young evangelists, the best of friends, had been studying the works of leading theologians who questioned the inspiration and reliability of the Bible. This created doubt in the minds of both men. One man left evangelism, returned to his home country, and began a career as a writer and television personality. The other also returned home, where he re-read Paul's message to his apprentice, Timothy, stating that "All scripture is given by inspiration of God" (II Tim. 3:16). He recalled that Jesus Himself quoted Scripture many times, including from the creation story (cf. Matt. 19:4-6), which was the portion of Scripture most in question in their studies. The young man stood at a crossroads (cf. Jer. 6:16). If the Bible was not the Word of God, he could not continue preaching.

In his own words, he described what happened next. "I walked out in the moonlight, my heart heavy and burdened. I dropped to my knees and opened my Bible on a tree stump. . . . 'Oh God,' I prayed, 'there are many things in this Book I do not understand. But God, I'm going to accept this Book as Your Word by faith. I'm going to allow my faith to go beyond my intellect and believe that this is Your Inspired Word.' From that moment on I have never doubted God's Word" (Busby, *Billy Graham: God's Ambassador,* Time-Life Books).

The first man was Charles Templeton. Brilliant and handsome, he became editor of The Toronto Star and a frequent guest on Canadian television. He espoused the worn-out intellectual arguments of the skeptics who had preceded him. One of his books was sadly entitled *Farewell to God.*

The second man was (as you no doubt have gathered) Billy Graham.

After his faith crisis, he became ever more confident in preaching the Bible. Thousands follow Jesus today because of his commitment to Scripture. He also wrote many books, each one based on Scripture. Until his death in 2018, he remained faithful to Jesus Christ and to God's Word, the Bible.

Paul reminded the divided Corinthian believers that the church of Christ is like a building (I Cor. 3:11). When the foundation of a building is unstable, serious problems result: cracks in the walls, doors that stick, windows that will not open, faults in the foundation, water seepage, and even the collapse of entire walls.

The church's foundation is Jesus Christ. When a church loses its commitment to biblical authority, its foundation becomes faulty because Jesus Himself is the Word of God (John 1:1).

True believers trust the Bible, teach the Bible, and live according to its precepts. One preacher put it this way, "Where the Bible is not believed, the church speaks with a stutter."

Charles Templeton lived for the temporary accolades that came with being important in the world. Admired as a leader among the agnostics, he became a poster-boy for scoffers (cf. Ps. 1:1).

Billy Graham looked beyond the temporary to the eternal. He said, "Someday you will read or hear that Billy Graham is dead. Don't you believe a word of it. I shall be more alive than I am now. I will just have changed my address. I will have gone into the presence of God."

The stories of these two men read like a modern-day parable that illustrates the necessity of trusting in the Lord, not our own understanding (cf. Prov. 3:5-6). Missionaries need to follow daily this passage in Proverbs.

—Rose McCormick Brandon.

The Jewish Aspect

The Hebrew Scriptures are replete with teachings about the importance of foundations, both physical and metaphorical. God and the foundation of His throne are extolled by David (Ps. 89:14; 97:2). David also spoke of God establishing the foundation of the earth. "Of old hast thou laid the foundation of the earth: and the heavens are the work of thy hands" (Ps. 102:25). The prophet Isaiah wrote of God as saying, "Mine hand also hath laid the foundation of the earth, and my right hand hath spanned the heavens: when I call unto them, they stand up together" (Isa. 48:13).

In the Lord's discourse with Job, He asked "Where wast thou when I laid the foundations of the earth? declare, if thou hast understanding. Who hath laid the measures thereof, if thou knowest? or who hath stretched the line upon it? Whereupon are the foundations thereof fastened? or who laid the corner stone thereof" (Job 38:4-6).

The importance of the foundation of a building was also a common theme in the Hebrew Scriptures. When Solomon built the first temple, huge blocks of the best stone were quarried, and great and costly stones were used to lay the foundation. "And the king commanded, and they brought great stones, costly stones, and hewed stones, to lay the foundation of the house" (I Kgs. 5:17).

Seventy years after the destruction of the first temple, the building of the second temple was completed on the same site, with the encouragement of the prophets Haggai and Zechariah. "And when the builders laid the foundation of the temple of the Lord, they set the priests in their apparel with trumpets, and the Levites the sons of Asaph with cymbals, to praise the Lord, after the ordinance of David king of Israel" (Ezra 3:10). The joyful scene was the result of the return of biblical worship.

The destruction of the temple in A.D. 70 brought great mourning and devastation to the Jewish people because it had been the center of Jewish life and the place of God's presence among His covenant people. "The temple also played a central role in the early history of Christianity. Jesus' family came to the temple after his birth to celebrate the redemption of the first born (Exodus 13:13, Numbers 18:15-16) and so that his mother could offer the sacrifice the Torah requires after childbirth (Lev. 12)" (www.bibleodyssey.org).

Speaking of the Messiah to come, Isaiah said, "Therefore thus saith the Lord God, Behold I lay in Zion for a foundation a stone, a tried stone, a precious corner stone, a sure foundation: he that believeth shall not make haste" (Isa. 28:16). When the Jewish leaders challenged Yeshua (Jesus), He quoted the words of the psalmist: "The stone which the builders refused is become the head stone of the corner" (Ps. 118:22).

When Paul wrote to the believers in Ephesus, he reminded them that, as believers in Jesus, they were no longer strangers, but members of the household of God (Eph. 2:19). Jesus, he said, was the chief cornerstone, "in whom all the building fitly framed together groweth unto an holy temple in the Lord: in whom ye also are builded together for an habitation of God through the Spirit" (vss. 21-22). Paul warned the believers at Corinth against their carnal thinking and the divisions among them. He said that they were the building of God. Jesus, he said, was the true foundation: "For other foundation can no man lay than that is laid, which is Jesus Christ" (I Cor. 3:11).

—Deborah Markowitz Solan.

Guiding the Superintendent

Paul is now ready to emphasize the main reason he is against all divisions in the church that are based on celebrated preachers (see lesson 1). It is because everything based upon mere human wisdom will ultimately lead to God's judgment (I Cor. 3:1-5, 17).

Using the analogy of a building and a temple, Paul explained why divided loyalties centered around merely human leaders is contrary to the nature of leadership in the church and contrary to the very nature of the church itself.

DEVOTIONAL OUTLINE

1. The church as building (I Cor. 3:10-15). By God's grace, Paul was a wise builder. He had laid the foundation of the Corinthian church that others later built upon. The church's only foundation is Jesus Christ, and this is the foundation that Paul had laid by preaching the gospel and teaching sound doctrine.

A building is only as reliable as its foundation. Because the church's foundation is Jesus Christ, those who build on that foundation should not depart from it as they erect the building's superstructure. Paul's point is that all the various cliques formed by the Corinthians around human preachers and teachers are folly, destructive to the life of their fellowship in Christ.

The buildings in ancient cities were very susceptible to fires. Only quality building materials will survive a fire. Only a church that is built on the foundation of Jesus Christ alone will survive God's judgment without loss when it comes.

One day, all service to Christ will be revealed for what it truly is. The judgment day will reveal the true quality of the materials used to build up the church. It is important to notice that in this particular passage Paul is only talking about rewards for faithful service in ministry, not about salvation. Those believers who are not rewarded will still be saved, but much like a person escaping a burning building.

2. The church as temple (I Cor. 3:16-23). Paul reminds his readers that the life of their church is too important for them to be sabotaging it by engaging in bickering, envying, and strife. Such things are not from God; they are devilish in their origins. The Corinthians have no reason to be proud of their conflicts. They should mourn over them instead and seek to repent of such destructive behavior!

In the Old Testament, the temple of God was a special building that housed God's glorious presence (cf. I Kgs. 8:29). In the New Testament, God's presence dwells in the "temple" that is the church, made up of believers indwelled by the Holy Spirit. Severe judgment from God awaits those whose actions lead to damage to this temple.

Paul used two Old Testament texts (cf. Job 5:13; Ps. 94:11) to warn the Corinthian believers that their divisions were both foolish and dangerous. Following the wisdom of mere humans is a vain exercise, for the Lord will bring all such prideful thinking to nothing. He reminds the Corinthian believers that all they have is because they are in Christ through the gospel. They have no reason to boast. The only foundation they need is Christ, because everything they are is because of Him.

CHILDREN'S CORNER

Children are just beginning to learn what church is all about. This lesson will emphasize that the church's foundation is Christ and that it is a temple in which God dwells.

—*Martin R. Dahlquist.*

SCRIPTURE LESSON TEXT

I COR. 6:12 All things are lawful unto me, but all things are not expedient: all things are lawful for me, but I will not be brought under the power of any.

13 Meats for the belly, and the belly for meats: but God shall destroy both it and them. Now the body *is* **not for fornication, but for the Lord; and the Lord for the body.**

14 And God hath both raised up the Lord, and will also raise up us by his own power.

15 Know ye not that your bodies are the members of Christ? shall I then take the members of Christ, and make *them* **the members of an harlot? God forbid.**

16 What? know ye not that he which is joined to an harlot is one body? for two, saith he, shall be one flesh.

17 But he that is joined unto the Lord is one spirit.

18 Flee fornication. Every sin that a man doeth is without the body; but he that committeth fornication sinneth against his own body.

19 What? know ye not that your body is the temple of the Holy Ghost *which is* **in you, which ye have of God, and ye are not your own?**

20 For ye are bought with a price: therefore glorify God in your body, and in your spirit, which are God's.

NOTES

Members of Christ

Lesson Text: I Corinthians 6:12-20

Related Scriptures: I Corinthians 5:1-13; 6:1-11;
I Thessalonians 4:3-8; Colossians 3:1-11; Romans 6:1-14

TIME: A.D. 55   PLACE: from Ephesus

GOLDEN TEXT—"What? know ye not that your body is the temple of the Holy Ghost which is in you, which ye have of God, and ye are not your own? For ye are bought with a price: therefore glorify God in your body, and in your spirit, which are God's" (I Corinthians 6:19-20).

Introduction

What are you living for? Perhaps a better question to ask is *who* are you living for? Many people are living for themselves with no consideration for the will of God. People seem to pay little attention to whether their actions are sinful or not. The concept of sin is either dismissed as irrelevant or laughed at altogether. This week's lesson teaches us, however, that the way we live matters to God.

Immorality is a problem both outside and inside the church. We all still commit sin in our daily lives, but it is important to repent and turn from it quickly. Otherwise, sin will take over our lives and dominate us.

Immorality cannot be tolerated in the church because we are the temple of the Holy Spirit, both individually and corporately. The way we live has an impact on those around us who do not know Christ.

LESSON OUTLINE

I. OUR BODY FOR THE LORD— I COR. 6:12-14

II. MEMBERS OF CHRIST— I Cor. 6:15-17

III. THE TEMPLE OF THE HOLY SPIRIT—I Cor. 6:18-20

Exposition: Verse by Verse

OUR BODY FOR THE LORD

I COR. 6:12 All things are lawful unto me, but all things are not expedient: all things are lawful for me, but I will not be brought under the power of any.

13 Meats for the belly, and the belly for meats: but God shall destroy both it and them. Now the body is not for fornication, but for the Lord; and the Lord for the body.

14 And God hath both raised up the Lord, and will also raise up us by his own power.

"All things are lawful" (I Cor. 6:12). "It is my body, and I can do with it whatever I choose!" This is a slogan that is shouted repeatedly in American society. Unfortunately, it is the rally cry of the rebel and is absolutely false, as we will see in this lesson.

Most cultures have slogans or clichés that become commonplace, whether they are true or not. We say things such as, "Live and let live," "What is true for you is not true for me," and "You made your bed, now you lie in it." These statements and many others like them become so familiar that many of us never question their validity.

The Corinthians also had slogans in their culture that they lived by until Paul challenged them. The first slogan Paul takes issue with was a popular saying among the Corinthians: "All things are lawful unto me." This was such a common refrain in Corinth that Paul quotes it twice in his address.

The Corinthian Christians used this phrase to argue that they could do as they pleased and there was no reason for them to stop indulging themselves in whatever gave them pleasure. {Paul responds by stating that while all things may be lawful, not all things are helpful.}ᑫ1 Just because we legally can do something does not mean that we should. The legality of an issue is not the only factor in determining whether it is right or wrong. The government allows many things, both historically and currently, that are absolutely abhorrent.

In the past, our government allowed the despicable practice of slavery. More recently, the government has redefined marriage unbiblically and allows abortion, the murder of an unborn child. Just because these things are legal does not make them acceptable. We should be interested in glorifying Christ and not in self-gratification. Unfortunately, too many professing Christians use their "Christian liberty" for sinful and destructive living.

Paul goes on to state that he would not be enslaved by anything. That sounds similar to the cry of the rebel discussed earlier, but it is the exact opposite. Paul realized that doing whatever pleases us at any given moment is a sure way to become a slave to that behavior. Indulging in the flesh can lead to terrifying addictions. Most addicted persons would be glad to be free from their addictions, but they cannot escape.

Interestingly, the very thing that the world looks at as bondage is the only thing that brings freedom. When we are living in obedience to Christ, we are set free to not indulge in these behaviors. Deliverance from sin is not only a matter of going to heaven or hell. It is a matter of living out holiness, something every Christian should be striving for and trusting God to produce in our lives.

"Food for the stomach" (I Cor. 6:13-14). {The next Corinthian slogan that Paul addresses is, "Meats for the belly, and the belly for meats." This is how the Corinthians justified their intention to satisfy any and all of their cravings.}ᑫ2 This expression was not limited simply to eating what they wanted. It was more a matter of *doing* what they wanted. Immorality ran rampant in Corinth. Sexual desire was as natural to them as the stomach craving food. A hungry man would not deny himself food, so why would one deny his sexual impulses? After all, they were natural.

{Paul responds by writing that God will destroy both the stomach and food in the end. These things are not eternal, and we should not live for them.}ᑫ3 Bodily urges may be "natural," but they are temporal and subject to God's judgment. Acting on our cravings or impulses is a terrible way to live our lives and ties us to a trainload of unwelcome consequences. Instead, we should seek higher desires like holiness.

The apostle goes on to state that the body is not meant for sexual immorality, but for the Lord. Just because something feels natural or right does not excuse sinful activity. Far too often people rationalize their sinful desires by saying, "It just feels so right." I have heard people say that God told them to leave their spouse and gave them a sign by sending someone else into their life that they fell in love with. "It felt so right," they said. This is, as we say in the South, "hogwash."

We exist for God's purposes, not our own. We owe our lives to God and are subject to Him because He has bought us with a price and prepares us for holiness. Paul states that God raised Jesus up and will also raise us by His power. Just as God raised Jesus from the dead, He will also raise us. What right do we have, then, to pollute a body that He owns and preserves for a glorious eternity? We are completely subject to Him, and our works will be judged. There will be no excuses.

MEMBERS OF CHRIST

15 Know ye not that your bodies are the members of Christ? shall I then take the members of Christ, and make them the members of an harlot? God forbid.

16 What? know ye not that he which is joined to an harlot is one body? for two, saith he, shall be one flesh.

17 But he that is joined unto the Lord is one spirit.

"Do you not know?" (I Cor. 6:15-16a). In the beginning of this letter, Paul alluded to the fact that the church is Christ's body and should not be divided (1:13). Just as there should not be any division in the corporate assembly of believers through favoritism or preference, there should also be no division internally in the believer because of sin.

Getting saved is not simply coming to an agreement with certain doctrinal principles. It is more than saying a prayer, going to church, and participating in sacraments (baptism and communion). {Becoming a Christian is to become a member of Christ, that is, to be united with Him in relationship and fellowship.}Q4 We love Him, obey His teachings, and repent when we fail and fall short.

{Twice in verses 15 and 16, Paul asks the Corinthians, "Know ye not?" This makes it clear that the Corinthians should have already known his teaching, but their practice implied a lack of understanding.}Q5 Paul was perplexed that they could be so defective in their understanding of such basic things. They should have already understood the sinfulness of sexual immorality and indulging in immoral pleasures. However, they continued to justify their actions.

In order to point out the error of their ways, Paul states that Christians are members of Christ. All of us are members of His body. This is a union that all believers have with Christ upon conversion. We are then indwelt by the Holy Spirit, who guides and convicts us of sin. We are in a very dangerous and vulnerable position if we no longer hear the voice of the Holy Spirit or sense His conviction when we knowingly sin.

Paul asked a question that was sure to shock the conscience of the Corinthian Christians, and the thought of it should shock ours today as well. He asked them if he should take the members of the body of Christ and then join them with a prostitute. The mere idea was inconceivable and reprehensible to Paul, and it should be to us as well.

In response to his own question, Paul emphatically states, "God forbid!" This is the strongest denunciation he could have given. {It was absolutely unthinkable that Christ, in His holiness, would ever participate in sexual activity with a prostitute, yet Paul indicates that the unthinkable is essentially what happens when a Christian commits sexual sin.}[Q6] Since a believer is a member of the body of Christ, he brings Christ into the unholy union.

The world does not see sexual deviancy as a big deal, but Paul vehemently argues otherwise. All sexual relations outside of biblical marriage—which is one man married to one woman for life—are sin. Premarital sex (fornication), extramarital sex (adultery), and homosexual sex are forbidden by God and are under His condemnation. This includes other perversions as well, such as pornography, bestiality, incest, polygamy, and bigamy. It is bad enough that the world engages in these practices, but to find them practiced among believers is an abomination of the worst sort.

One flesh (I Cor. 6:16b-17). The intimate nature of a sexual relationship makes two people one flesh. In order to establish his point, Paul refers to God's creative order and takes the Corinthians back to the creation of human beings. It was there when God created male and female that He said the two shall become one flesh (Gen. 2:24).

This is not just Paul's opinion on this matter. He has often been mischaracterized and falsely accused in modern times of being a prude, a misogynist, and a homophobe who tried to foist his own agenda on other people. That is absurd, and Paul repeatedly shows that his theology is not rooted in his own opinion but rather in the Word of God that was established in the beginning.

{The reference to the two being one flesh shows that sexual intimacy has a spiritual as well as a physical aspect.}[Q7]

Sex is a beautiful union within biblically defined marriage, but it is destructive outside of marriage.

THE TEMPLE OF THE HOLY SPIRIT

18 Flee fornication. Every sin that a man doeth is without the body; but he that committeth fornication sinneth against his own body.

19 What? know ye not that your body is the temple of the Holy Ghost which is in you, which ye have of God, and ye are not your own?

20 For ye are bought with a price: therefore glorify God in your body, and in your spirit, which are God's.

Flee from sexual immorality (I Cor. 6:18). {The only way to avoid sexual sin is to flee from it.}[Q8] This is Paul's only instruction on the matter. Sexual temptation is so strong that the only way to deal with it is to remove yourself from the situation immediately. Otherwise, you are likely to be completely overtaken by desire, leading you to give in to the temptation (cf. Jas. 1:14-15).

{Sexual sin is more damaging than other sins because of the ramifications. Disease, unwanted pregnancy, and a false sense of intimacy are just a few of the long-lasting, if not lifelong, problems that come with sexual sin.}[Q9] And ironically, in a society that applauds sexual freedom, the social stigma is still very intense for people caught committing sexual sin. Many celebrity scandals revolve around it. The list goes on almost endlessly of people and families who have been ruined by sexual sin and perversion. It is in this respect that a person sins against his own body, as Paul states.

The apostle's warning to the Corinthian believers is to run away from sexual sin. At the first hint of temptation, get out of the situation that you are in. Do not stand around and fight it. Run away! Joseph is a stellar example of a man who fled when faced with sexual temptation. Joseph stalwartly resisted multiple advances, but as soon as he found himself facing them alone, he fled the scene (Gen. 39:7-12).

Your body is the temple of the Holy Spirit (I Cor. 6:19-20). Again, Paul asks the question, "Know ye not?" Again, what follows is something the Corinthian Christians should already have understood. There is nothing wrong with needing to be taught basic Christian doctrines, but there comes a time when we are expected to move beyond foundational issues and get into deeper teaching (cf. Heb. 5:11-14).

Paul informed the Corinthians that they were the temple of the Holy Spirit. Just as we learned in last week's lesson, the believer individually and the church corporately comprise the temple of the Holy Spirit. God no longer resides in a building made with human hands. Instead, He lives in every believer. The church is a gathered assembly of redeemed sinners, which means the Holy Spirit is in us all whether we are alone or gathered together.

With a statement that refutes much modern-day thought, Paul writes that we are not our own. We do not belong to ourselves, but to God. We are accountable to Him for our actions. This flies in the face of the modern chant that insists, "It is my body, and I can do with it whatever I choose." That is the rallying cry of the pro-choice movement. Well, the Holy Spirit says otherwise.

{We are not our own, because we have been bought with a price.}^Q10 Jesus shed His blood on Calvary's cross so that we can be free from sin. He gave His life as a ransom (Matt. 20:28) to redeem us from sin (cf. Eph. 1:7). Since Christ is both our Creator (cf. John 1:3; I Cor. 8:6; Col. 1:16) and Redeemer, we belong to Him and will answer to Him for the way we live our lives. Therefore, our bodies should be used to glorify God, not to satisfy ourselves.

Whenever you are faced with the opportunity or temptation to engage in any kind of questionable conduct, remember that your body is the temple of the Holy Spirit. Sexual sin especially should never be permitted in His temple. Your morals and conduct should reflect who you belong to, giving no cause for shame or disgrace to His name. Instead, your aim should always be to bring Him glory and delight.

Our bodies do not exist for our own pleasure, and we are not to do just anything we want with them. We do not belong to ourselves, but to God. This should be seen as liberating because God will resurrect our bodies and give us eternal life.

—Robert Ferguson, Jr.

QUESTIONS

1. How did Paul respond to the claim that "all things are lawful"?
2. What was meant by the expression, "Meats for the belly, and the belly for meats"?
3. How did Paul respond to this claim?
4. What did Paul mean when he said that we are members of Christ?
5. Why did Paul ask the Corinthians, "Know ye not"?
6. What picture did Paul use to demonstrate how reprehensible sexual sin was?
7. What is meant by "they shall be one flesh" (Gen. 2:24)?
8. How did Paul say we are to deal with sexual temptation?
9. Why is sexual sin so much more damaging than other sins?
10. Why can we not say that our bodies belong to ourselves?

—Robert Ferguson, Jr.

Preparing to Teach the Lesson

Paul has just addressed two specific problems within the church at Corinth. The first was a matter of extreme sexual immorality. He admonished the Christians there for allowing such an offense go on in their midst with impunity. He commanded them to ostracize the offender so that he perhaps might be purged from his corruption by the trials Satan would visit on him.

The second was an issue between believers who were bringing each other into the civil courts. They brought shame on the church by publicly displaying the strife and contentions among them.

Paul then points them to the foundational truths that disallow all such shameful behaviors: they are members of Christ's holy body and a holy temple to God, indwelled by the Holy Spirit.

TODAY'S AIM

Facts: to see that all believers have been set apart and dedicated to the Lord.

Principle: to understand what holiness means in our daily lives.

Application: to seek holiness in our daily behavior, avoiding immoral and corrupt behavior and replacing it with devotion to the Word, to prayer, and to serving others as they have need.

INTRODUCING THE LESSON

In this week's lesson, Paul develops two main truths. First, although in Christ we have been liberated from the guilt and condemnation of the law, we have been set apart—made holy—as members of Christ's own body. Second, we stand together as a holy temple to God, each of us indwelled by the Holy Spirit. We must therefore avoid immorality and pursue holiness in all we do.

DEVELOPING THE LESSON

1. A higher calling (I Cor. 6:12-14). Although no longer bound by the detailed regulations of the Mosaic law, and although delivered through faith in Christ from the law's sentence of death, Christians should recognize that not everything that is allowed is either wise or appropriate.

Many things that are not specifically prohibited under Christian liberty nevertheless have dire physical, mental, and emotional consequences. It is so easy for various actions to lead to addictions. Christians must practice self-control in all things.

Paul quotes a proverb in verse 13: "Meats for the belly, and the belly for meats." The point of this proverb is that food is intended to be eaten, just as one's body is intended to eat it. In other words, God intended us to delight in eating the foods that our body happens to need to sustain itself. God has created both the need and the pleasure in meeting that need.

But Paul adds a serious qualification to this proverbial truth: both food and our stomachs are merely temporary; they are not more important than what is spiritual and eternal.

Paul then further qualifies this principle, warning that even though there are divinely ordained physical necessities, sexual immorality is not one of them! The overriding principle here is that our physical bodies are intended to serve and glorify the Lord who created them.

In verse 14, Paul drives his point home by reminding his readers that what really matters is that we are to live as people who serve the resurrected Lord Jesus Christ. Our lives should consistently reflect this reality. Rather than be preoccupied with the desires of our material existence, our focus should be on a higher calling: the pursuit of holiness.

2. Christ's own members (I Cor. 6:15-18). Next, Paul pointedly queries his readers. Do they not realize that their bodies are the members of Christ's holy body, His church? It is unthinkable that holy members of Christ's body would be defiled with a prostitute! Paul refers his readers back to the book of Genesis, reminding them that sexual union carries with it the unavoidable union of two people as one. Rather than be so united with corruption, believers are to be joined spiritually to the Lord Himself.

Adding weight to his admonition, Paul warns that sins of sexual immorality carry an added degree of defilement beyond other sins. Every other sin is primarily spiritual and therefore has spiritual consequences that can be remedied through genuine repentance. But the defilement of sexual sin permanently defiles the physical body, and its consequences may oppressively linger for an entire lifetime.

3. Bought with a price (I Cor. 6:19-20). Paul now calls his readers' attention to the reality of their status individually as the temple of the Holy Spirit. Not only are they members of Christ's body corporately, but the Spirit indwells them each as individuals, making them into a holy temple to the Lord.

The corollary to this truth is that, because we are the temple of the Holy Spirit, we no longer belong to ourselves. Christ Himself paid the price for our redemption from sin. We are therefore owned by Him entirely. This means that we have been dedicated and sanctified unto God's holy purposes for our lives. Therefore, we must henceforth devote our bodies and our spirits to God's glory alone!

ILLUSTRATING THE LESSON

The illustration shows that believers are both members of Christ's own body, the church, as well as the living temple of the Holy Spirit. We are therefore holy unto the Lord and must refrain from being corrupted by the world.

MEMBERS OF CHRIST'S BODY, THE TEMPLE OF THE HOLY SPIRIT!

Members of Christ's body

The temple of the Holy Spirit

CONCLUDING THE LESSON

Since we are no longer under the strict regulations of the law of Moses, we enjoy spiritual liberty in Christ. But not everything is appropriate for our standing as Christians.

Because we are all actual members of Christ's body, we have been dedicated to the holy purpose of serving Christ with our lives. In addition, because we are each indwelt by the very Holy Spirit of God, we are also the holy temple of God. Since we are so doubly sanctified and joined to both Christ and His Holy Spirit, we dare not defile ourselves with profane behaviors. We are holy; we must therefore pursue holiness in all that we do.

ANTICIPATING THE NEXT LESSON

Next week's lesson will focus on being sensitive toward other members of Christ's body, the church.

—*John Lody.*

PRACTICAL POINTS

1. God does not free us from the power of sin to have us brought under its power again (I Cor. 6:12).
2. God's people find ultimate fulfillment in pleasing Him (vs. 13).
3. The power that raised Christ from the dead is at work today to free believers from the bondage to sin (vss. 14-15).
4. Sexual immorality is acceptable in our culture, but it still offends God (vss. 16-17).
5. Sexual sin holds men and women in bondage; God desires that they be free (vs. 18)!
6. God has paid the price for believers to glorify Him with their bodies (vss. 19-20).

—Cheryl Y. Powell.

RESEARCH AND DISCUSSION

1. What are some Scriptures that Christians often misapply, taking them out of context? Discuss.
2. Are sexual sins worse than other sins? Why or why not? Discuss.
3. Is it possible for a believer to maintain sexual purity in today's culture?
4. What are some similarities between the sexual attitudes and practices of the Corinthian culture of Paul's day and the culture in which we live today?
5. What does it mean that your body is the temple of the Holy Spirit?

—Cheryl Y. Powell.

ILLUSTRATED HIGH POINTS

Not be brought under the power of any (I Cor. 6:12)

Paul is not so much interested in the permissibility of human behaviors as in the power they have to dictate to or even destroy us.

It is well-documented that many mood and mind-altering substances have the power to enslave their users. The temporary highs they experience will take them down a seemingly rosy path—but the end is despair.

Many addicts will fail to recognize addictions until significant harm has already been done. Paul wants us to nip such habits in the bud and stop dangerous behaviors before they take hold.

Not for fornication, but for the Lord (vs. 13)

A once impressive vessel, the Sam Ratulangi PB 1600 was found drifting near Yangon in Myanmar. This mysterious ghost ship was void of both cargo and personnel. Large and functional as she still was, authorities were baffled as to how this 580 ft. vessel, built in 2001, had ended up in a state of abandonment.

They soon learned that the vessel was being towed by a tugboat called *Independence* to a scrapyard for its final destruction. Before arriving, the towlines broke in a storm, and the vessel was lost.

Are we keeping our lives filled with His Holy Spirit, and are we using the precious cargo of His spiritual gifts? Or are we steering toward the scrapyard? Have we engaged the tugboat of "Independence" in order to get out of life what scraps we can salvage for our own selfish ends, or are we allowing the true Captain to steer the ship—bought with the precious blood of Christ?

—Therese Greenberg.

Golden Text Illuminated

"What? Know ye not that your body is the temple of the Holy Ghost which is in you, which ye have of God, and ye are not your own? For ye are bought with a price: therefore glorify God in your body, and in your spirit, which are God's" (I Corinthians 6:19-20).

Paul spends the second part of chapter six instructing the Corinthians on the proper use of the body. Learning that some members are involved in sexual immorality, he compellingly reminds them of their identity in Christ.

Many people believe that Christianity is opposed to sex, but scripturally literate believers know that sex is a good and precious gift from God. After the Lord created Adam and Eve, He told them, "Be fruitful, and multiply" (Gen. 1:28). The Song of Solomon extols the beauty of marital relations in lush, poetic imagery. In the New Testament, Jesus declares that God created male and female so that they might become "one flesh" (Mark 10:6-8).

Sexuality is good, but since God created us, He has the right to tell us how it should be used. Sadly, some in the Corinthian church were taking God's commands about sex lightly. For instance, a man in the church was actually having relations with his mother-in-law! Instead of disciplining them, the congregation actually was proud about it—perhaps patting themselves on the back for their misguided sense of tolerance and inclusion. Paul scathingly writes that this sin was so heinous that even the pagans would not speak of it (I Cor. 5:1)!

The city of Corinth was infamous as a center for sexual immorality. These loose morals of the city had apparently made their way into the church.

Because they had been purchased with the blood of Christ, Paul urged the believers at Corinth to use their bodies for the glory of God. But Paul goes further—he reminds them that they are the temple of the Holy Spirit.

Recall that the first temple, built by King Solomon in the tenth century B.C., was a breathtaking structure of stone, cedar wood, and gold. When Solomon dedicated the temple, divine fire fell, consuming his burnt offering. The Shekinah glory of the Lord filled the place with such awesome splendor that the priests themselves could not enter it (II Chr. 7:1-3).

Paul tells the Corinthians that the true temple, the one that God now indwells, is the body of the believer. He specifically uses a Greek word that means an inner shrine or sanctum where God Himself resides. Paul is alluding to the Holy of Holies. This is where the ark of the covenant resided, the golden chest that contained the tablets of the Ten Commandments. Once a year only, the Jewish High Priest entered this sacred place to atone for the sins of the people of Israel.

Paul never tells the Corinthians that their immoral behavior has removed their status as God's sanctuary. They are still the Holy Spirit's temple, but they have polluted it. They have grieved the Holy Spirit and quenched His fire (cf. Eph. 4:30; I Thess. 5:19). To become clean again, they must live according to their identity as people who have been washed, sanctified, and justified in the name of the Lord Jesus Christ (I Cor. 6:11).

—*Mark Winter.*

Heart of the Lesson

Jesus' death and resurrection have set believers free from the punishment for sin, which is spiritual death (cf. Rom. 8:2). That liberty, however, does not give us a free pass to commit sin without consequences. Rather, we have the freedom to choose obedience motivated by love and reverence for God.

In Corinth, the pagan temple of Aphrodite attracted many worshippers. This pagan worship centered around illicit sex with temple prostitutes. In the midst of this illicit sexuality, many Corinthian Christians interpreted their freedom as a license to sin rather than as an opportunity to submit to God.

1. A Christian's freedom (I Cor. 6:12-14). Through Christ, believers have received the promise that God will never condemn them for their sin (cf. Rom. 8:1). Some of the Corinthians, however, had misconstrued this truth to mean that believers were free to engage in any activity they desired. Paul gave them two questions to consider to determine if they were using their freedom in the right way. First, did their actions help or hurt themselves or others? Second, did their choice stem from a desire to exert power over others or result in slavery to sin?

Two of the most powerful bodily cravings are hunger and sexual desire. But not all sinful indulgence is equally damaging. Eating is a necessary and purely physical process. Sexuality, however, involves both the body and soul. While eating too much may cause indigestion and other physical problems, sexual sin will be a much more direct cause of emotional and spiritual damage, as well as possible physical harm.

Paul also reminded the Corinthians to evaluate their choices based on God's promise of resurrection. The bodies of believers will one day be raised imperishable (cf. I Cor. 15:54). This hope should influence how believers make decisions each day, including how they deal with their desires.

2. Christ's body (I Cor. 6:15-17). Jesus is the Head of the church, and each believer is part of His body (cf. Col. 1:18). If Christians commit sexual sin, they involve Christ in that sin and negatively affect the church, His body. Jesus died to pay for our sin, so to commit sexual sin mocks the cross and cheapens God's costly grace.

In the Old Testament, a marriage certificate or a licensed pastor did not unite a man and woman in marriage. When Isaac and Rebekah were married, they did not have an elaborate wedding ceremony. Their sexual union bonded them as husband and wife. If a person has multiple sexual partners, it is like marrying multiple spouses, which is polygamy and adultery. Each sexual union connects two people, soul and body. When that relationship ends, it is like getting a divorce. It causes deep pain to the people involved and profanes the name of Jesus.

3. God's dwelling place (I Cor. 6:18-20). Sexual immorality not only causes spiritual and emotional damage; it also can lead to venereal disease, sickness, and death. That is why Paul called sexual sin an attack on one's own body.

Paul reminded the Corinthians that just as the tabernacle and temple in the Old Testament signified the place where God dwelled (cf. Ex. 40:34), each Christian, body and soul, is God's dwelling place. God is holy, so His dwelling place must be holy. When Christians, in whom God's Spirit lives, engage in illicit sex, they are profaning God's temple.

—*Malia E. Rodriguez*

World Missions

The pursuit of happiness and the belief that we have a right to happiness has led some Christians to adopt a semi-hedonist philosophy. For example, a pastor's wife had an affair. She soothed her conscience and explained her actions to others by saying that her husband simply did not meet her needs. Her listeners nodded as if to say this reason made sense because everyone has the right to be happy.

In his book, *Of God and Men,* A. W. Tozer wrote, "The doctrine of man's inalienable right to happiness is anti-God and anti-Christ, and its wide acceptance by society tells us a lot about that same society."

The church at Corinth was infected by the gross sexual sin of one of its members. That particular sin was shocking even to outsiders, yet the church leaders not only did not address the issue, they were proud of their tolerance of it (I Cor. 5:1-5).

A blatant, unrepentant sinner, especially one tolerated by the church leadership, taints the whole church and brings outrage from outsiders. In *Life Together,* Dietrich Bonhoeffer writes, "Reproof is unavoidable. God's Word demands it when a brother falls into open sin. The practice of discipline in the congregation begins in the smallest circles. Where defection from God's Word in doctrine or life imperils the family fellowship and with it the whole congregation, the word of admonition and rebuke must be ventured" (HarperOne).

Correcting a brother or sister is no small matter. It must be prefaced by prayer, accompanied by godly wisdom, and grounded in Scripture. The goal of the corrector must be to rescue the sinner and to be faithful to God's Word. Bonhoeffer describes correction as a "ministry of mercy." If it is given and received in humility, it restores the sinner to a right relationship with God and with the church (Jas. 5:20). "Nothing can be more compassionate than the severe rebuke that calls a brother back from the path of sin" (Bonhoeffer).

How a Christian lives matters. When we were born again, we became the dwelling place of God; we are His temple. This sets us apart. We no longer belong to ourselves but to Him (I Cor. 6:19-20).

Sexual sin was not the only disturbing activity going on in the Corinthian church. Members who had grievances against one another took their cases before the civil courts. Thus, they made a mockery of God's love, the glue that binds the church together (John 13:35). It is better to be defrauded, Paul declared, than to cause outsiders to have contempt for the church (I Cor. 6:7-8).

A godly business owner was threatened with a lawsuit by a member of his church. The owner tried to settle the issue with the person, but he insisted on having his day in court. After prayer, the owner went to the man again and told him that if a court case ensued he would tell the judge to give the man whatever he wanted; he refused to participate in the grievous practice of one believer taking another to court. In the end, the plaintiff agreed to settle the matter out of court.

We were once slaves to sin, but Christ has made us servants of righteousness (Rom. 6:17-18). We are called to purity in speech, actions, and morals (Col. 3:1-17).

As missionaries spread the gospel around the world, they also must help those who struggle with sin, all the while watching that their own behavior does not grieve God (Gal. 6:1).

—*Rose McCormick Brandon.*

The Jewish Aspect

When Paul admonished the believers in Corinth about sexual immorality within the church, he used terminology that would help the Jewish believers understand the gravity of what was taking place. According to the Torah (the first five books of the Hebrew Scriptures), there were numerous sexual practices that were punishable by death, including incest and adultery. In Judaism, sex is permissible only within the context of a marriage. "Therefore shall a man leave his father and his mother, and shall cleave unto his wife; and they shall be one flesh" (Gen. 2:24). Two of the Ten Commandments warn against sexual immorality (Ex. 20:14, 17). "If God created man, woman, and their marriage relationship; and if the creation of man and woman is good and marriage a blessing; then God is a conscious, albeit silent, partner in the marriage. Thus the ideal Jewish marriage is a triangle composed of two human beings and their Creator" (www.myjewishlearning.com). The Lord also said that His people should be joined together with Him.

The Hebrew Scriptures have many accounts of the consequences of sexual immorality. One of the most notable is the adulterous relationship between David and Bathsheba, which resulted in conspiracy, murder, the death of David's infant son, and the eventual rebellion of David's son Absalom and his death as well (cf. II Sam. 12:10-11; 16:21-22).

"In Judaism, sexuality is viewed as having both positive and negative potential, depending on the context in which it is expressed. According to medieval Rabbinical enumerations of the 613 commandments, the commandment to procreate is the first mitzvah [commandment] in the Torah" (www.wikipedia.org). "The Jewish sages recognized that the sexual need of mankind (also known as Yitzra De'arayot) is essential for perpetuating society, despite having its negative sides which may lead to sins. For this reason, the classical rabbis' attitude and statements on the matter are dual, and they recognize two inclinations in mankind, the Yetzer hatov (the 'Good inclination') and the Yetzer hara (the 'evil inclination'), that can both influence sexuality and sexual behaviours" (www.reddit.com).

The admonition against sexual sin was a common warning throughout the Hebrew Scriptures and the New Testament (Matt. 5:28; Mark 7:22-23; Rom. 6:11-14; II Cor. 12:21; Eph. 5:3; Col. 3:5; Gal. 5:19; Heb. 13:4). This made it clear that sexual sin was a sin against God.

Paul's strong admonition to the church at Corinth used another analogy that the Jewish believers would have taken seriously. "What? know ye not that your body is the temple of the Holy Ghost which is in you, which ye have of God, and ye are not your own?" (I Cor. 6:19). The temple was the most important structure in ancient Judaism, the center of Israelite religious, cultural, and intellectual life. "The Holy Temple was the place where [God's] presence throughout the universe could be physically sensed. When the Temple stood, [God] was real to everyone. You didn't have to find Him—you just traveled to Jerusalem and connected to Him at His Temple. The Temple was a symbol of [God]: majestic, grand and awe-inspiring because [God] is majestic, grand and awe-inspiring. It was a shrine to [God] and all the things that ['God'] means: responsibility, morality, ethics, love, compassion, humility" (www.jattitude.net).

—Deborah Markowitz Solan.

Guiding the Superintendent

It would be very hard to distinguish the difference between the immorality of ancient Corinth and that of modern America. Paul would deal with the situation by focusing on the importance that the physical human body has in the Christian worldview.

DEVOTIONAL OUTLINE

1. Slogans (I Cor. 6:12-14). The apostle refers to two slogans that the believers were apparently using to justify their immoral behaviors.

"All things are lawful unto me" was the first slogan. Paul quotes this slogan as generally true, but with two essential qualifications. First, just because something is lawful does not mean it is beneficial, especially in regard to growing in holiness. A Christian should focus his behavior on those things that advance devotion and dedication to the service of Christ. Second, Christians should never indulge in a practice if it is likely to lead to a sinful addiction. Liberty should never become slavery.

"Meats for the belly, and the belly for meats" was the second slogan. This is also generally true. Hunger prompts us to sustain ourselves nutritionally, while the desire for sexual pleasure prompts us to multiply and sustain the human race. But both of these desires need God-ordained boundaries to keep them from becoming harmful or enslaving. In the case of food, we need to exercise moderation and wisdom. In the case of sexual desire, God has ordained the institution of marriage between one man and one woman.

Our physical bodies have been given to us to worship and glorify the Lord, not for immoral purposes. God raised Christ's body, not just His spirit.

2. Members of Christ (I Cor. 6:15-17). Paul reminds the believers of two key truths about the relationship between believers and Christ. The first truth is that, because believers are united to Christ, we are all members of Christ's own body, the church, His holy bride. Therefore, it should be obvious that it would be unconscionable for members of Christ's own body to defile themselves by engaging in sexual immorality.

The second truth is that, since the Scriptures clearly teach that sexual union also makes the two participants one flesh before God, believers who dare to engage in illicit sexual unions are blaspheming Christ Himself! Paul is not saying that such illicit unions qualify as true marriage; rather, he is showing the profound gravity of such sinful behaviors.

3. The temple of the Spirit (I Cor. 6:18-20). Paul next gives two commands to emphasize the importance of living a clean, moral life. The first command is, "Flee!" When faced with any temptation to commit sexual immorality, believers should react as Joseph of old did (Gen. 39:12)—flee the tempting situation and put it far away from you!

The second command is, "Honor!" Since believers have been bought with the price of Christ's own precious blood. They are to dedicate their bodies to honoring God alone since they are now the temple of the Holy Spirit.

CHILDREN'S CORNER

Some material in this lesson is too mature for young children to fully understand. For them, the emphasis should be on the importance of remembering that every part of our lives belongs to God.

—*Martin R. Dahlquist.*

SCRIPTURE LESSON TEXT

I COR. 8:1 Now as touching things offered unto idols, we know that we all have knowledge. Knowledge puffeth up, but charity edifieth.

2 And if any man think that he knoweth any thing, he knoweth nothing yet as he ought to know.

3 But if any man love God, the same is known of him.

4 As concerning therefore the eating of those things that are offered in sacrifice unto idols, we know that an idol *is* **nothing in the world, and that** *there is* **none other God but one.**

5 For though there be that are called gods, whether in heaven or in earth, (as there be gods many, and lords many,)

6 But to us *there is but* **one God, the Father, of whom** *are* **all things, and we in him; and one Lord Jesus Christ, by whom** *are* **all things, and we by him.**

7 Howbeit *there is* not in every man that knowledge: for some with conscience of the idol unto this hour eat *it* as a thing offered unto an idol; and their conscience being weak is defiled.

8 But meat commendeth us not to God: for neither, if we eat, are we the better; neither, if we eat not, are we the worse.

9 But take heed lest by any means this liberty of yours become a stumblingblock to them that are weak.

10 For if any man see thee which hast knowledge sit at meat in the idol's temple, shall not the conscience of him which is weak be emboldened to eat those things which are offered to idols;

11 And through thy knowledge shall the weak brother perish, for whom Christ died?

12 But when ye sin so against the brethren, and wound their weak conscience, ye sin against Christ.

13 Wherefore, if meat make my brother to offend, I will eat no flesh while the world standeth, lest I make my brother to offend.

NOTES

Concern for a Weaker Brother

Lesson Text: I Corinthians 8:1-13

Related Scriptures: Matthew 25:31-46; Romans 14:1-23;
I Corinthians 10:23-33; Galatians 5:1-15

TIME: A.D. 55   PLACE: from Ephesus

GOLDEN TEXT—"Wherefore, if meat make my brother to offend, I will eat no flesh while the world standeth, lest I make my brother to offend" (I Corinthians 8:13).

Introduction

Concern for other people should be a high priority for all Christians. We are called to serve others before ourselves (cf. Phil. 2:3-4). Sacrificial love should be one of the great hallmarks of the church, and people will be able to see our love for the Lord by the way we love one another (cf. John 13:35).

Sadly, this is not always a real practice with some believers. We still wrestle with sins such as selfishness even after we get saved, to the detriment of the church as well as those on the outside who are watching our lives. It is easy to get frustrated with others at times, especially if we feel like someone is holding us back.

This week's lesson reminds us that love is greater than liberty and that it is better to lay down our rights as Christians than to trample on the faith of a brother or sister in the Lord. This is difficult in our individualized society, but it is what Christ calls us to do.

LESSON OUTLINE

I. LOVE IS GREATER THAN KNOWLEDGE—I COR. 8:1-3

II. LOVE IS GREATER THAN IDOLATRY—I Cor. 8:4-6

III. LOVE IS GREATER THAN LIBERTY—I Cor. 8:7-13

Exposition: Verse by Verse

LOVE IS GREATER THAN KNOWLEDGE

I COR. 8:1 Now as touching things offered unto idols, we know that we all have knowledge. Knowledge puffeth up, but charity edifieth.

2 And if any man think that he knoweth any thing, he knoweth nothing yet as he ought to know.

3 But if any man love God, the same is known of him.

The issue of food (I Cor. 8:1). This letter from Paul to the Corinthians is actually a continuation of correspondence that had already been taking place between himself and some of the leaders of the church. Some have called I Corinthians an "occasional" document, meaning that it was written, at least in part, to address specific issues, or occasions, raised by the church.

{The eighth chapter begins with Paul considering a question raised concerning food, particularly meat, that had been offered to idols.}Q1 To a twenty-first century Christian, this is a non-issue, but to a first-century Christian living in a culture saturated with paganism, it was a huge deal. Greco-Roman culture was extremely polytheistic, meaning the people worshipped many gods instead of just one.

Meat that was sold in the marketplace and served at feasts and other social gatherings bore a strong likelihood of having been sacrificed in the temples to various pagan gods. This raised a serious question in the minds of some of the Christians in Corinth, who considered it a sin against God to eat food that had been offered to a false god. Not knowing how to handle this situation, they turned to Paul for guidance.

While some felt it was improper to eat food offered to idols, others felt it was perfectly fine to do so. Issues like this can be a source of division, as the church debated with whether or not it was permissible to eat this food and probably judged one another for their various opinions.

Many in Corinth were confident that they had sufficient knowledge to handle the issue. Paul did not argue with that. Lack of knowledge was not the issue, but rather how some were using their knowledge in their relationships with one another.

{Paul points out that knowledge by itself "puffeth up." It can lead to arrogance and selfishness. Love, on the other hand, builds up and seeks the benefit of others.}Q2 {Knowledge without love looks impressive at first, but it quickly becomes unattractive as the one who is puffed up uses his knowledge to tear down other believers rather than encourage them.}Q3 Knowledge without love creates pride in a person, causing him to look down on those he considers ignorant.

The issue of knowledge (I Cor. 8:2-3). Have you ever thought you knew something, only to find out later that you were wrong? That has probably happened to everyone at some time or another, and it is never a good feeling. In fact, it is downright humbling.

Paul states that knowledge apart from God is incomplete. This does not mean that unbelievers are unintelligent. It just means that they do not have a true framework for their knowledge because of their rejection of God. Knowledge should always be applied in love. Jesus said everything hangs on one's love for God and neighbor (Matt. 22:36-40). Knowledge is good and important, but only if used to love others.

Many among the educated elite do not know as much they think they do. They are smart people, but they can often be proud and arrogant because of their perceived knowledge and academic achievements. Their arrogance prevents them from seeing the truth and learning from it. For example, the scientist fully committed to Darwinism loathes any teaching that exposes his false philosophical presuppositions. This sometimes leads to personal attacks on the one who brings biblical truth to the argument. They have some knowledge, but not the greatest knowledge.

The greatest knowledge is the knowledge of God. This is not just knowing about God but knowing Him personally. {The greatest blessing of loving God is the fact that those who love Him are known by Him.}Q4 The intellects of the world are sure to think we are foolish, but as we have already learned, the wisdom of the world is foolishness to God. It is much better to love God and be known by Him than to appeal to the ever-shifting theories and opinions of man.

LOVE IS GREATER THAN IDOLATRY

4 As concerning therefore the eating of those things that are offered in sacrifice unto idols, we know that an idol is nothing in the world, and that there is none other God but one.

5 For though there be that are called gods, whether in heaven or in earth, (as there be gods many, and lords many,)

6 But to us there is but one God, the Father, of whom are all things, and we in him; and one Lord Jesus Christ, by whom are all things, and we by him.

The emptiness of idols (I Cor. 8:4). Paul now turns his attention back to the issue of food offered to idols, but only after having established love as the proper context for the question. He does not hide the fact that he claims to know something that pagans do not know, namely God. This means he not only has knowledge of the truth, but he also has love for his brother. Knowing God leads one to love others because God is love (cf. I John 4:8).

{Paul's knowledge that came from knowing God told him that idols were simply man-made objects with no authority.}[Q5] Christians agree that idols have no substance. Pagans, however, do not possess this knowledge, not because they are stupid, but because they do not love God. They are wrapped up in worship of false deities, which leads them away from the truth. Idols and false gods were merely figments of man's imagination.

There is only one God, and He has no rival or equal. {Man has created a multitude of gods in his own image, but the one and only true God has made man in His image. A god made in the image of man is no god at all.}[Q6] It has no power, no authority, and no voice. It can do nothing. Jesus Christ, God in the flesh, has all power, all authority, and a voice that is heard through all places in all times by those who love Him.

The sovereignty of God (I Cor. 8:5-6). False claims of deity do not supplant God. There are many forms of gods and idols in the world today. Along with these are a wide variety of philosophies, doctrines, and religions. The fact that other religions have their own gods or reject the existence of any god does not change the fact that there is only one true God.

Our faith in or rejection of God does not negate the truth of His existence. Truth does not hinge on whether we agree with it or not. People who do not believe in gravity do not float away. Gravity exists whether we acknowledge it or not. Likewise, God exists whether we acknowledge Him or not. Faith in God does not make Him more real. It is simply a submission to His authority and will for our lives.

Our Father God is the Creator and Sustainer of the universe and all life, even those who reject Him. We exist because of and for Him. We have one Lord, who is Jesus Christ, God's only Son. {Everything and everyone owe their existence to Jesus,}[Q7] and all humans are accountable to God the Father and God the Son. God is sovereign over all things, even those who reject and hate Him.

LOVE IS GREATER THAN LIBERTY

7 Howbeit there is not in every man that knowledge: for some with conscience of the idol unto this hour eat it as a thing offered unto an idol; and their conscience being weak is defiled.

8 But meat commendeth us not to God: for neither, if we eat, are we the better; neither, if we eat not, are we the worse.

9 But take heed lest by any means this liberty of yours become a stumblingblock to them that are weak.

10 For if any man see thee which hast knowledge sit at meat in the idol's temple, shall not the conscience of him which is weak be emboldened to eat those things which are offered to idols;

11 And through thy knowledge shall the weak brother perish, for whom Christ died?

12 But when ye sin so against the brethren, and wound their weak conscience, ye sin against Christ.

13 Wherefore, if meat make my brother to offend, I will eat no flesh while the world standeth, lest I make my brother to offend.

Understanding fellow believers (I Cor. 8:7). Because not everyone loves God, not everyone possesses the knowledge that Paul has just described. It is important not to judge these people by a modern, "enlightened" viewpoint. These were not stupid, dimwitted people. They were just indoctrinated by the pagan system that dominated their culture. Until Paul came along and planted the church in Corinth, paganism was the only thing they knew.

But the people Paul had in mind were Christians, so he knew they loved God. There was a subconscious issue at play here. Paul never condemned any of them for their hesitation. He was simply trying to teach the church the truth about their Christian freedoms in love.

The knowledge that idols are lifeless and meaningless allowed Paul and many of the Corinthian believers to have a clear conscience regarding eating food sacrificed to them. However, the consciences of many others were plagued by deep-seated convictions regarding idols, and some of these believers may not even have been totally convinced that idols had no power at all. They struggled to have free consciences regarding idolatry because false gods had been a huge part of their old lifestyle.

Paganism taught that there were multiple gods that all had to be worshipped. These gods controlled different things, such as weather, fertility, fire, water, and more. People had to pray to and appease each of them to get what they wanted. Paul then came to town with a message that there is only one God, which ran counter to everything the Corinthians understood.

{It is easy to see how the Corinthians' past belief in the power of idols could still affect their consciences. They had genuinely trusted in Christ, but for many of them, eating food that had been offered to idols still felt like idolatry and was a great stumbling block to their newfound faith.}[Q8]

Many in the church today who have been strongly influenced by bad philosophy and wrong teaching struggle to walk away from what they have believed their whole lives. It takes time for the truth of the gospel to sink in and transform all areas of life.

Loving fellow believers (I Cor. 8:8-11). The most important thing here to Paul is not food. In fact, food was of little consequence to him. We are not more spiritual because we abstain from certain foods or less spiritual because we eat certain foods. Our diet does not bring us closer to God. To Paul, food—and the question that had been raised about it—was not the actual issue. He knew well enough that the people who ate the food in question were no worse off than those who abstained—and vice versa.

What was important to Paul was the way those with strong faith treated those with weaker faith. Some of the Corinthian Christians really struggled with food offered to idols; it was a crisis of faith for them. Instead of pushing them to act on their liberties, Paul sternly instructed those who felt free to eat this meat not to become a stumbling block for a brother or sister whose faith was not as strong. We may exercise our Christian liberty, but what good is it if it damages another person's faith?

The knowledge we have in Christ should never be used as a weapon against weaker brothers or sisters. It is important to be patient with them, not denying the freedom we have in Jesus but not pushing them to violate their consciences, either.

I once knew a young man who had struggled with drugs and alcohol since he was a boy. He later became a Christian. Our group of friends took him in and invited him to every get-together we had. One of our favorite things was to meet and play games on Friday and Saturday nights. One game in particular, though, brought his thoughts and emotions back to his partying days, and he began to struggle with old habits.

There was nothing immoral or inappropriate about this game. It just brought back bad memories for him. Instead of telling him to get over it and that there was no need for him to feel that way, we put the game away and did not play it again. His faith was more important than the freedom we felt in playing it. Our brother was more important than our liberty.

Caring for fellow believers (I Cor. 12-13). There is never an excuse to neglect loving another person. There is no question that we have freedom in Christ, but we must understand that everyone has a different level of maturity and understanding of spiritual things.

The world has influenced each of us in different ways, and we will not be free of the effects of sin on our minds and hearts until we reach heaven. {Just because a brother may be "weak" in one area never merits disrespect. In fact, if we judge them, it shows that we are weak in Christian love, which is even worse.}Q9 People are all at dif-ferent places in their walk with Christ.

Jesus does not love those who are mature more than others who seem to be lagging behind. This is not to say that God does not expect us to grow and mature, but He sets the pace for each of us, and we need to trust Him in that.

Preferring personal liberty over another person's soul is sin. Christian liberty should never be used in a selfish way. {We should always be willing to help a weaker brother or sister mature in their faith, even if it means laying aside some of our rights.}Q10 That is the attitude of love, and love is greater than liberty.

—Robert Ferguson, Jr.

QUESTIONS

1. What was the main consideration Paul deals with in this chapter?

2. What is the main difference between knowledge and love?

3. What is the problem with having knowledge without love?

4. What is the greatest blessing of loving God?

5. What did Paul understand about idols that the pagans did not?

6. What is the main difference between the pagan "gods" and the one true God?

7. To whom do we owe our existence?

8. Why was eating food offered to idols such a stumbling block for some Christians in Corinth?

9. How do other people's weaknesses often show us our own weaknesses?

10. What does it sometimes cost us as Christians to help a brother or sister mature in faith?

—Robert Ferguson, Jr.

Preparing to Teach the Lesson

In chapter 7, Paul has been addressing issues concerning whether or not a Christian should marry or remain single. This was the first of many practical applications he makes throughout his epistle to the church at Corinth concerning what it means to be holy members of the body of Christ.

Now Paul turns his attention specifically to the question of eating food that previously had been offered to pagan deities and then resold in the marketplace. Some at Corinth held that it was their right to eat such food, since idols are actually just nonentities that only matter to unbelievers. But others held that to eat such food made one a collaborator with the idol worshippers. They were horrified that any Christian would have anything to do with anything that had been used as part of such worship.

Paul's constant priority since the initial chapter of this epistle is for the church to be unified in love and humility, not divided by strife and controversy. Its witness before the world needs to remain clear and compelling.

TODAY'S AIM

Facts: to learn the difference between just having knowledge and having love for the brethren.

Principle: to understand that although knowledge can be helpful, being proud of your knowledge does not show love for fellow believers.

Application: to strive above all for genuine humility and love in our behavior toward others.

INTRODUCING THE LESSON

Some at Corinth valued their superior knowledge more than the spiritual welfare of those whose consciences were sensitive. Paul admonished these prideful people, declaring that their values were topsy-turvy. The conscience of a fellow Christian is worth infinitely more than anything we may think we know.

DEVELOPING THE LESSON

1. Knowledge versus love (I Cor. 8:1-3). In turning his attention toward the issue of whether it was OK to eat food offered to idols, Paul first establishes the superior importance of Christian love ("charity") to knowledge. He addresses those who rely on their erudition to hold prominent status in the church.

In short, he tells these know-it-alls that they actually know nothing as they ought to know it. Their insistence on their personal liberty at the expense of those with weak consciences reveals the true deficiency in their thinking. They need to make loving God and being truly known by Him their first priority.

2. Only one God (I Cor. 8:4-6). Paul readily concedes that in reality, all idols are vain fictions that have no power to do anything for their worshippers. Although the multitudes of the world may pretend that there are many gods and goddesses, Christians understand that this is all so much nonsense. There is only one God and one Lord Jesus Christ; all other so-called gods are nothing but empty and impotent products of the imaginations of those who remain in spiritual darkness.

3. Love for the weak (I Cor. 8:7-13). Having conceded this point, Paul points out that those who know this should also realize that they cannot assume universal understanding of this principle. Many still abhor the idea of having contact with anything that is associated with idols and see the consumption of food offered to an idol as participation in idol worship.

If someone who had that conviction were to go ahead and partake of such food, their conscience would be convicted of having committed the sin of idolatry. The guilt they would feel over their sin might even cause them to stumble and fall away from the faith!

Paul challenges those who are so proud of their knowledge to ponder this: Is any food or drink worth the spiritual ruin of a soul? Does eating any food or drink gain favor with God? If a fellow believer sees eating such food as idolatry, is it worth alienating him or leading him morally astray by eating it and setting a questionable example?

Paul then makes it clear in verse 12 that using one's liberty in such a reckless way is a sin against the Lord Jesus Christ. To do anything that induces a believer to wander back into the moral corruption of the world is an affront to Christ's sacrificial death. He endured that death to make the believer holy unto God.

For the sake of a brother in Christ (and, by reasonable implication, for the sake of a potential future brother in Christ as well!), Paul affirms that it would be better to never eat meat at all "while the world standeth" (vs. 13) than to stubbornly insist on exercising Christian liberty by eating it. Paul would rather forgo any behavior until the end of the world for the sake of a fellow believer's weak conscience. Would you?

We are called to "let nothing be done through strife or vainglory; but in lowliness of mind let each esteem other better than themselves" (Phil. 2:3).

Of course, it would be missing the point here to interpret this verse as somehow recommending vegetarianism or veganism. The particular context plainly places Paul's emphasis on refraining from *anything* (not just meat) that might cause a fellow Christian to be led astray from the path of holiness to which we are all called in Christ.

ILLUSTRATING THE LESSON

How we use our knowledge shows whether we love our fellow believers. Flaunting our freedoms is hurtful.

NOT ARROGANT KNOWLEDGE, BUT LOVE AND HUMILITY

Proudly flaunting our knowledge may spiritually hurt fellow believers

Love, compassion, and humble service build up others in the faith

CONCLUDING THE LESSON

Paul's highest priority throughout this epistle to the church at Corinth is their unity in true Christian love. He recognized another force that had been dividing the believers there: arrogance based on knowledge and sophistication. The issue of whether to eat foods that had been offered to idols was just one more area in which some Corinthians were big on brains but lacking in heart.

Whenever we face controversial issues within the body of Christ, we must retain Paul's priorities of love, humility, and unity in the faith. Pray for the leadership of your church that they would always make these Christian virtues paramount.

ANTICIPATING THE NEXT LESSON

In next week's lesson, Paul instructs his Corinthian readers about the Lord's Supper. Some of the believers there were not taking this sacred ordinance seriously, and thereby were incurring God's judgment on themselves.

—*John Lody.*

PRACTICAL POINTS

1. Unity in God's kingdom is built on love, not on pride in knowledge (I Cor 8:1).
2. God honors those whose lives are shaped by love for Him and His people (vss. 2-3).
3. The false gods of this world have only the power that men give them (vss. 4-5).
4. Believers find value and purpose in living for the one true God (vs. 6).
5. Mature believers help others grow in faith by choosing love over liberty (vss. 7-9).
6. Be aware that young Christians look to mature Christians for their examples (vss. 10-13).

—Cheryl Y. Powell.

RESEARCH AND DISCUSSION

1. What risks do believers take when they rely on knowledge above other considerations?
2. How does a believer's love for God impact his or her approach to conflict with others? Discuss.
3. What Bible passages are often misinterpreted to suggest that there are other gods?
4. What responsibility do mature believers, who are more knowledgeable about Christian liberty, have toward those who are weaker in faith and knowledge? Discuss.
5. How can Christians avoid legalism (cf. Gal. 2:1-21; 5:1-14)? Why should we avoid legalism? Discuss.

—Cheryl Y. Powell.

ILLUSTRATED HIGH POINTS

Knowledge puffeth up, but charity edifieth (I Cor. 8:1)

Jerry Jesch was educated and knowledgeable regarding social psychology. His uncle, Commander Dale Barnes, was a retired naval officer, a gentle, contemplative man of great intelligence.

The younger man understood the value of his elder's advice and would visit him twice a week just to discuss the questions of life. Together, they came to this insightful conclusion, "Wisdom is knowledge and understanding, compassionately brought to bear." In other words, wisdom is about how much like Christ we actually apply our knowledge to life.

As someone so wittily put it, "Knowledge is knowing that a tomato is actually a fruit; wisdom is not putting it in a fruit salad!"

Stumblingblock to them that are weak (vs. 9)

The Indians called it "Manisses," or "island of the little god," while the maps label it "Block Island." Sailors have nicknamed this tiny Long Island Sound mass "The Stumbling Block."

The island's history can teach us an important lesson. Homes were built to resemble England's Victorian era, and tourists flocked there on weekends reminiscing of simpler days. Sadly, a few years after this seemingly successful transformation, a 1938 hurricane destroyed most of the structures on Block Island.

The things we allow, that we justify as Christians, may seem nothing more than workable, pleasant, personal choices. They may seem ever so small in our estimation—but what of our brethren? Are we content to let their lives be ravaged by our tiny pet privileges?

—Therese Greenberg.

Golden Text Illuminated

"Wherefore, if meat make my brother to offend, I will eat no flesh while the world standeth, lest I make my brother to offend" (I Corinthians 8:13).

Would you eat a halal steak?

Halal, an Arabic word meaning "permissible" or "lawful," is meat prepared according to strict Islamic standards. Before slaughtering an animal, a Muslim butcher must face Mecca and invoke the name of Allah.

Some Christians might feel uneasy consuming meat that has been consecrated to Allah, while others might simply view it as a tasty steak with no spiritual connotations. Now you have a sense of what was going on in the church of Corinth.

The ancient Greeks and Romans worshipped a pantheon of gods, which included regular sacrifices to their patron deities. One notable site was Caesarea Philippi, where Peter made his famous confession about Christ. This city was known for its dedication to Pan, the goat-footed deity of the desolate woods and wilds. Sacrifices to Pan occurred here, as well as pagan fertility rituals.

Pagans who had converted to Christianity knew all about these heathen practices, rejecting anything to do with idols. Jews who had become believers also eschewed meat that had been sacrificed to pagan gods. This, of course, was deeply ingrained in their collective conscience. The second of the Ten Commandments forbade the manufacture or worship of any graven image (Ex. 20:4-6). A Jewish Christian in Corinth would know all this, and therefore he would be diligent in avoiding any hint of idolatry.

In those days, a shopper might buy meat that had been sacrificed to an idol. In I Corinthians 8:10, we read that some Christians ate such meat in the pagan temple itself. This offended their fellow Christians who believed that such food was forbidden; yet the Christians who consumed such consecrated meat insisted that it was permissible. Paul actually agreed with the latter group: "We know that an idol is nothing in the world, and that there is none other God but one" (vs. 4).

Though Paul believed that an idol is not really any deity at all, he cautioned those who would violate the conscience of another for the sake of liberty. What was important in this matter was not how much knowledge one had, but how much love one had for fellow believers.

Paul repeats this principle in Romans 14:1-4, warning Christians not to judge others over their eating preferences. In Galatians 5:13, the apostle writes that freedom in Christ is no excuse for provoking doubt or temptation in fellow believers.

Though Paul admits that he finds no food unclean, this does not mean he or anyone else has the right to violate someone else's conscience over such a matter. If he knew that certain Christians will not eat meat for moral reasons, neither will he in their presence.

Spiritual knowledge and Christian liberty are good things, but they should not be used to place a stumbling block in the path of a brother or sister in Christ. Paul admonished that such action is to sin against Christ Himself (I Cor. 8:12). We must be careful to temper our knowledge and liberty with the love of God.

—Mark Winter.

Heart of the Lesson

There were many temples to the Greek and Roman gods in Corinth. When food was sacrificed in these pagan temples, the leftover food would be sold in the market place. Many who had become Christians at Corinth still thought that these leftovers were defiled by being part of the sacrifices to pagan deities. They would have nothing to do with such leftovers.

Other Corinthian Christians realized that the pagan gods were really nothing at all. They understood that the leftovers that were sold in the market place were just food; there was nothing morally wrong with eating it. These Christians felt that their liberty in Christ allowed them to freely eat such food.

1. True liberty (I Cor. 8:1-6). In order to address the misunderstandings and conflicts at Corinth over this issue, Paul started with this principle: knowledge without love is prideful (cf. I Cor. 13:1-3). As the Corinthian believers pursued holiness before God and fellowship with each other, the apostle reminded them that love is first of all humble and considerate of the needs of others.

When Paul had established the Corinthian church, he had taught them that there is only one God, and that idols, or so-called gods, have no power (cf. Ps. 115:4-8). When it came to the issue of eating food that had been sacrificed to such idols, Paul rightly taught that everything was created good by God the Father through Jesus Christ. Christians, therefore, had the freedom to eat food from any source, as long as they received it as a gift from the true and living God. But not every Christian at Corinth understood this, resulting in arrogance on the one hand and accusations of sin on the other instead of love, patience, and consideration for one another.

2. Limited liberty (I Cor. 8:7-8). Some of the more mature believers in Corinth knew that nothing that they ate could spiritually defile them (cf. Matt. 15:11), especially since Christ's death and resurrection had cleansed them from all sin. Even though they used to participate in feasts featuring food offered to idols, these mature believers had repented of their former foolishness, which freed them to eat this food with a clear conscience.

There were some Corinthian Christians, however, who still believed it was a sin to eat such idol-associated food. Even though Paul had taught that believers are justified only by their faith in Jesus, not by what they eat, some Corinthians struggled with how to live in a pagan culture.

3. Loving liberty (I Cor. 8:9-13). When it came to the issue of food offered to idols, mature (strong) and immature (weak) Christians in Corinth clashed. The strong believers held to their freedom in Christ, causing weak believers to stumble in their walk with God. Paul reminded the mature believers that although their consciences allowed them to eat meat sacrificed to idols, love for less mature believers should motivate them to refrain from flaunting their freedom to the spiritual detriment of their brothers and sisters in Christ.

Knowledge without love is pride. A Christian should never place his or her freedom in Christ above the needs and limitations of weaker sisters and brothers in Christ. As an illustration of this principle, Paul was willing to forgo all meat in order to show brotherly love to others. Paul did not ask believers to deny their knowledge, maturity, or liberty in Christ, but to exercise them in love.

—*Malia E. Rodriguez.*

World Missions

One of the most difficult Christian disciplines is putting others ahead of ourselves. A missionary must have an especially tender heart for the lost, living by a love that rises above their own needs and desires.

A pastor once confessed to me that when he was young, he preached an unbalanced message focused on the freedom we have in Christ. While spiritual freedom is an important truth, he realized he had failed to consider how one believer's freedom might affect another in an adverse way. He changed his emphasis and now balances Christian freedom with the obligation to reflect on how our actions might hurt others.

Paul taught that our freedom should not lead us to value our physical desires over spiritual concerns. So adamant was he about this that he pledged never to eat meat again if doing so offended the conscience of another. The context of Paul's pledge was the eating of meat that had been offered to idols. Some believers, former idol worshippers, had pledged never to have anything to do with idols again, including the eating of meat offered to them. Others recognized that idols are not really gods but mere inanimate objects with no life in them. Therefore, they had no qualms about eating such meat.

There was no real right or wrong concerning the eating of meat or the honoring of one day over another, which was another area of dispute at Corinth. The real offense was found in the lack of love and consideration that exercising such freedoms might entail in tempting believers with less knowledge, enticing them perhaps to follow the lead of a stronger Christian and thus causing them to violate their own consciences.

The freedoms Paul cites here are nonessential ones to the Christian life. That is why he says that neither the weaker nor the stronger should look down on the other (Rom. 14:13). However, if we believe an act to be sinful, then for us it is (vs. 14). The weaker believer should not exult in his abstinence and the stronger one should not flaunt his liberty.

One thing is clear: there should be no quarrels over these nonessential differences, as they run the risk of causing division in the church. In essential matters, as when the Judaizers insisted on circumcision, Paul was inflexible in his assertion that these people were false teachers. In the strongest language he repudiated them, using the expression, "Let him be accursed" (Gal. 1:8-9).

If a believer is deterred in his walk with Jesus, or is filled with sorrow because we flaunt our freedoms, whatever they may be, then we have not acted in the love of Christ. Now that we are set free from slavery to sin, we are free to honor God in everything we do (I Cor. 10:31).

John Piper writes, "The great foundation for our forbearance of one another is that God has accepted us in Jesus Christ. The weak and the strong believe in Christ who died for them. They are accepted by God in Christ. We should accept them with all their differences" ("How to Welcome a Weak Brother," desiringgod.org).

There is joy in mentoring a new believer. All care should be taken to nurture them in love. Sometimes a misguided comment or a critical word can do harm. Young Christians look to mature ones for guidance, and their disappointments in us can be serious or even faith-damaging. Our freedom should always be tempered by love. Paul did his best to be considerate of everyone's feelings, and he instructed the church to do the same (I Cor. 10:31-33).

—*Rose McCormick Brandon.*

The Jewish Aspect

Idolatry was forbidden by the Lord throughout the Hebrew Scriptures. The first and second commandments spoke directly against idolatry (Ex. 20:3-4); however, the history of the Israelites was filled with it. "Israel's calling was to the worship of the one true God. God's election separated the people from unholiness and to himself as his special possession. The covenant provided legal parameters for this unique relationship, and the limitation of exclusive worship was a significant part of the covenant" (www.biblestudytools.com).

Idol worship, in ancient times, consisted of performing pagan rituals, bowing down to idols, and bringing food and drink offerings to them. Eating the sacrifice was an important part of the ritual. The issue of food sacrificed to idols was discussed, in detail, by the apostle Paul to the believers at Corinth (I Cor. 8:1-13; 10:23-33). "Even the relatively ordinary household duties of buying meat from the butcher or going out to dinner with friends were fraught with problems. Some butchers bought their produce wholesale from the pagan temples where it had been ritually slaughtered or partially offered as a sacrifice to idols. Christians in Corinth were unsure whether or not to buy such meat, or to eat it if it was set in front of them" (J. A. Thompson, *Handbook of Life in Bible Times,* InterVarsity Press).

The Council of Jerusalem retained Jewish dietary restrictions for Gentile believers, including eating food contaminated by idols (Acts 15:20, 29; 21:25). Paul also specifically addressed this issue with the new, formerly pagan, believers at Corinth. "The former pagans of Corinth who became believers knew that even though they once worshipped idols, offering similar sacrifices in the same shrines, God has forgiven their past sins. Further, as believers they do not offer such sacrifices now; rather they know that the idols to which they sacrificed have 'no real existence' at all" (David H. Stern, *Jewish New Testament Commentary,* JNT Publications). Hebrew Scriptures also confirmed the worthlessness of idols (Isa. 45:20; Jer. 51:17-18; Ps 106:28).

Paul's emphasis, however, was on something far greater than food, regarding which he said, "But meat commendeth us not to God: for neither, if we eat, are we the better; neither, if we eat not, are we the worse" (I Cor. 8:8). Paul was more concerned with the spiritual welfare of believers who are weak in faith. Any knowledge regarding food sacrificed to idols or the liberty to eat it paled in comparison to concerns about becoming a stumbling block to those with a weak conscience. Paul recognized that eating food sacrificed to idols might cause harm to those who are weak in faith (Rom. 14:1-6). "Paul lays the groundwork for them resolving their conflicting ideas toward idols by stressing not what they know but how much they love" (www.biblicalresearchresources.com).

Paul emphasized that concern for the brethren is more important than knowledge, and that the fulfillment of the law was to love your neighbor as yourself (Gal. 5:13-14). Love builds up the body of Christ; knowledge, unless it is governed by love, creates selfish pride.

—*Deborah Markowitz Solan*

Guiding the Superintendent

A believer is allowed freedom of conscience in matters not specifically forbidden by Scripture. But a specific situation had arisen in the Corinthian church that required a careful interpretation of this principle. It involved the question of whether it was lawful for a Christian to eat meat that had been offered to idols.

In a city filled with pagan temples, some of the best deals on food would have involved the sale of meat left over from pagan sacrifices. Because idols are false gods and therefore really nothing, Paul advised the Corinthian believers that it was technically lawful for them to eat such food. But there was another consideration that had to be addressed regarding this issue. There are cases when a believer should abstain from such liberties. In dealing with this issue, the apostle would elaborate upon the principle of Christian love to arrive at his answer.

DEVOTIONAL OUTLINE

1. Love, not knowledge (I Cor. 8:1-3). Every believer has some knowledge; some have more than others. But because of the propensity of increased knowledge to engender pride, Paul asserts the superiority of love over knowledge. Paul is not rejecting sound doctrine. He is merely saying that the accumulation of knowledge in and of itself can easily lead to arrogance and conceit if it is not tempered with Christlike love for fellow Christians.

2. Idols are vain (I Cor. 8:4-6). Because there is only one true God, idols are nothing. All the other things that people worship as gods are falsehoods, and those who worship them are deceived. Therefore, it was, in principle, lawful to eat meat that had been offered to something that in actuality does not exist.

The only true God is the heavenly Father of our Lord Jesus Christ. All things exist because He created them, and the reason we exist is to honor and glorify Him. The Father created all things through Christ.

3. Love over liberty (I Cor. 8:7-13). With this knowledge of who God is and that idols are nothing, it is little wonder that some in the church at Corinth had not hesitated to eat the sacrificial meat from pagan temples, giving little thought to other considerations.

However, there were some members of the church who had been so steeped in idolatry before their conversion to Christ that they still felt that eating meat offered to idols was the same as worshiping pagan gods.

Before Paul goes on to offer his pastoral instruction on the issue, he reminds his readers that whether or not we eat certain foods has nothing to do with pleasing God or serving Him. Neither is God favorably impressed by the pride we take in our knowledge or the lack of consideration we might show in exercising our freedoms.

Paul does not discount the value of godly learning or freedom per se, but he warns the Corinthians that using their freedom in a manner that could cause a fellow believer to sin is itself a sin against Christ Himself.

Love is the priority of the Christian life. For the sake of the conscience of a weaker Christian, Paul would abstain from eating such food forever.

CHILDREN'S CORNER

Like adults, children often like to exercise their freedoms regardless of who gets hurt. This lesson should focus on learning to become sensitive to the feelings of others.

—*Martin R. Dahlquist.*

SCRIPTURE LESSON TEXT

I COR. 11:20 When ye come together therefore into one place, *this* is not to eat the Lord's supper.

21 For in eating every one taketh before *other* his own supper: and one is hungry, and another is drunken.

22 What? have ye not houses to eat and to drink in? or despise ye the church of God, and shame them that have not? What shall I say to you? shall I praise you in this? I praise *you* not.

23 For I have received of the Lord that which also I delivered unto you, That the Lord Jesus the *same* night in which he was betrayed took bread:

24 And when he had given thanks, he brake *it,* and said, Take, eat: this is my body, which is broken for you: this do in remembrance of me.

25 After the same manner also *he took* the cup, when he had supped, saying, This cup is the new testament in my blood: this do ye, as oft as ye drink *it,* in remembrance of me.

26 For as often as ye eat this bread, and drink this cup, ye do shew the Lord's death till he come.

27 Wherefore whosoever shall eat this bread, and drink *this* cup of the Lord, unworthily, shall be guilty of the body and blood of the Lord.

28 But let a man examine himself, and so let him eat of *that* bread, and drink of *that* cup.

29 For he that eateth and drinketh unworthily, eateth and drinketh damnation to himself, not discerning the Lord's body.

30 For this cause many *are* weak and sickly among you, and many sleep.

31 For if we would judge ourselves, we should not be judged.

32 But when we are judged, we are chastened of the Lord, that we should not be condemned with the world.

33 Wherefore, my brethren, when ye come together to eat, tarry one for another.

34 And if any man hunger, let him eat at home; that ye come not together unto condemnation. And the rest will I set in order when I come.

NOTES

74

Thoughts on the Lord's Supper

Lesson Text: I Corinthians 11:20-34

Related Scriptures: Matthew 26:26-28; Mark 14:22-24;
Luke 22:17-20; I Corinthians 10:14-22

TIME: A.D. 55   PLACE: from Ephesus

GOLDEN TEXT—"For as often as ye eat this bread, and drink this cup, ye do shew the Lord's death till he come" (I Corinthians 11:26).

Introduction

One of the great privileges of the Christian life is our participation in the Lord's Supper, or communion. It is where we, as a body of believers, observe and remember the death of Jesus on the cross. Jesus gave us this in order that we would never forget the sacrifice He made for us.

Communion is an important part of our walk with Christ. It should never be done in such a way that it loses its significance in our hearts. It should not be seen as just a part of our church service. It should be done, every time, as a memorial of the sacrifice Jesus made for us on the cross.

Communion is reserved for believers in Christ. There is no saving power in it.

We are not saved because we eat the bread and drink the cup. We do so because we are saved. There *is* a unifying effect on those who come together in love and remember what Christ did for us on the cross. Without the death of Jesus, there would be no resurrection and we would be dead in sin.

LESSON OUTLINE

I. REBUKE FOR SELFISHNESS—
   I COR. 11:20-22

II. THE BODY AND THE BLOOD—
   I Cor. 11:23-26

III. SELF-EXAMINATION—
   I Cor. 11:27-34

Exposition: Verse by Verse

REBUKE FOR SELFISHNESS

I COR. 11:20 When ye come together therefore into one place, this is not to eat the Lord's supper.

21 For in eating every one taketh before other his own supper: and one is hungry, and another is drunken.

22 What? have ye not houses to eat and to drink in? or despise ye the church of God, and shame them that have not? What shall I say to you? shall I praise you in this? I praise you not.

Paul's contention (I Cor. 11:20-21). Division was an ongoing problem in the Corinthian church in more ways than one. As we have studied, some were divided over their favorite preachers while others were divided over the exercise of Christian liberty when it came to eating food offered to idols.

Another area of division came in the observance of the Lord's Supper (vs. 18). Not surprisingly, economic status varied in the church, as the gospel was preached to both the wealthy and the poor. {Dividing lines were drawn between the rich and the poor at the Lord's Supper, with the rich gorging themselves while the poor were being shut out.}[Q1] Word got back to Paul that they were not serving the Lord's Supper in a loving way, and this caused him to issue a stern rebuke to the church.

When the church would gather, there would typically be a common meal served for everyone to enjoy and participate in. The meal that was served was called the "Lord's Supper," as the bread and the cup were featured in it. {But Paul points out that the people were not really eating the Lord's Supper, regardless of what they called it. Nothing about what the Corinthians were doing even closely resembled what Christ would have approved of or practiced Himself.}[Q2]

The problem with the way the Corinthians were observing the meal was that every person was out for himself. Each person treated the meal as though it were his own instead of the communal meal it was intended to be. Those who had plenty to bring had plenty to eat, but those who had little or nothing to bring were left out and went hungry. Others were using the time as an opportunity to get drunk. Drunkenness was a common feature of pagan worship feasts, and this may have been a hold-over for some of the Corinthians.

The church's community meal was a perfect opportunity for the poor to have a feast. For some, it might have been the best meal they had all week. Sadly, the poor were treated with contempt by the wealthy, who should have been looking out for them and sharing with them.

Paul's rebuke (I Cor. 11:22). Paul was alarmed at what he had heard concerning the observance of the Lord's Supper. He asked the church why they were using this community meal as an opportunity to eat like they would at home. He points out that when they gathered together, it was supposed to be for a greater purpose than a regular meal. They were to share so that everyone could partake equally.

If the meal was to be called the "Lord's Supper," it should be conducted in a way that was consistent with the Lord's character and example. Jesus would never have gorged Himself and let the poor go hungry. Instead, He would have rebuked anyone who did so.

To treat the poor in such a contemptible way was to despise the church of God and humiliate the poor. God had always commanded that those with means should care for the poor and not treat them as second-class citizens (cf Jas. 2:1-7). {In Paul's mind, the Corinthians' selfish practices were repulsive, and he set out to remind them of what the Lord's Supper was really all about.}[Q]

THE BODY AND THE BLOOD

23 For I have received of the Lord that which also I delivered unto you, That the Lord Jesus the same night in which he was betrayed took bread:

24 And when he had given thanks, he brake it, and said, Take, eat: this is my body, which is broken for you: this do in remembrance of me.

25 After the same manner also he took the cup, when he had supped, saying, **This cup is the new testament in my blood: this do ye, as oft as ye drink it, in remembrance of me.**

26 For as often as ye eat this bread, and drink this cup, ye do shew the Lord's death till he come.

The revelation entrusted to Paul (I Cor. 11:23). As upset as Paul may have been with the Corinthians' behavior, he was not content with just shaming them with his rebuke and leaving them to their sin. They needed to be instructed on how to conduct themselves at the Lord's table. This is not to say that he had never given them proper teaching on this issue, but he felt it necessary to teach them again.

{Paul had received instructions on the Lord's Supper from Jesus Himself.}Q4 He was not taught this by anyone else, nor did he formulate his own directives. Christ taught him, and he passed that teaching on to the Corinthians. For them to disobey Paul was the same as disobeying God, since this was Jesus' own teaching on this matter.

The Lord's Supper originated with Jesus the night He was betrayed by Judas Iscariot. None of the events of that night or the following day caught Jesus off guard, and He showed the church through the apostles how He wants us to remember Him.

Jesus never lost sight of the purpose of His death. Onlookers may have thought it resulted from the demands of an angry mob. Jesus knew it was always about purchasing and securing the redemption of sinners and reconciling fallen man with a holy God. Jesus was not preoccupied with His suffering and death. The most important thing to Him was our redemption.

The body (I Cor. 11:24). At the very first communion service, Jesus gave thanks and broke the bread apart (cf. Luke 22:19). Just as He gave thanks to God for the bread, we must give thanks to God for giving us His only Son, the

Bread of Life (John 6:35). It is this Living Bread that sustains us throughout our lives and gives us life eternal.

{The bread that was broken was symbolic of the fact that Jesus' own body would be ravaged just hours later.}Q5 This body that never inflicted pain on anyone would be riddled with pain. Hands that held the hurting and feet that walked on water to rescue the frightened disciples were nailed to a cross. Eyes that were filled with love were filled with blood from a crown of thorns. A heart full of compassion was pierced by the end of a spear. All of this, Jesus said, was for us. He gave His body for us, and we are to eat the bread in remembrance of Him.

The blood (I Cor. 11:25-26). After distributing the broken pieces of bread, Jesus then took the cup. {The cup represents the blood of Jesus and introduces the new covenant between God and His people, one which we are still under today.}Q6 Jesus made a new covenant and ratified it with His blood.

The blood of Jesus is precious because God used it to redeem us from sin (cf. I Pet. 1:18-19). The Innocent took the place of the guilty so the guilty could go free. Jesus shed His blood and died so we could live. We have the blessed promise of living with Him forever because He rose from the dead (I Cor. 15:20).

Just as we eat the bread in remembrance of Jesus, we also drink the cup in remembrance of Him. {We proclaim the death of Christ by eating the bread and drinking the cup, and the church is to continue this practice until Christ returns.}Q7 When we partake of communion, our minds must be focused on Jesus and the sacrifice He made for us. Our minds should not be wandering or thinking about anything else. It is a holy moment meant for our reflection on Christ's work on the cross.

SELF-EXAMINATION

27 Wherefore whosoever shall eat this bread, and drink this cup of the Lord, unworthily, shall be guilty of the body and blood of the Lord.

28 But let a man examine himself, and so let him eat of that bread, and drink of that cup.

29 For he that eateth and drinketh unworthily, eateth and drinketh damnation to himself, not discerning the Lord's body.

30 For this cause many are weak and sickly among you, and many sleep.

31 For if we would judge ourselves, we should not be judged.

32 But when we are judged, we are chastened of the Lord, that we should not be condemned with the world.

33 Wherefore, my brethren, when ye come together to eat, tarry one for another.

34 And if any man hunger, let him eat at home; that ye come not together unto condemnation. And the rest will I set in order when I come.

Reverence in communion (I Cor. 11:27-28). Communion is an event so holy that one must partake in it carefully. {To partake in communion unworthily is to treat it as ordinary food and drink without giving any thought to what it means.}[Q8] To eat and drink unworthily in this way is to totally disrespect Christ, making one guilty of despising the body and blood of Jesus. Disrespecting others at the Lord's Supper is bad enough, but disparaging the sacrificial work of Jesus on our behalf is horrendous.

In order to avoid such a disgrace from occurring, Paul calls on each person to examine himself, to make sure he is remembering and honoring the Lord for what He did. Communion should also be seen as an opportunity to discover any unconfessed sin and to repent of it. To save us from sin, after all, is the very reason Jesus gave His life.

Notice that Paul is not telling the Corinthians to give up partaking at all. He is not trying to frighten anyone into not sharing in communion. He is simply stating that entering into this event must be done with reverence and worship. He is telling us not to participate in an unworthy manner. In other words, before you take the bread and the cup, take the time to recognize and honor Jesus' sacrifice, and confess any sin you become aware of.

Purpose of communion (I Cor. 11:29-30). Communion itself does not bring salvation. In fact, taking communion without being saved brings judgment, not salvation. Communion is reserved for those who are saved, not for the unrepentant sinner.

The negative consequences of taking communion in an unworthy manner are more than just spiritual. Paul points out that there were physical consequences in the Corinthian church. {Many in the church had become sick and even died for partaking in a sinful way.}[Q9] This was the way the Lord disciplined the Corinthians for their disrespect, and we should not think that we modern Christians are immune to such discipline, although it does not always happen that way.

Communion must always be seen exactly as what it is. It is a holy observance of the death of Jesus. It is inexcusable to observe it in any other fashion than as prescribed by Christ and taught by Paul. We must be grateful in action, not only in speech, for what Jesus has done for us.

Evaluation for communion (I Cor. 11:31-32). There is an element of personal responsibility involved here that cannot be overlooked. The warning against not partaking in communion in an unworthy manner is not a suggestion that we should not participate at all. In fact, God wants us to come to His table and enjoy the blessings He has prepared for us.

We are blessed when we participate in communion in a worthy manner. We are blessed when we worship the Lord in gratitude for what He has done for us. We share in the great love that He has for us when we remember His sacrifice on the cross. Paul does not want us to stay away from the table, but to approach it with reverence for the Lord.

If we are honest in our judgment of ourselves, we will not be considered unworthy by God. It is wrong to think that God is just waiting to punish us when we make mistakes. He wants to forgive us, but we must repent. That is why the time of self-examination and honest judgment prior to communion is so important.

When God judges a believer this way, it does not mean he is sent to hell. {Judgment in this case refers to God's discipline. As a loving parent, He disciplines us in order to correct wrong behavior or a bad attitude. The idea is to bring us to repentance and obedience, not to cast us away.}^{Q10} God's discipline itself is a blessing, as it brings us back into right fellowship with Him and keeps us from having hard hearts like the world. As Paul says, believers are not judged the same as the world (vs. 32). Because of our faith in Jesus, believers are not condemned (cf. Rom. 8:1).

Those who have repented do not need to be afraid to take communion. If you have confessed your sin and take the bread and the cup in remembrance of the Lord, you are free to enjoy the benefits of this blessed event.

Love in communion (I Cor. 11:33-34). After reminding the church what the Lord's Supper was all about, Paul then instructs them to wait for one another when they share the meal. It was not wrong for them to have the meal, nor was it wrong for them to enjoy the meal, since it was customary at that time. They were simply to enjoy it to-gether in love, humility, and harmony.

Then Paul gives a fairly practical suggestion. He says that if a person is so hungry that he cannot wait for the rest of the church to gather together, that person should eat at home. When we gather as a church, we should do everything we can to be prepared for serving others, whether this means making sure we are not hungry and focused on that or just getting enough sleep the night before. These practical things will make us better servants in the body of Christ.

The Lord's Supper is about the Lord, not us. When we partake of it, we should do so in a way that will bring glory to Him.

—Robert Ferguson, Jr.

QUESTIONS

1. What was causing division in the Corinthian church regarding the Lord's Supper?

2. Why does Paul tell the Corinthian church they were not actually eating the Lord's Supper?

3. What was Paul's attitude toward those who were being selfish at the Lord's Supper?

4. Where did Paul receive his instructions concerning the Lord's Supper?

5. What is represented by the bread?

6. What is represented by the cup?

7. What do we proclaim when we partake of the bread and the cup?

8. What does eating and drinking in an unworthy manner mean?

9. What was the consequence of the Corinthians' partaking of communion unworthily?

10. What is the purpose of God's discipline of a believer?

—Robert Ferguson, Jr.

Preparing to Teach the Lesson

The first-century church at Corinth must have indeed been a troubled one. As we read through Paul's first epistle to this church, we see a troublesome pattern of behavior that points to an equally worrisome wrong set of priorities.

Over seemingly every issue, the believers in Corinth tended toward contention and strife. They were divided over human leaders, over knowledge, over church discipline, over Christian liberty—and now we see that they were even divided over the celebration of the Lord's Supper!

Their underlying problem stemmed from clinging to carnality in large swaths of their lives (cf. 3:1-4); that is, they were still in many cases holding on to the priorities of the unsaved culture around them rather than replacing that worldly set of values with a corresponding set of new Christian values. Instead of living like the pagans around them, they should have been pursuing humility, holiness, and loving unity in the Holy Spirit. Those are pursuits to which all believers are called.

TODAY'S AIM

Facts: to learn about the right way to observe the Lord's Supper.

Principle: to understand that the Lord's Supper is a holy witness to the death of the Lord Jesus Christ until He comes again; it is not a dinner party.

Application: to rightly prepare our hearts and minds to celebrate the Lord's Supper in a sober, solemn, humble, and worthy manner.

INTRODUCING THE LESSON

In chapter 11 of his first epistle to the church at Corinth, Paul turns to the issue of the proper celebration of the Lord's Supper. As with most of their issues, even this holy ordinance had become a point of contention and strife among them.

It is easy to sit in judgment on the Corinthian believers for their waywardness, but that is not what this passage calls us to do. Instead, we must examine ourselves: Of what does the Lord want to cleanse us?

DEVELOPING THE LESSON

1. Not the Lord's Supper (I Cor. 11:20-22). Paul begins by informing his readers in no uncertain terms that because of their fleshly indulgence and arrogance toward one another, whatever they gathered to celebrate was definitely not the Lord's Supper! As it seemed in quite a few areas of life, many were using even communion to exalt themselves—in this case as an occasion to flaunt their own affluence in the face of those who were hungry and needy. Some were apparently even abusing the elements of the Lord's table to make themselves drunk!

Paul rightly admonishes them that such disgraceful wantonness was completely foreign to the holy celebration they supposedly were observing. If they were so hungry, why did they not eat in the privacy of their own homes before coming to the gathering? What they were currently doing was a dishonor to Christ's church and an affront against the poor and needy! Did they think that Paul would approve of such behavior? He most vehemently did not!

2. The true Lord's Supper (I Cor. 11:23-26). To lay a solid foundation so that there would be no misunderstanding about his admonitions, Paul next gives the Corinthians a detailed description of the origin and meaning of the holy ordinance of the Lord's Supper. Paul declares that he received this instruction from the risen Christ (either through the apostles or by direct revelation, or both).

Paul places emphasis on Christ's blessing and breaking of the bread as His body offered up in sacrifice, His sharing of the cup as His blood of the new covenant, and His commending of this ordinance as a continuing, solemn memorial to His death.

Concluding his exposition of communion, Paul stresses that this celebration is intended as a graphic testimony to the central position of Christ's saving sacrifice in the life of His church; it would serve that purpose until the day that He returns.

3. Chastening to avoid condemnation (I Cor. 11:27-34). Paul's warning here is stated in the gravest of terms. Because the Lord's Supper is such an essential, sacred ordinance in the life of the church, those who defile it with wanton feasting and drinking, as if they were somehow rejoicing in Jesus' suffering and death, are "guilty of the body and blood of the Lord."

But Paul also provides a remedy against incurring such condemnation: self-examination. Thus, Paul is recommending that those who partake of communion first prepare themselves in all reverence and solemnity.

It is important to note that the Greek word rendered "damnation" (vs. 29) is a general term for any judgment or condemnation, not necessarily for eternal punishment. But apparently, there were many who were weak, sick, or had even died among the members at Corinth, and Paul's diagnosis is that this was because of their unworthy behavior concerning the Lord's Supper.

In verse 31, Paul begins to establish the principle of self-chastening to avoid the Lord's chastening. He says that the reason the Lord brings correction and chastening upon His church is to purify it, so that it will not be condemned along with the world. If

a believer is wise enough to exercise self-restraint, he will thereby give God less cause to chasten him.

ILLUSTRATING THE LESSON

The illustration contrasts partaking of the Lord's Supper unworthily with worthily sanctifying the ordinance in our hearts and rightly discerning that it represents the body and blood of the Lord Jesus Christ Himself.

UNWORTHY VERSUS WORTHY

The Lord's Supper is not an occasion for feasting and drunkenness!

The Lord's Supper is holy, showing forth the Lord's death until He comes!

CONCLUDING THE LESSON

Attitude matters! There are many matters in the life of the church that call for godly rejoicing. Easter, Christmas, a conversion, a baptism, a birthday, or any other noteworthy blessing that comes upon a fellow Christian may be a cause for celebration.

But the occasion of the Lord's Supper is a different matter. Though we rejoice that Christ's death has cleansed us from our sins, we should remember His death in utmost reverence and solemnity.

ANTICIPATING THE NEXT LESSON

Next week's lesson focuses on the paramount importance of Christ's resurrection as God's provision and guarantee that we too shall be raised bodily to new life at His second coming.

—*John Lody.*

PRACTICAL POINTS

1. Be careful to honor God with pure motives in worship, service, and fellowship (I Cor. 11:20-22).
2. Our faith grows deeper whenever we remember Christ's sacrifice for our sins (vss. 23-24).
3. Our faith and worship look forward to Christ's coming in glory (vss. 25-26).
4. Instead of being drawn away from Him by guilt, believers should always draw closer to Christ for forgiveness and restoration (vss. 27-29).
5. Believers invite unintended consequences when their worship is careless (vss. 30-32).
6. We should gather for worship in love and consideration for all our fellow believers (vss. 33-34).

—Cheryl Y. Powell.

RESEARCH AND DISCUSSION

1. How might the issues raised by Paul in I Corinthians 11:1-19 have contributed to the problems in their love feasts and their observances of the Lord's Supper? Discuss.
2. What atmosphere is appropriate for observing the Lord's Supper today? Discuss.
3. How should we confront the issue of selfishness in a congregation?
4. What does it mean to partake of the Lord's Supper unworthily? What does it mean to partake of it worthily? Discuss.

—Cheryl Y. Powell.

ILLUSTRATED HIGH POINTS

This is not to eat the Lord's supper (I Cor. 11:20)

The architecture of the Old West is famous for its towns made up of false fronts (or facades). The word "facade" comes from the French and means "frontage," or "face." The purpose of the facade was to hide a cheap building behind a decorative face.

Paul says that what the Corinthian church was calling "The Lord's Supper" was, in fact, not the Lord's Supper. People were greedy, rude, and even drunken. They shamed the poor by their excesses.

One wonders what other so-called "Christian" activities we are doing that do not pass muster. Is our "worship" really worship? Is our "prayer" really prayer? Is our "church growth" really church growth? Are we actually invested in living for Christ, or do we only appear to be?

Have ye not houses to eat and to drink in? (vs. 22)

It seems every industry has its version of "best of the year" awards. One such award in the advertising industry is the AME award for "Advertising and Marketing Effectiveness." In 2004, this award went to International House of Pancakes' chief marketing officer, Gregg Nettleton. He did this with a simple slogan, "Come Hungry, Leave Happy!"

What are we hungry for when we come to church? Food for our bellies or approval or recognition? Paul would suggest that these are not the things we should be seeking.

When you come to church, open your heart for an encounter with the almighty God. Yes, by all means; come hungry, and leave happy!

—Therese Greenberg.

Golden Text Illuminated

"For as often as ye eat this bread, and drink this cup, ye do shew the Lord's death till he come" (I Corinthians 11:26).

Paul is outraged as he writes these time-honored words about the Lord's Supper. Twice in this chapter he tells the Corinthians, "I praise you not" (vss. 17, 22).

Why is Paul so angry? The situation he is addressing involved gluttony, elitism, and drunkenness, all set within a "love feast" of the church! This banquet (sometimes called the agape feast after the Greek word for the highest love) was a communal meal that incorporated the Lord's Supper. Jude 1:12 also mentions an abuse of this meal, referring to ungodly people, masquerading as Christians, who eat at the sacred table without qualms. Outside of the Bible, the love feast is mentioned in a letter from Pliny the Younger, a Roman administrator, to the emperor Trajan. He writes that after meeting "on a stated day" in the morning to "address a form of prayer to Christ, as to a divinity," the Christians would reassemble later to "eat in common a harmless meal."

Because there were no church buildings then, it is likely that believers gathered in the homes of wealthy members, since those dwellings would be large enough to accommodate the gatherings. Appallingly, some at Corinth were getting drunk during the love feast! Paul also had learned that others were going hungry. Either the rich were devouring the food before the poorer members arrived, or they were excluding the poor from access to their sumptuous meals.

Against these abuses, Paul reiterates what he had already taught the Corinthians, which Christ himself had revealed: "For I have received of the Lord that which also I delivered unto you" (I Cor. 11:23). Paul stresses the solemnity of the Lord's Supper by mentioning the betrayal of Jesus on the night that He took the bread and cup. In stark contrast to the selfishness of the Corinthians at their feasts, Jesus generously shared food and wine with His disciples. The bread represents His body to be offered on the cross, while the cup symbolizes the blood of the new covenant, which was shed for the forgiveness of sins.

Paul sounded a stern warning about the abuse of the Lord's Supper. In the previous chapter (vs. 7), he reminded them of the story in Exodus 32:1-6, when the Israelites offered sacrifices in the midst of practicing idolatry and then engaged in debauchery: "And they rose up early on the morrow, and offered burnt offerings, and brought peace offerings; and the people sat down to eat and to drink, and rose up to play" (vs. 6). As a result of their wantonness, God punished the Israelites by sending destroying angels and venomous snakes among them. Paul cautioned the Corinthians that their immoral behavior at the Lord's Table would bring similar divine judgment upon them. This is why he urges them to examine their consciences before they receive the bread and the cup.

The Lord's Supper is actually a visible sermon to the world. In sharing the bread and cup, the church preaches the sacrificial death of Jesus, as well as His future glorious return. Because of this, Paul forcefully reminded the Corinthians that they needed to eat the Lord's Supper in a worthy manner.

—Mark Winter.

Heart of the Lesson

When the first-century Corinthians participated in the Lord's Supper, it was quite different than the simple communion ceremonies of many churches today. In Corinth, the Lord's Supper was often part of a love feast, a potluck style meal in which every believer brought food and drink to share.

Unfortunately, what was happening at Corinth was that the wealthier members of the church were consuming all of their food and drink while refusing to share any with the poorer members. The communion meal should have demonstrated mutual love, humility, and generosity, motivated by Christ's sacrificial death for all who believe in Him. Instead, gluttony and drunkenness characterized the love feasts held in the church at Corinth.

1. The problem (I Cor. 11:20-22). The cliques that divided the Corinthian church profoundly affected how they related to one another and dealt with conflict. Prideful factions had so divided the church that they even disrupted the Lord's Supper. Many Corinthians cared more about their own desires than their brothers and sisters in Christ.

When partaking of the Lord's Supper, the Corinthians should have focused their attention on remembering what Jesus had done for them on the cross and looking forward to His return. Instead, what should have been a holy gathering looked more like a Friday night at the bar!

2. The purpose (I Cor. 11:23-26). The apostle Paul had received instructions for the communion meal from the Lord Jesus Himself. On his first trip to Corinth, he had instructed the church about how and why to celebrate the Lord's Supper.

Paul reminded the Corinthians about Christ's final meal with His disciples before the crucifixion, in which He broke bread and shared a cup with them. The bread symbolized His body, about to be broken on the cross, and the cup symbolized His blood of the new covenant.

The Lord's Supper, like the Passover meal, is a multisensory experience that looks both backward and forward. When we eat food that symbolizes Christ's body, we remember His substitutional death on the cross and we look forward to His glorious return when He will raise us with glorified bodies just like His. When we drink the cup that symbolizes Christ's blood, we look back at the perfect Lamb of God, whose blood removed our sin and fulfilled the old covenant, initiating the glorious new covenant.

3. The solution (I Cor. 11:27-34). Since the Lord's Supper celebrates Jesus' costly death on the cross to grant believers forgiveness and the promise of resurrection, Paul warned the Corinthians not to participate in it in an unworthy manner. In other words, believers should observe communion with gratitude, and also by reflectively searching their hearts and confessing their sins in the light of Jesus' sacrifice.

As a result of Christ's shed blood and the offering of His body on the cross, those who follow Him have been united in one body—Christ's body, the church. Believers who took part in the Corinthian love feast with pride, selfishness, and unconfessed sin were in danger of God's judgment, including sickness and death. Love and humility, not greed and selfishness, will show the world that we are Christ's followers and that God's love is real (cf. John 13:35).

—Malia E. Rodriguez.

World Missions

Missionaries can attest to the fact that the closest thing to heaven on earth is the deep connection we have with other Christians, no matter where they are from. We have a natural longing for companionship with them. This longing springs from our mutual love for Jesus and our realization that He binds us together (Col. 3:14).

The Greek word used to describe this heavenly fellowship is *koinonia*, which points to a close-knit family living in harmony, sharing resources, and loving one another. In *Life Together,* Dietrich Bonhoeffer writes, "The fellowship of the Lord's Supper is the superlative fulfillment of Christian fellowship. As the members of the congregation are united in body and blood at the table of the Lord so will they be together in eternity. . . . The life of Christians together under the Word has reached its perfection in the sacrament" (HarperOne).

As members of Christ's body, we belong to one another. May we strive to attain the rich fellowship of the first-century believers, who devoted themselves to the apostles' teaching, to prayer, to the Lord's Supper, and to mutual commitment (Acts 2:42).

"Breaking of bread" refers to participating in the Lord's Supper, which Jesus instituted before He went to the cross (Matt. 26:26-28). When Jesus took the bread, broke it, and shared it with His disciples, He was doing two things: showing that His body would be offered up for them and that they should practice the breaking of bread amongst themselves to remember His sacrifice (Luke 22:19).

Bread, a product of rain from heaven and grain from earth, is useless unless it is shared and partaken. As members of Christ's body, which was offered up for us, we too are to be willing to sacrifice for one another. From the first century until the present day, countless missionaries have suffered, and many have died, for the cause of Christ. When we mourn with the grieving and rejoice with the joyful, we are forsaking self-centeredness for the greater good of God's family (Rom. 12:15).

The Lord's Supper is a source of joy, for there is nothing else on earth like the communion of the redeemed. As we drink of the cup, we joyfully remember that all our sins have been washed away by the blood of our Lord Jesus. The words of Isaiah echo through the millennia, reminding us that our sins, which were once bright scarlet, have been erased by a blanket of purity, like fresh fallen snow (1:18). The footprints of past sins are gone. We are unmarked in God's sight, as if we had never sinned at all. Even more, all our future sins are likewise cleansed away by the blood of Christ.

The Lord's Supper is accompanied by the warning that no one should eat and drink without examining themselves for sins and wrong attitudes. Since in communion we are remembering Christ's body and blood, we must come to the table in holy awe. The Corinthian church had failed at this. They enjoyed eating and drinking so much that they turned communion into an occasion for selfish gluttony and drunkenness. Paul scolded them for trivializing the act of the Lord's Supper and pointed out that this behavior could result in sickness and even death among them (I Cor. 11:27-30).

Churches may vary in how they celebrate the Lord's Supper. Some use whole loaves and a shared chalice. Others dispense wafers and individual cups. What matters most is that we remember our Lord's death until He comes again (I Cor. 11:26).

—*Rose McCormick Brandon*

The Jewish Aspect

When Yeshua (Jesus) instructed Peter and John to find a place to prepare the Passover on the day of unleavened bread (Luke 22:7-13), they had no idea that the annual historical commemoration of Israel's deliverance from slavery in Egypt would take on an entirely new dimension with the imminent death of the Lord Himself.

As commanded by the Lord, in the first Passover each family in ancient Israel slaughtered a lamb and placed the blood of the lamb upon their doorposts (Ex. 12:3-7), thereby sparing their firstborn children from death. Yeshua fulfilled the words of the prophet Isaiah, who said, "He was oppressed, and he was afflicted, yet he opened not his mouth: he is brought as a lamb to the slaughter, and as a sheep before her shearers is dumb, so he opened not his mouth" (Isa. 53:7).

Comparing the events surrounding the Passover with the days that led up to the crucifixion of Yeshua is instructive. The Passover lamb was set apart on the tenth day of the first month of Nisan—the same day that Yeshua rode into Jerusalem on the foal of a donkey. The lamb was inspected for four days (until the 14th day of Nisan) to ensure that it had no spot or blemish—Yeshua taught openly for four days. On the same day that Yeshua was slain, Passover lambs were being slaughtered (dayofrepentance1.org).

In celebrating the Passover with His disciples before His death, Yeshua applied the meaning of the Jewish feast to Himself. The drinking of four cups of wine was a part of the Passover that Yeshua celebrated with His disciples. Each cup had a name—first cup, sanctification; second cup, plagues; third cup, redemption; fourth cup, praise.

In drinking the cup, Yeshua said, "This cup is the new testament in my blood, which is shed for you" (Luke 22:20). The prophet Jeremiah said, "Behold, the days come, saith the Lord, that I will make a new covenant with the house of Israel, and with the house of Judah" (Jer. 31:31). During the Passover meal, Yeshua broke the unleavened bread and gave it to His disciples to eat and said that the bread represented His body (Luke 22:19). The unleavened bread signified the purity of the sinless Messiah.

Following Yeshua's command to remember His death (Luke 22:19), the early church continued the memorial of the Lord's Supper. However, the believers in the Corinthian church were filled with idolatry, strife, division, pride, and immoral behavior, and they were making a mockery of the Lord's Supper. The Lord's Supper was partaken in connection with a fellowship meal called a love feast. The believers brought what they could to the meal—fish, cheese, poultry, milk, honey, fruit, etc. However, the wealthy members of the church were gorging themselves and getting drunk during these meals. By the time the slaves and the poor people arrived, the food was already gone.

Paul confronted this selfishness and gluttony and said that what they were doing was not representative of the sacrifice being commemorated by the Lord's Supper. He said they were bringing public reproach upon Christ and admonished them to not eat the Lord's Supper unworthily. They were supposedly celebrating the giving of Jesus' body for their sins, but they were sinning against the very ones for whom He gave His body!

—*Deborah Markowitz Solan.*

Guiding the Superintendent

The Bible does not prescribe many religious rites or ceremonies for believers. The Lord's Supper is one notable exception.

The subject of disunity in the church dominated Paul's entire first letter to the Corinthians. The church was filled with strife, partisan spirit, and tolerance toward grossly immoral behavior. Yet another great problem in Corinth was how the church was observing the Lord's Supper. In fact, Paul could no longer even call what they were doing the Lord's Supper. The believers in the church had become very inconsiderate of one another. This observance was intended to unify the church; instead, the people had turned it inside-out by turning it into an occasion to divide the body.

DEVOTIONAL OUTLINE

1. Not the Lord's Supper (I Cor. 11: 20-22). The early church often ate shared meals together, which would commonly conclude with the Lord's Supper (cf. Acts 2:46). But at Corinth, the communion service that was meant to remember and honor Christ's selfless sacrifice had been turned into a manifestation of selfish gratification.

The privileged would eat first, leaving little or nothing for the poor who had arrived hungry. Others would abuse the availability of wine and become drunk. By this behavior, they were disgracing the church of God and humiliating the poor. Because of their selfish and wanton lack of consideration for others, Paul was not able to praise them; rather, they received his severe rebuke!

Paul instructed those who desired to so indulge in food to at least have the consideration to eat their own food at home before they came to the church to celebrate the Lord's Supper.

2. The Lord's Supper (I Cor. 11:23-26). Now Paul reminded them of what he had taught them about the Lord's Supper—and this teaching had come directly from Jesus. Paul emphasized three aspects that constitute a worthy observance of the Lord's Supper:

First, the historical aspect. When they partook of these elements, they were to remember His death.

Second, the salvation aspect. The cup represented Christ's blood, which had established the new covenant of their salvation.

Third, the prophetic aspect. Every time they ate the bread and drank from the cup, they were to do it as a way of looking forward to Christ's future return.

Mindful recognition of these key aspects was essential to partaking of the Lord's Supper in a worthy manner.

3. The consequences of unworthiness (I Cor. 11:27-34). To emphasize the seriousness of partaking unworthily of the Lord's Supper, Paul warned them of the strict judgment that awaited those who did so. Some have understood this warning as a reference to personal sins in a believer's life. But the context of Paul's entire letter is concerned with discord in the church. The focus of the Lord's Supper is the Lord Himself and His death, which all had in common as a unifying bond. To partake of the Lord's Supper in a careless fashion, failing to recognize this unity, was to dishonor the Lord Jesus. Thus, many in Corinth had been struck with weakness, illness, and even death.

CHILDREN'S CORNER

The key principle of the Lord's Supper that children need to understand is that we observe it in serious remembrance of Jesus and His death on the cross for us.

—Martin R. Dahlquist.

SCRIPTURE LESSON TEXT

I COR. 15:1 Moreover, brethren, I declare unto you the gospel which I preached unto you, which also ye have received, and wherein ye stand;

2 By which also ye are saved, if ye keep in memory what I preached unto you, unless ye have believed in vain.

3 For I delivered unto you first of all that which I also received, how that Christ died for our sins according to the scriptures;

4 And that he was buried, and that he rose again the third day according to the scriptures:

5 And that he was seen of Cephas, then of the twelve:

6 After that, he was seen of above five hundred brethren at once; of whom the greater part remain unto this present, but some are fallen asleep.

7 After that, he was seen of James; then of all the apostles.

8 And last of all he was seen of me also, as of one born out of due time.

9 For I am the least of the apostles, that am not meet to be called an apostle, because I persecuted the church of God.

10 But by the grace of God I am what I am: and his grace which *was bestowed* **upon me was not in vain; but I laboured more abundantly than they all: yet not I, but the grace of God which was with me.**

11 Therefore whether *it were* I or they, so we preach, and so ye believed.

NOTES

Witnesses to Christ's Resurrection

(Easter)

Lesson Text: I Corinthians 15:1-11

Related Scriptures: Matthew 28:1-9; Mark 16:1-13; Luke 24:1-49;
John 20:1-18; Acts 1:3-4; I Corinthians 15:12-28

TIME: A.D. 55   PLACE: from Ephesus

GOLDEN TEXT—"For I delivered unto you first of all that which I also received, how that Christ died for our sins according to the scriptures; and that he was buried, and that he rose again the third day according to the scriptures" (I Corinthians 15:3-4).

Introduction

The foundational doctrine of the Christian faith is the resurrection of Jesus. The resurrection is the single most important event in human history, as man's salvation depends on it. This is not just an intellectual, philosophical, or even theological concept to agree with. It is a historical event that one must believe and trust in.

The world thinks it is absurd to claim that a man who was dead and buried could be alive again. That is not a problem, however, if God exists. God has the power to give life, which includes resurrecting a dead body. It is established, historical fact that Jesus was crucified on a Roman cross and buried in a tomb. Three days later, that tomb was found empty.

God raised Him from the dead! Let us rejoice in our risen Saviour!

LESSON OUTLINE

I. TESTMONY OF THE GOSPEL—I COR. 15:1-2

II. TESTIMONY OF EYEWITNESSES—I Cor. 15:3-7

III. TESTIMONY OF PAUL—I Cor. 15:8-11

Exposition: Verse by Verse

TESTIMONY OF THE GOSPEL

I COR. 15:1 Moreover, brethren, I declare unto you the gospel which I preached unto you, which also ye have received, and wherein ye stand;

2 By which also ye are saved, if ye keep in memory what I preached unto you, unless ye have believed in vain.

The fifteenth chapter of I Corinthians is the greatest defense of the resurrection of Jesus Christ as well as the resurrection of the believer in all of literature. The first eleven verses focus on the historical reality of this event.

To precede his defense of the resurrection of Jesus, Paul first reminds the Corinthians of the power of the gospel that he had preached to them and that they had received. {We all need to be reminded of the basics of the gospel from time to time because, as Paul stated elsewhere, "it is the power of God unto salvation to every one that believeth" (Rom. 1:16).}[Q1] We are saved by God, not ourselves.

Just as Paul devoted his life to preaching the gospel, the church must do the same today. We have been commissioned to take the gospel to the ends of the earth because people cannot receive the gospel unless it is told to them (cf. Acts 1:8; Rom 10:14-17).

Once we receive the gospel, we stand on it for the rest of our lives. The gospel never goes out of date, never becomes irrelevant, and never loses its power. It is the foundation of our lives, and any other ground we stand on is equivalent to quicksand. The gospel of Jesus Christ is the only thing that brings eternal life. Without it, we would remain dead in our sins (cf. Eph. 2:1-3).

There are numerous false religions and perversions of Christianity that promise some form of eternal bliss and their own way to God. Jesus Christ is the only one who can make good on that offer, since He died for our sins and rose again for our justification (Rom. 4:24-25). No other religious leader can come close to matching what Jesus did for us. They cannot even save themselves, much less their own followers. They are lost in their sins and need Him as much as anyone else.

{Paul's entire preaching ministry, as well as the proclamation of the other apostles, centered around the focal point of the gospel—the resurrection of Jesus Christ.}[Q2] It is the single most important aspect of Christianity. In fact, Paul states that if Christ has not been raised from the dead, then we are still in our sins and our faith is futile (I Cor. 15:14, 17). We are to always cling to the truth of the resurrection, as it is fundamental to our faith and there is nothing else to hold on to. Simply put, if there is no resurrection, there is no salvation.

TESTIMONY OF EYEWITNESSES

3 For I delivered unto you first of all that which I also received, how that Christ died for our sins according to the scriptures;

4 And that he was buried, and that he rose again the third day according to the scriptures:

5 And that he was seen of Cephas, then of the twelve:

6 After that, he was seen of above five hundred brethren at once; of whom the greater part remain unto this present, but some are fallen asleep.

7 After that, he was seen of James; then of all the apostles.

8 And last of all he was seen of me also, as of one born out of due time.

The gospel news (I Cor. 15:3a). As already stated, the most important thing to Paul was preaching the resurrection of Jesus. We cannot keep this information to ourselves. We are not saved by leading better lives, by becoming better neighbors, or by any type of moral improvement. These things are not bad, nor should they be discouraged, but none of these things can make us holy enough for God to save us.

In order to be saved, we must believe that God has raised Jesus from the dead (Rom. 10:9). We must further see it as of utmost importance that the news of the resurrection of Jesus be delivered to all people. That is the top priority in the ministry of the church to the world.

The entire gospel rests on the fact that Jesus has been raised from the dead. Without the resurrection, there is no gospel to preach. The gospel, which means "good news," is good news only if Jesus actually rose from the dead—not in concept only, but in reality. Jesus really did die on a cross, He really was buried in a tomb, and He really did get up and walk out of that tomb in a glorified, resurrected body that is no longer susceptible to pain, suffering, or death.

The gospel creed (I Cor. 15:3b-4). {The news of Jesus' resurrection was so important to the early church that they quickly formulated a creed that was easy to memorize and recite.}[Q3] This was essential because many people in the first century were illiterate and needed something they could easily learn and remember. Paul's recording of this creed in I Corinthians dates to around A.D. 55, only twenty-five years after the events themselves. That does not allow time for it to be relegated to a legend, as some modern critics have tried to do, and it is clear that the creed existed long before the writing of this letter.

The creed Paul taught the Corinthians was the same one that he had been taught after Jesus appeared to him on the road to Damascus. Paul was saved likely around two years after the resurrection of Jesus, and he met with Peter in Jerusalem three years after that, staying with him for fifteen days (cf. Gal. 1:18). At some point very soon after Paul's salvation experience, he was taught this creed, which he then delivered to the Corinthians when he first came to their city.

{The creed that was taught by the church very succinctly yet truthfully defines the gospel in three statements: Christ died for our sins in accordance with the Scriptures (Isa. 53:4-8); He was buried (53:9); and He was raised on the third day in accordance with the Scriptures (Ps. 16:10; cf. Acts 13:32-37).}[Q4] The resurrection was the culmination of God's plan of redemption.

Resurrection appearance to Peter (I Cor. 15:5). The resurrection of Jesus Christ is not something mystical or imagined. It was not conjured up by Jesus' followers. {In fact, the disciples were skeptical of it and doubted the first claims that Jesus had been seen alive (cf. Mark 16:9-11; Luke 24:10-11).}[Q5] Some even doubted when they saw Him themselves (Matt. 28:17).

The Bible does not hide behind some mysterious claims made by certain followers of Jesus who wanted to keep His memory alive and start a new religion. The disciples never tried to claim with no evidence that Jesus had risen from the dead. They had the greatest proof possible: they had seen Him with their own eyes!

Eyewitness testimony is a powerful line of evidence in any case, and Paul lines up witnesses in this passage. He begins with Peter, to whom Jesus made a special appearance (Luke 24:34; cf. Mark 16:7). In Mark's account, after Jesus has risen, the women are told to tell the disciples *and Peter* that Jesus would meet them in Galilee. Did you notice that Peter is singled out specifically?

{Peter had denied knowing Jesus three times, something detailed in all four Gospels (Matt. 26:69-75; Mark 14:66-72; Luke 22:54-62; John 18:15-18, 25-27). But Jesus showed that He had not given up on Peter by appearing to him personally after He had been raised from the dead.}[Q6] Peter was forgiven and restored by the risen Jesus (John 21:15-19).

Jesus also appeared to the principal disciples after His resurrection. Each of the disciples had a personal testimony of seeing Jesus in His post-resurrection body. None of them had to go by the testimony of another.

Resurrection appearance to five hundred (I Cor. 15:6). {In addition to Peter and the rest of the Twelve, Jesus also appeared to over five hundred men at the same time. None of their names are given, but this detail prevents the assertion that the resurrection was made up by the disciples of Jesus.}Q7 The Twelve were not the only ones to see Jesus alive after He had been declared dead and was buried.

Jesus appeared to this large body of men all at the same time in one place. Paul now has listed over five hundred eyewitnesses to the resurrected Jesus. The One they knew was dead was now alive again, and there is overwhelming evidence that supports this claim.

Paul states that most of these five hundred men were still alive at the time he penned I Corinthians, which means that Paul's story could be corroborated by witnesses. If Paul and the other apostles were not telling the truth, their story could have been easily discredited. Many of Jesus' enemies even admitted the undeniable truth of the resurrection.

Resurrection appearance to James (I Cor. 15:7). The people Paul mentioned up to this point were believers in Jesus before His death and resurrection. He now brings up a man who was not a believer during the life of Jesus and certainly not a follower of Christ. This man is James, the brother of Jesus. During the Lord's ministry on earth, James expressed embarrassment and even anger that Jesus was claiming to be the Son of God (cf. John 7:1-5; Luke 8:19-21).

James grew up in the same house as Jesus, probably shared a room with Him, and ate at the same table as Him. They were probably educated together, studied the Law together, and maybe even worked side by side in Joseph's carpenter shop. But James still failed to see who Jesus really was.

What changed James's mind? Jesus appeared to him after He had been raised from the dead. {The resurrection convinced James that Jesus was the Son of God. It changed him from an unbeliever to a believer.}Q8

Jesus also appeared to the rest of the apostles. Though we typically reserve the word "apostle" for one of the Twelve, in this instance it refers to a group that was larger than the Twelve. Their names are not mentioned in the text, but they would have been well known in the early church. We do know of one. This larger group would have included Matthias, who was named as the replacement for Judas Iscariot (cf. Acts 1:21-26).

Any of these sources could have refuted Paul's story, but they did not. The fact of the resurrection still stands today. The claims Paul is making in this passage did not originate with him, however. They were already the established teaching of the church, in effect even before Paul's conversion. He is simply passing on information that he received from others.

TESTIMONY OF PAUL

8 And last of all he was seen of me also, as of one born out of due time.

9 For I am the least of the apostles, that am not meet to be called an apostle, because I persecuted the church of God.

10 But by the grace of God I am what I am: and his grace which was bestowed upon me was not in vain; but I laboured more abundantly than they all: yet not I, but the grace of God which was with me.

11 Therefore whether it were I or they, so we preach, and so ye believed.

Grace fosters humility (I Cor. 15:8-9). The last eyewitness Paul calls forward is himself. As "one born out of due time," that is, as one who did not have three years of training as the Twelve did,

Paul experienced his sighting of Jesus after He had ascended to heaven (Acts 9:3-6). While the twelve disciples were studying at the feet of Jesus, Paul was studying under the Jewish rabbi Gamaliel (cf. Acts 22:3). Jesus appeared to Paul in bodily form, however, and commissioned him to preach the gospel.

Paul considered himself to be the least of the apostles. This was not false humility on his part. {He listed himself last and considered himself the least because he had persecuted the church.}[Q9] He was qualified to be an apostle only because Jesus appeared to him and called him.

Grace fosters good works (I Cor. 15:10-11). After seeing Jesus in His resurrected glory, Paul went immediately from antagonist to apostle by the grace of God. {God's grace did not lead Paul to laziness, however, but caused him to work harder than anyone else.}[Q10] He did not work *for* salvation, but *because* of salvation.

Paul is not boasting in what he was doing for Christ, but rather in what Christ had done in and for him. Grace was at work in his life, and that is what enabled him to preach the gospel the way he did. Paul was not out on a self-help mission but was empowered by the Holy Spirit to do what God had called him to do. Previously, he thought he was doing God's will by persecuting those who proclaimed the name of Jesus. He had considered Jesus a dead blasphemer who caused more trouble for Jews than anyone else. But when Jesus appeared to him, he learned that he himself was the one in the wrong.

Paul is not saying he worked harder than others in order to brag about himself. He is simply saying that the fire that was in him would not go out. Paul did not care about human recognition (cf. I Cor. 4:3). He rejoiced in the fact that the gospel was being preached and that people believed.

The gospel proclamation revolved around the preaching of the resurrection. Paul was absolutely convinced that he had seen the risen Jesus, just as over five hundred other men had, including the apostles. The resurrection changed his life, just as it changes the lives of believers today.

Has the resurrection changed your life, or is it just something the pastor preaches about every Easter? Has it impacted you deeply, or is it just another story? May the realization that Christ is alive help you resolve to trust Him completely.

—Robert Ferguson, Jr.

QUESTIONS

1. Why is it important to be reminded of the basic elements of the gospel from time to time?

2. What is the focal point of the gospel?

3. Why did the early church formulate the truth of Jesus' resurrection into a creed?

4. According to Paul (I Cor. 15:3-4), what three statements summarize the gospel?

5. How did Jesus' disciples react when they first heard that He had been resurrected?

6. What was significant about Jesus' personal appearance to Peter?

7. What was significant about Jesus' appearance to over five hundred men at one time?

8. What was significant about Jesus' appearance to His brother James?

9. Why did Paul consider himself to be the least of the apostles?

10. What was the result of God's grace in Paul?

—Robert Ferguson, Jr.

Preparing to Teach the Lesson

Paul has nearly reached the end of his first letter to the church at Corinth, and he has just concluded an admonition for them to conduct themselves during worship in a decent and orderly manner as an appropriate witness to their unity in the gospel of Christ (14:40).

By way of summarizing his letter thus far, Paul begins chapter 15 with a succinct statement of the essential tenets of the true, scriptural gospel message that is the foundation of our faith down to the present day.

TODAY'S AIM

Facts: to learn the essential truths about Christ's resurrection.

Principle: to understand and be grounded in the truth that Christ's resurrection is a surely attested historical event.

Application: to consciously live daily in the realization that Christ's resurrection is the foundation of our unshakable hope.

INTRODUCING THE LESSON

In this lesson, Paul reminds us of what the gospel is, as well as the supreme importance of Christ's resurrection.

DEVELOPING THE LESSON

1. The gospel according to the Scriptures (I Cor. 15:1-4). Paul prefaces his statement of the gospel by reminding his readers that this gospel is the same one that they originally received from him. (Galatians 1:6-9 tells us that already there were false gospels making the rounds at the time. It was important for people to discern which gospel they were listening to.) The gospel Paul proclaimed is the very basis for their (and our) faith and right standing before God.

Note the emphasis on the phrase "according to the scriptures" (vss. 3-4). Paul wants these Corinthian believers to keep in mind that their source of truth for salvation is the inspired Scriptures alone.

Paul's summary contains three essential points: Christ died for our sins, Christ was buried, and Christ rose again on the third day. There are many other propositions that define the fullness of the gospel, but these are its most central and indispensable elements.

2. Witnesses to Christ's resurrection (I Cor. 15:5-8). As verifiable proof of the historical truth of the gospel, Paul lists the main eyewitnesses to Christ's resurrection. This is one characteristic that sets Christianity apart from all other religions, namely, its historicity. While other religious writings are full of vague visions and unverifiable fables that may or may not be intended as historical facts, Christianity is supremely conscious of the solid, historical basis of its truths. The writers of Scripture are keen on making clear that they are relating to their readers real events that really happened in real history.

The first witness to Christ's resurrection whom Paul lists is Peter ("Cephas" is the Aramaic form of his name, which means "rock"). Peter was actually with John at the time (cf. John 20:3-8), but for whatever reason, Paul does not mention him here. That may have been because of Peter's more prominent reputation among the churches of that day.

Also, although the women who went to anoint Christ's body were given the honor of being the true first witnesses to Christ's resurrection (cf. Matt. 28:1-10; Mark 16:1-10; Luke 24:1-10; John 20:1-2), Paul was likely making a cultural accommodation by mentioning a male disciple as the first indisputable witness. It may be noteworthy that at the actual time of the event, the men did not accept the women's testimony without first going to the tomb to see for themselves (cf. Mark. 16:11; Luke 24:11-12; John 20:3-8).

Paul lists the Twelve as the next set of witnesses to Christ's resurrection (cf. Matt. 28:16-17; Mark 16:14; Luke 24:33-48; John 20:19-20). Of course, counting Peter, there were only eleven apostles at that time since Judas Iscariot was already dead. Paul used the term "twelve" simply as a convenient and standard label for the whole group.

In I Corinthians 15:6, Paul alludes to an occasion when the risen Christ Himself appeared to over five hundred witnesses at once! Although none of the scriptural writers specify a time when there were over five hundred witnesses present, this most likely happened just preceding Christ's ascension into heaven (cf. Mark 16:15, 19; Luke 24:50-51; Acts 1:2-11).

The subsequent appearances of the risen Lord to James (most likely the Lord's brother, known as "James the Just," the head of the Jerusalem church) and "all the apostles" (presumably an extended number who were at Jerusalem along with James) are not recorded in the Gospels or Acts. But Paul was readily in a position to have been told personally by these individuals about these other appearances of the risen Christ.

Last of all among the witnesses to Christ's resurrection, Paul mentions himself. He is undoubtedly referring to his encounter with the risen Christ on the road to Damascus (Acts 9:1-6). Paul's phrase, "one born out of due time," is actually the Greek term for a miscarriage. But contextually, Paul clearly does not mean this in any literal sense. Rather, he refers to his spiritual birth as an apostle as being beyond the time when the original apostles had been commissioned by Christ.

3. Least of the apostles (I Cor. 15:9-11). Paul humbly declares that his own status as an apostle occupies the lowest level in prestige and that he himself is not even worthy to be rightly called an apostle, since he once persecuted the church.

ILLUSTRATING THE LESSON

The illustration diagrams the historical witnesses to the resurrection of the Lord Jesus Christ.

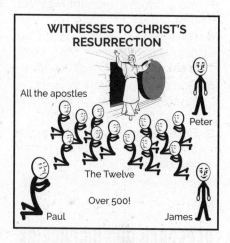

WITNESSES TO CHRIST'S RESURRECTION

All the apostles

Peter

The Twelve

Over 500!

Paul

James

CONCLUDING THE LESSON

Paul was always haunted by his ignominious past, even though all his sins, like every other true believer's sins, had been atoned for by Christ's sacrifice.

But note that Paul never allowed his deep regrets to hold him back in service to the Lord. Rather, he "labored more abundantly than they all" (vs. 10), that is, the other apostles. But even in this, he admits that it is not to his own credit.

ANTICIPATING THE NEXT LESSON

In next week's lesson, we move on to Paul's second epistle to the Corinthian church. The lesson will focus on how God's comforting us enables us in turn to comfort other fellow believers.

—*John Lody.*

PRACTICAL POINTS

1. The faith that saves is the same faith that enables believers to stand firm in their Christian walk (I Cor. 15:1-2).
2. Our witness for Christ must be anchored in the gospel (vss. 3-4).
3. Our faith in Christ has been confirmed by ample evidence, but many choose to doubt Him (vss. 5-8).
4. Rejoice that past sins do not disqualify believers from doing great works for Christ (vs. 9).
5. God's grace at work in us as believers transforms us beyond all human expectation (vs. 10).
6. Believers are saved by the power of the gospel—not by any human teacher (vs. 11).

—*Cheryl Y. Powell.*

RESEARCH AND DISCUSSION

1. Where in your community do people most need the gospel?
2. What does it mean to you that many at Corinth remained faithful to the gospel in spite of all the problems? Discuss.
3. What does it mean that Jesus died for our sins (cf. Isa. 53:3-6; John 3:16-18; I Cor. 1:23)?
4. What would it mean for our faith if Jesus had not risen from the dead?
5. What made Paul such a dynamic witness for the gospel (cf. I Cor. 15:10)? Discuss.

—*Cheryl Y. Powell.*

ILLUSTRATED HIGH POINTS

The gospel which I preached unto you (I Cor. 15:1)

Paul reminds the Corinthians of the enduring quality of the gospel. The gospel that was presented to him, he preached to them. This gospel must never be changed.

God has been careful to preserve the contents of the Bible. It has been faithfully preserved through multiple copies over thousands of years. Illustrating this truth is the story of a young Bedouin shepherd who made an amazing discovery. One day as he was throwing stones into a dark cave, he heard one of his stones break a clay vessel. This led to the greatest archeological find of the twentieth century—the Dead Sea Scrolls. It was found that these older documents were virtually identical to the manuscripts from which our modern Bibles were translated.

Wherein ye stand (vs. 1)

The term "diehard" is linked to the men of the British Army's 57th Regiment in the 1811 Battle of Albuera during the Napoleonic Wars. Though British officer William Inglis was wounded, he nevertheless remained in the battle, shouting to his men, "Stand your ground and die hard! Make the enemy pay dear for each of us! Die hard, 57th! Die hard!" From that day forward, his regiment became known simply as the "The Die Hards."

The gospel we preach will suffer constant attack. Many will be tempted to compromise it, soften its edges, or even abandon it altogether. Yet Paul, though often wounded himself in the Lord's service, would shout to us all even today, "Stand your ground, believers! The true gospel will live forever!

—*Therese Greenberg.*

Golden Text Illuminated

"For I delivered unto you first of all that which I also received, how that Christ died for our sins according to the scriptures; and that he was buried, and that he rose again the third day according to the scriptures" (I Corinthians 15:3-4).

Harry A. Ironside, who pastored Moody Church in Chicago from 1929-1948, wrote, "The Gospel is not good advice to be obeyed; it is good news to be believed."

The apostle Paul would undoubtedly agree. The fifteenth chapter of I Corinthians is a soaring summary of the gospel, the good news that transformed his heart and for the spread of which he risked life and limb. Paul told the church that he delivered the gospel "first of all" (that is, of primary importance). The gospel is no minor teaching; it is the very heart and soul of the Scriptures.

First, the gospel is centered on the atoning death of "Christ," a Greek term corresponding to the Hebrew title "Messiah," meaning "Anointed One." Only God the Son could have accomplished the task of atonement for the sins of the world. He lived a sinless human life, and therefore could become our Sin-bearer.

An early Christian heresy called *Docetism* (from the Greek, "to seem") denied that Jesus came in human flesh. Appalled by the idea that Almighty God would become human, the Docetists asserted that Jesus only appeared to be human. His human form was merely an illusion—it looked genuine to observers, but was only a facade to conceal that He was purely spirit. To the Docetists, Christ's suffering and death were illusory. But Paul makes it clear that the gospel includes the physical death burial, and resurrection of Jesus, who came in real human flesh (cf. John 1:14, I John 4:2-3).

Though the gospel's foundation is the sacrificial death of Christ, it would hardly be good news if His story ended at the tomb. Thanks be to God, it did not! Jesus also rose again! In fact, in this same chapter, Paul asserts that if Christ's resurrection had not happened, then our faith would be in vain and we would all die in our sins with no hope of being raised in Christ. If this were the case, then Christians ought to be pitied above all people, for our trust would be placed in a mere human who still lies in the grave (cf. I Cor. 15:12-19).

"But now is Christ risen from the dead" (vs. 20). Paul backs up this astounding statement with eyewitness accounts. The resurrection of Jesus is not a myth, but a historical fact, witnessed by Peter, the Twelve, and over 500 believers at once. The risen Christ also appeared to Paul.

All of this occurred according to the Scriptures, which repeatedly foretold the death and resurrection of Messiah (cf. Ps. 16:10; 22:16-18; Isa. 52:13—53:12). Even the story of Jonah was revealed by Jesus to be a foreshadowing of His own burial: "For as Jonas was three days and three nights in the whale's belly; so shall the Son of man be three days and three nights in the heart of the earth" (Matt. 12:40).

The gospel is not some afterthought, but God's plan from before Creation to bring sinners from death to eternal life.

—*Mark Winter.*

Heart of the Lesson

The bodily resurrection of Jesus from the dead forms the foundation of the gospel and Christianity. Without the truth of Christ's resurrection, our faith crumbles into a pile of false hope. When believers stand firm on the truth of the resurrection, however, we can live to honor God today, with hope beyond the grave for tomorrow.

Unfortunately, in Corinth there were some who denied the resurrection and, as a result, their lives began to crumble. So the apostle Paul devoted a large section of his letter to defending Christ's resurrection.

1. Remember the gospel (I Cor. 15:1-2). The gospel not only saves us; it shows us how to live as well. Paul encouraged the Corinthians to remember the pure, simple gospel he had taught them. When deceptive teachers threatened to distort the truth of Jesus' sacrificial death and victorious resurrection, Paul told the Corinthian church to stand firm on the gospel they had believed.

Many believers in Corinth lived their lives as if Christ's resurrection had not happened—as if Jesus' victory over the grave had no consequences for their lives. Lying, cheating, sexual immorality, greed, gluttony, and pride plagued the church and called into question the power of the gospel in their lives.

2. Understand the gospel (I Cor. 15:3-8). When Paul first traveled to Corinth, he shared with the people there the simple truth that Jesus had fulfilled many Old Testament prophecies by dying to pay for our sins and rising from the dead (cf. Ps. 16:8-11; 22:1-21; Isa. 52:13—53:12).

To further authenticate the amazing message of the gospel, the resurrected, glorified Jesus appeared to at least five hundred other believers. Later, Jesus appeared to Paul, both on the road to Damascus (cf. Acts 9:1-9) and in a special vision (cf. II Cor. 12:1-10).

In the Old Testament, eyewitnesses played an important part in authenticating a truth. To convict someone of a crime, the law required at least two eyewitnesses (cf. Deut. 19:15). When Jesus faced questions about His identity and message, in addition to referring to John the Baptist's witness and the witness of His own works, He called God the Father as His witness against the unbelieving Jewish leaders (cf. John 5:36-39).

While the Old Testament required two witnesses, the resurrected, glorified Jesus had hundreds of eyewitnesses. In either an ancient or modern legal setting, hundreds of eyewitnesses overwhelmingly validates the truth of an event.

3. Live the gospel (I Cor. 15:9-11). Finally, Paul shared one more way to authenticate the truth of the gospel—the transforming power of the gospel in his life. In Acts 26:1-19, Paul recounted his earlier life as a Pharisee and persecutor of Christians. But that all changed when the resurrected Jesus appeared to Paul on the road to Damascus. The hope of bodily resurrection, which had motivated Paul as a Pharisee, was fulfilled and resulted in his complete transformation into a Christ-follower when he met the risen Jesus. The resurrection hope of the gospel transformed Saul, the angry terrorist, into Paul, the loving evangelist.

The gospel completely changed Paul's life, just as it had transformed Jesus' disciples from a sad, scared bunch of men into a group of joy-filled, fearless evangelists. Only the power and hope of the gospel, authenticated by the risen Christ, could result in such a transformation in so many lives!

—*Malia E. Rodriguez.*

World Missions

On one of his Friday night visits to inmates on death row, Bob McAlister, tired after a long week and having seen all his regulars, peered into one last cell. On the dirty cement floor sat Rusty Woomer, surrounded by garbage and filthy walls, and smelling like a sewer. Rusty was the color of death and unresponsive. Cockroaches swarmed the cell, crawling over his matted hair and dirty clothes. He did not even try to swat them away. Gazing at this sight, Bob felt a strong presence of evil. He called Rusty's name. No response. He pleaded, "Rusty, just say the name of Jesus." Silence. Then a whisper, "Jesus. Jesus." With the mention of this name, a door opened in Rusty's heart. He bowed his head like a child and followed Bob's instruction to ask Jesus to forgive his sins.

The following Monday, Bob returned to Rusty's cell and received one of the greatest surprises of his life. The cell had been scrubbed clean, and the garbage had been removed. "I figured that's what Jesus wanted me to do," Rusty said (Colson, *Being the Body,* Thomas Nelson).

As surely as the disciples and others were witnesses to Christ's resurrection, Rusty Woomer in his death row cell became a witness to the power of the living Jesus.

Eleven men in one room saw the resurrected Jesus, among them a noted doubter, Thomas, whom Jesus invited to touch the wounds on his hands and side. His response: "My lord and my God." Seeing was believing for Thomas. Jesus then pronounced a blessing on those who, like Rusty Woomer, would centuries afterward believe without seeing (John 20:28-29). In our complex world, Jesus is still asking the question He posed to Mary Magdalene at the empty tomb: "Who are you looking for?" (cf. John 20:15).

One of the important truths that missionaries, and in fact all Christians, must not lose sight of is that nothing is too hard for God. We must never think that any person is beyond the reach of God's grace. If we start feeling that way, perhaps we are allowing pride to creep in. After all, the fact that God regenerated us was a big miracle, was it not? Paul called himself the chief of sinners (I Tim 1:15), and adopting his attitude will make us more effective witnesses to God's grace.

Jesus is still setting free the hopeless and the helpless. Wherever broken hearts reside, He asks, "Who are you looking for?"

When Jesus took His last breath on the cross, an incredible event occurred. Long-dead saints rose from their graves and were seen walking the streets of Jerusalem (cf. Matt. 27:52-53). Barely a sentence is devoted to this miraculous occurrence that foreshadows the future resurrection of all the dead in Christ. This is the effect Jesus has on the dead—He brings them to life!

On April 26, 1991, death in the electric chair propelled Rusty Woomer into the everlasting arms of Jesus Christ. Christians should love to tell about how Jesus has transformed them. We were not among the 500 who saw the resurrected Christ, yet we believe. Therefore, we have His promise that we too will one day rise from dead (Rom. 8:11).

Charles Wesley, in his long-beloved hymn "And Can It Be That I Should Gain?", expressed the joy of salvation with these words, "My chains fell off, my heart was free; I rose, went forth and followed Thee."

Jesus sets the captives free indeed!

—*Rose McCormick Brandon.*

The Jewish Aspect

Although Yeshua (Jesus the Messiah) had repeatedly told His disciples that He would be betrayed, arrested, crucified, and raised from the dead (cf. Matt. 16:21; 17:22-23; 20:17-19; 26:32; Mark 8:31; 9:30-32; 10:32-34; Luke 9:22, 43-45; 18:31-34), they did not understand what He was saying and were too afraid to ask Him about it. Yeshua also explained that His death, resurrection, and glorification were necessary so that many Jews and Gentiles could come to eternal life.

The Hebrew Scriptures often refer to an afterlife. "The Torah indicates in several places that the righteous will be reunited with their loved ones after death, while the wicked will be excluded from this reunion" (www.jewfaq. org). It speaks of many noteworthy people as being "gathered to their people" (cf. Gen. 25:8, Abraham; 25:17, Ishmael; 35:29, Isaac; 49:33, Jacob; Deut. 32:50, Moses and Aaron; II Kings 22:20, King Josiah) (www.jewfaq.org). Throughout the history of Judaism, however, the actual nature of the afterlife has been interpreted differently and is considered ambiguous.

When Yeshua told His disciples about His death and resurrection, He said it would yield a great harvest. "And Jesus answered them, saying, The hour is come, that the Son of man should be glorified. Verily, verily, I say unto you, Except a corn of wheat fall into the ground and die, it abideth alone: but if it die, it bringeth forth much fruit" (John 12:23-24). He was referring to Himself as the firstfruits of those who would be raised from the dead. He was relating His resurrection to the Feast of the Firstfruits (cf. Num. 28:26; Ex. 23:16; 34:22). "The concept of firstfruits derives from God's creation work. Because God created everything that exists, all of creation belongs to him (Psalm 24:1). Consequently, that which is first and best belongs to him and is to be given to him" (www.biblestudytools. com). "The Feast of Firstfruits marked thanksgiving to God for the firstfruits of the harvest—in this case, the grain and cereal harvested in the spring in ancient Palestine. . . . Somewhere around A.D. 30, the firstfruits of an even greater harvest issued forth, for it was on the first day after the Sabbath that occurred in the midst of the Passover celebration that Jesus rose from the dead" (www. ligonier.org).

Many people saw Yeshua following His resurrection (cf. Matt. 28:1-9; Mark 16:1-13; Luke 24:1-49; John 20:1—21:14; Acts 1:3-4). These same accounts, however, reveal that Yeshua's disciples and followers did not expect Him to be resurrected.

Paul went to great lengths to speak to the believers in the church at Corinth about the resurrection from the dead. No one seems to have been denying the resurrection of Jesus, but there were some false teachers who denied the reality of resurrected bodies for believers. They "did not deny Jesus' resurrection; they denied our resurrection. They were influenced either by Greek philosophy (which considered the resurrection undesirable, thinking the state of 'pure spirit' superior), or by the thinking of the Sadducees (which thought the world beyond to be just wishful thinking). . . . we lived forever, but not in resurrected bodies" (enduringword.com).

As a result, Paul provided the details about many who witnessed the risen Christ, and he emphasized the importance of the resurrection of all believers. He also spoke of Christ as the firstfruits of all those who had died.

—Deborah Markowitz Solan.

Guiding the Superintendent

Without the bodily resurrection of Christ, Christianity is only so much wishful thinking: "If Christ be not raised, your faith is vain; ye are yet in your sins . . . we are of all men most miserable" (I Cor. 15:17-19). But the most verified and reliable event from ancient history is the physical resurrection of Jesus Christ from the dead. In our text for this week, the apostle reminds his readers of the simple gospel according to the holy Scriptures and of the historical eyewitnesses to that profoundly decisive event.

DEVOTIONAL OUTLINE

1. The gospel (I Cor. 15:1-4). Paul begins this chapter by declaring to the Corinthian believers the saving gospel message that he first preached to them when he established them as a local body of Christ. Having received this saving message, it was the foundational truth on which their salvation stood before the holy God and Father of the Lord Jesus Christ. He warns that those who have forgotten this saving message or have disgraced it by their disobedience to it have given evidence that their faith was never genuine.

This is the gospel: Christ died for our sins, He was buried, and on the third day He rose from the dead. All this happened according to the prophetic Scriptures of the Old Testament.

2. First eyewitnesses (I Cor. 15:5-7). In a court of law, one of the most reliable forms of evidence is the testimony of responsible and honest eyewitnesses. The Gospels are filled with such eyewitness accounts of Jesus appearing many times to many different people after His resurrection. First, He appeared to Peter (Cephas), then to all the Twelve, and then to over 500 people at once, many of whom were still alive when Paul

was writing this epistle. Christ also appeared to His brother James (known as James the Just, who became the head of the church at Jerusalem), and again to all the apostles. This number of eyewitnesses is just too many to dismiss as anything other than testimonies to an historically reliable fact.

3. Paul as witness (I Cor. 15:8-11). No doubt the most reluctant (at least at first) witness to the resurrected Jesus was Paul himself. The last thing Paul had intended was to become a follower of Christ. He had at one time been among the most zealous of those who persecuted Christians. It was while he had been on his way to persecute Christians in Damascus that the risen Jesus had confronted him and sovereignly saved him (cf. Acts 9:1-20).

Paul humbly saw himself as the least of the apostles, undeserving of the title. He never ceased to be amazed that Christ had graciously saved him, a persecutor of the church of God, and called him to such an undeservedly high honor. Later, he even referred to himself as the chief of sinners (I Tim 1:15). Paul credited everything that he had ever accomplished to the grace of God.

This saving message of the gospel has always been the foundational message of the church. It has been the testimony of every faithful evangelist and preacher, and the unshakable fact of the resurrection of Jesus from the dead is the historic justification for our faith.

CHILDREN'S CORNER

Children need to understand that Christ's resurrection is not wishful imagining. It is based on solid, historical, eyewitness testimony. Jesus' resurrection is just as real as George Washington being our first president.
—*Martin R. Dahlquist.*

SCRIPTURE LESSON TEXT

II COR. 1:1 Paul, an apostle of Jesus Christ by the will of God, and Timothy *our* brother, unto the church of God which is at Corinth, with all the saints which are in all Achaia:

2 Grace *be* to you and peace from God our Father, and *from* the Lord Jesus Christ.

3 Blessed *be* God, even the Father of our Lord Jesus Christ, the Father of mercies, and the God of all comfort;

4 Who comforteth us in all our tribulation, that we may be able to comfort them which are in any trouble, by the comfort wherewith we ourselves are comforted of God.

5 For as the sufferings of Christ abound in us, so our consolation also aboundeth by Christ.

6 And whether we be afflicted, *it is* for your consolation and salvation, which is effectual in the enduring of the same sufferings which we also suffer: or whether we be comforted, *it is* for your consolation and salvation.

7 And our hope of you *is* stedfast, knowing, that as ye are partakers of the sufferings, so *shall ye be* also of the consolation.

8 For we would not, brethren, have you ignorant of our trouble which came to us in Asia, that we were pressed out of measure, above strength, insomuch that we despaired even of life:

9 But we had the sentence of death in ourselves, that we should not trust in ourselves, but in God which raiseth the dead:

10 Who delivered us from so great a death, and doth deliver: in whom we trust that he will yet deliver *us*;

11 Ye also helping together by prayer for us, that for the gift *bestowed* upon us by the means of many persons thanks may be given by many on our behalf.

NOTES

God's Comfort in Trouble

Lesson Text: II Corinthians 1:1-11

Related Scriptures: I Peter 4:12-19

TIME: probably A.D. 56   PLACE: from Macedonia

GOLDEN TEXT—"[God] comforteth us in all our tribulation, that we may be able to comfort them which are in any trouble, by the comfort wherewith we ourselves are comforted of God" (II Corinthians 1:4).

Introduction

Have you ever needed to be comforted? I am not talking about just being soothed, but rather to be strengthened and empowered to rise above your struggles. In a world that is vehemently opposed to the God we represent, we go through trials and even persecutions as we serve Christ. If the Christian life is all roses, it is only because of the many thorns in the rose bush.

Many people go through suffering and are desperate for comfort. What we need to realize is that Christ has suffered too, and He knows what we go through (cf. Heb. 4:15). It is futile to try to receive comfort from things such as alcohol, drugs, cigarettes, food, or anything else the world throws at us. Some try to read the latest books by popular self-help gurus, only to find that nothing works. The ways of the world provide no help for the child of God.

The only one who can provide the comfort that will help us through the hardest trials and tragedies of life is Jesus Christ.

LESSON OUTLINE

I. COMFORT—II COR. 1:1-7

II. AFFLICTION—II Cor. 1:8-9

III. DELIVERANCE—II Cor. 1:10-11

Exposition: Verse by Verse

COMFORT

II COR. 1:1 Paul, an apostle of Jesus Christ by the will of God, and Timothy our brother, unto the church of God which is at Corinth, with all the saints which are in all Achaia:

2 Grace be to you and peace from God our Father, and from the Lord Jesus Christ.

3 Blessed be God, even the Father of our Lord Jesus Christ, the Father of mercies, and the God of all comfort;

4 Who comforteth us in all our

tribulation, that we may be able to comfort them which are in any trouble, by the comfort wherewith we ourselves are comforted of God.

5 For as the sufferings of Christ abound in us, so our consolation also aboundeth by Christ.

6 And whether we be afflicted, it is for your consolation and salvation, which is effectual in the enduring of the same sufferings which we also suffer: or whether we be comforted, it is for your consolation and salvation.

7 And our hope of you is stedfast, knowing, that as ye are partakers of the sufferings, so shall ye be also of the consolation.

Introductory words (II Cor. 1:1-2). Paul begins II Corinthians the same way he began I Corinthians. He identifies himself as the author and establishes from the outset his apostolic calling and authority.

As we have learned in previous lessons, Paul did not seek apostleship on his own. In fact, prior to his conversion to Christ, being an apostle would have been the last thing he aspired to. Paul no doubt had his eyes set on rising up the ranks of the Sanhedrin, perhaps even becoming its president one day. He considered the believers to be blasphemous enemies of God and sought to eradicate them through severe persecution.

{It was Christ who called Paul to be an apostle to the Gentiles,}[Q1] and this calling was initiated suddenly as he traveled to Damascus for the sole purpose of arresting Christians and bringing them back to Jerusalem for punishment. Becoming an apostle could not have been further from Paul's mind, but God had other ideas.

Many of the Corinthian believers did not respect Paul's apostolic position. There were better speakers who were more impressive in their appearance and presentation. In the minds of these Corinthians, Paul was not up to par with their preferred philosophers.

Paul's relationship with the Corinthian church was testy, to say the least. However, he constantly addressed them as brothers and did not allow personal disappointment and frustration to tempt him to abandon them. He did, however, find himself regularly defending his ministry.

{The only difference from his personal salutation in his first letter is the mention of Timothy instead of Sosthenes.}[Q2] The writing of II Corinthians came not too long after the sending of I Corinthians, but by the time he wrote his second letter, Paul had joined up again with Timothy, whom he considered to be his son in the faith (cf. I Cor. 4:17; Phil. 2:19-22).

The letter is addressed to the saints in Corinth and is part of an ongoing correspondence with the Corinthian church. As is usual for Paul's epistles, he includes a prayer for grace and peace through God our Father and our Lord Jesus Christ. Although there has been much dispute between Paul and the Corinthians, he still has tender affection for them.

The source of comfort (II Cor. 1:3-4). After greeting the Corinthians, Paul then directs his attention to the praise of God. He was thankful *for* the Corinthian church, but he was thankful *to* God.

As Paul often did in his teachings, he makes the connection between God the Father and Jesus Christ. He praises the Father of our Lord Jesus Christ, which also shows the relationship between Jesus and His people, with Him being our Lord. What a wonderful relationship we have with God the Father and Christ. We have both a Heavenly Father and a Living Lord who love us unconditionally.

Paul also recognizes God as the Father of mercies. It is sad to see that some people see God as a dictator who is only interested in punishing people any time they make a mistake. That certainly is not how the Bible describes God, and Paul's presentation of Him as the Father of mercies shows that he sees God as tender and loving, not mean and domineering. This does not mean that He is going to give us everything we want but rather that He does not use His power to harm us. God loves us and spares us from His wrath.

{Paul then turns toward what is going to be the major theme of this passage. He is going to discuss comfort in affliction.}Q3 {But before getting to that, he affirms that God is the source of all comfort.}Q4 The world can give us things to make us temporarily numb to our problems, but only God can provide true comfort.

{God comforts us in *all* of our afflictions, not just some of them.}Q5 Nothing we go through is so bad that God cannot comfort us. His comfort does not come after the affliction is over, but while we are going through it. If you are suffering or hurting right now, you can turn to your Father; in Him you will find mercy and comfort.

God's comfort is often shown through His saints. When God comforts us, it is so that we can in turn comfort another person. Because of the power of the Holy Spirit, we can bring comfort to other people. We know how it feels to suffer, and we can comfort others because God has comforted us.

The need for comfort (II Cor. 1:5-6). When we are going through times of suffering, it is often difficult to understand why it is happening to us. Honestly, sometimes the answers never become clear, even after the trial comes to an end. We often look back and try to figure out why we went through that particular affliction, and it remains a puzzle. Keep in mind that some of the answers to our questions may not become clear until we are in eternity with the Lord.

Instead of focusing on the suffering, it is good to focus on the God of all comfort, as Paul has described. Paul was not writing from a fancy office with a world-class view of a big-city skyline or an oceanfront resort. He was a man who suffered a great deal and never enjoyed a life of luxury or complacence. He was imprisoned, beaten, threatened, chased out of town, hunted, shipwrecked, and even left for dead on one occasion.

Paul understood suffering, and he also understood comfort. He is a very qualified expert to speak on this subject, so we are wise to pay close attention to what he has to say. As Christians, we are not shielded from suffering, just as Christ was not shielded from suffering. Jesus said that the world hates us because it hated Him (John 15:18-21). According to Paul, we share abundantly in Christ's sufferings. What may seem somewhat surprising is that Paul does not resent this fact at all but embraces it (cf. Phil. 3:10-11).

Paul's assurance to those who suffer is that Jesus knows how to comfort us because He has suffered more than anyone. {The peace that comes with knowing Christ gives us the solid assurance that if we share in His suffering, then we can also expect to share in His comfort.}Q6

Your suffering is also intended to help you bless others who are suffering, just as Paul helped the church through his own suffering. He was not writing a manual or a self-help book on how to get rid of our suffering. He wrote to comfort us and help us endure it. He wrote from sympathy as one who knew what it was like to endure severe hardships repeatedly. {God may bring someone who is going through a real battle into your life someday, and you will be able to help him or her because you have been through something similar.}[Q7] It may seem like little consolation now, but God can use your suffering for His glory.

The hope in comfort (II Cor. 1:7). No one enjoys suffering, but it cannot shake the hope of a person who is sold out for God. The Spirit-filled believer knows that God is with him in the fire of tribulation. That does not mean it is good or right to seek suffering, but when it comes, we are not left alone to collapse under the weight of it.

God has given us the Holy Spirit to guide us through the hard times of life and to navigate our course to make sure we stay in step with the Lord. The danger is not in suffering, but in straying from Christ. We never want to be out of the Lord's revealed will, even in search of relief from pain. Our hope is in our merciful Father, who is the God of all comfort.

AFFLICTION

8 For we would not, brethren, have you ignorant of our trouble which came to us in Asia, that we were pressed out of measure, above strength, insomuch that we despaired even of life:

9 But we had the sentence of death in ourselves, that we should not trust in ourselves, but in God which raiseth the dead:

Paul's personal sufferings (II Cor. 1:8). In order to deal effectively with our trials, it is important to be honest about them. It is wrong to exaggerate them but it is also a mistake to downplay them. It is best to face up to them and seek the Lord's help to get us through.

Remember that God works through His church, so it is good to enlist the help of our brothers and sisters in Christ to counsel us through times of affliction. It can be a great help to listen to others tell their story about how God brought them through a rough time.

Paul's sufferings in Asia may point back to persecution he endured in Ephesus; he mentioned in I Corinthians that he had "fought with beasts" there (15:32). However, in our passage, he does not cite the exact location or occurrence, so we cannot know for certain. The Corinthians, on the other hand, would have been very familiar with what he was talking about.

While Paul does not go into specific details concerning the suffering he faced in Asia, he does say that it was so severe that he despaired of life itself. He literally thought he was going to die. The pressures or burdens he faced in Asia made him feel as though he was going to collapse under their weight.

Paul's fight for life (II Cor. 1:9). {The suffering Paul endured felt like a death sentence to him.}[Q8] At times it may seem like there is no way out of our suffering and that the end result must be death. In those moments, do not despair of life. Jesus Christ, who has conquered death, has promised to give you abundant life, but you must persevere in faith.

Persecution and suffering come to all believers (cf. Acts 14:22; II Tim. 3:12). {God allows these things to come to us in order to keep us close to Him.}[Q9] Truth be told, we often learn more from suffering and failure than we do from victory and success. It is in the fire of suffering that we see the power of God at work.

DELIVERANCE

10 Who delivered us from so great a death, and doth deliver: in whom we trust that he will yet deliver us;

11 Ye also helping together by prayer for us, that for the gift bestowed upon us by the means of many persons thanks may be given by many on our behalf.

Deliverance from death (II Cor. 1:10). In writing about his personal suffering, Paul does not try to act brave or pretend that he was not afraid. In fact, he was so afraid at one point when living in Corinth that Jesus Himself had to actually come to him to assure him that no harm was going to come to him (cf. Acts 18:9-10).

Courage is not the absence of fear. It is pushing through in spite of fear. Paul was courageous not because he was fearless, but because he was faithful. The more he suffered, the more he was delivered. The more he was delivered, the more confident he became that God would deliver him again and again, no matter what he went through.

No matter what kind of suffering you may have gone through or may be going through right now, God is actually building up your faith. He will see you through. If you have been delivered before, know that He can handle your current problems as well. Nothing is too hard for the Lord.

Our hope is set on God, and our faith in Him is fixed. Suffering cannot steal our peace and joy. We can surrender them by giving in to temptation or negative thinking, but they cannot be stolen from a child of God. Remember that hope in the Lord is not wishful thinking—it is a sure thing.

Deliverance through prayer (II Cor. 1:11). What we have learned in this lesson is that God promises to comfort us in suffering and that He gives us strength to endure. The word translated "comfort" and "consolation" (the same word in Greek) appears ten times in verses 3-7. Your afflictions are serious, but so is God's commitment to comfort you.

Suffering seems to be endless when we are in the midst of it, but be assured that at the right time, God will deliver you completely from all suffering. Paul encourages us all to take courage in the Lord because He will comfort us and give us the strength to endure until His purposes are fulfilled.

{The key to perseverance is not to try harder or to wrestle more with our issues, but rather to turn to God in prayer.}[Q10] There is no shortcut for this. It is vital that we all pray for one another, because suffering is universal. It comes to everyone in varying degrees. No one is immune to suffering.

Just as Paul prayed for the church, he needed the church to pray for him. Our spiritual leaders, such as pastors, elders, evangelists, teachers, and deacons, are all expected to pray for the people they preside over. The people likewise need to pray for their leaders. Suffering comes to everyone, but so does deliverance to those who keep moving forward in faith.

—*Robert Ferguson, Jr.*

QUESTIONS

1. How did Paul end up in the apostolic ministry?

2. Who replaced Sosthenes from I Corinthians as Paul's companion (II Cor. 1:1)?

3. What is the overall theme of this week's passage of Scripture?

4. Who does Paul say is the source of all comfort?

5. How many of our afflictions does God comfort us in?

6. What assurance do we have about sharing in Christ's sufferings?

7. How can your suffering help another person?

8. How severe were Paul's personal sufferings?

9. What is one reason why suffering comes to all believers?

10. What is the key to perseverance?

—*Robert Ferguson, Jr.*

Preparing to Teach the Lesson

How do you respond to troubles in your life? Is your first response to worry, to become fearful, or perhaps to lash out in anger? Do you exhaust all your "practical" options first? Or do you begin by humbling yourself before the Lord in prayer? Most of us would have to admit that we often fall into one of the first responses noted above rather than the one involving prayer.

But we should remember that God always has a redemptive purpose for the trials He brings into our lives, even if most of the time we fail to understand it. God is also mighty and abundant in bestowing comfort on believers who are facing trouble. This is the focus of our lesson for this week.

TODAY'S AIM

Facts: to recognize that God comforts us in our troubles.

Principle: to understand that as we are comforted in our troubles by God, we become equipped to comfort others in their troubles.

Application: to seek opportunities to comfort others in their troubles as God has comforted us in ours.

INTRODUCING THE LESSON

In his second epistle to the church at Corinth, Paul takes a much milder tone than in his previous letter. Absent are the pointed pleas to forsake divisive behavior. In their place, he instructs them in the gentle virtue of comforting one another and consoling each other in their trials.

DEVELOPING THE LESSON

1. Greetings (II Cor. 1:1-2). In contrast to the opening of his first letter to the church at Corinth, Paul's greeting in this second letter is much more cordial. It would seem that the severe admonitions of his first epistle had achieved their desired effect in reforming the conduct of the Corinthian believers.

The greeting is from both Paul and his beloved companion Timothy. Those in Corinth are addressed as "saints" (holy ones) without reservation or further comment, unlike the greeting of his previous letter, in which these same Corinthians were merely "called to be saints" (cf. I Cor. 1:2), after which Paul felt compelled to launch quickly into a series of admonitions. But here he merely bids them grace and peace from God their Father and His beloved Son, their Lord Jesus Christ.

2. Being comforted, we comfort (II Cor. 1:3-6). Paul now sets up the principle of God's abundant comfort toward believers in their tribulations. He blesses God as the "Father of mercies, and the God of all comfort." Paul has had much need of comfort at this juncture of his ministry (cf. vss. 8-9).

He testifies that in whatever affliction we may find ourselves, God is more than able to give us the comfort we need. God does this to prepare us to in turn comfort others in their afflictions, using the same comfort that God Himself revealed to us when He comforted us.

Verse 5 may remind us of Paul's declaration about the relationship between sin and grace in Romans 5:20. He declares that as our sufferings for Christ abound, God's consolation and comfort also abound in Christ. The sufferings of this life cannot outperform God's power to comfort us and provide for our needs in the midst of our sufferings (cf. I Cor. 10:13).

Paul next declares that whether he is enduring affliction or being comforted, both his affliction and his consolation are for the sake of his readers' salvation. God intended for them to be consoled by observing Paul's endurance in affliction and also by observing the abundant manner in which he received comfort from the Lord.

3. Deliverance from death (II Cor. 1:7-11). Paul next testifies of his assured hope about the Corinthian believers. As they endure similar sufferings to his in their service for Christ, they will likewise be partakers of the abundance of God's comfort and provision.

Starting in verse 8, Paul begins to tell the Corinthians about a specific affliction that he has been suffering, one that began while he was in Asia. Commentators are unsure what the specific affliction was. Some think it might have been linked to the rebellion in Ephesus (Acts 19:23-35). Others believe it was some persecution event that is not recorded in Scripture. Still others believe it was a debilitating illness that had brought Paul nearly to death's door.

Whatever it was, it must have been extremely serious for him to use such exceptionally strong language to describe it. Wording such as "we despaired even of life" (vs. 8) and "we had the sentence of death in ourselves" (vs. 9) are uncharacteristic of Paul (cf. 4:8-10), whose resiliency under trials is well attested throughout the book of Acts.

Even in the midst of such grave affliction, Paul clearly sees its divine purpose in disciplining him not to trust in himself, but in God. He is even able to raise the dead to fulfill His purposes if He sovereignly chooses to do so (1:9).

Apparently, whatever Paul's suffering was about, God did indeed deliver him from it, even if it had brought him close to death. From this divine instance of deliverance, Paul took renewed faith that God would continue to deliver him from whatever came next.

In verse 11, Paul acknowledges his debt of gratitude to the Corinthians for their support in praying for him, and he encourages them now to praise God and give Him abundant thanksgiving for the Lord's answer to their prayers on his behalf.

ILLUSTRATING THE LESSON

The troubled believer on the left is being comforted by God. On the right, that same believer moves on to comfort another in his troubles.

GOD COMFORTS US SO THAT WE MAY COMFORT OTHERS

CONCLUDING THE LESSON

Although Paul was sorely afflicted throughout his years of service to the gospel, he always understood a key divine purpose for his sufferings, namely, to train him not to trust in himself but to trust in God alone. God's priorities for our good are primarily eternal, not temporal.

ANTICIPATING THE NEXT LESSON

Next week's lesson focuses on the glory of the new covenant in contrast to the merely temporary types and shadows of the old covenant.

—John Lody.

PRACTICAL POINTS

1. God sovereignly chooses each of His servants for a specific time and place to accomplish His purposes (II Cor. 1:1).
2. God gives His people the grace and peace they need to fulfill their purpose (vs. 2).
3. God's comfort toward us has multiplied benefit; it is used through us to help others (vss. 3-4).
4. Patience and endurance in trials are evidence of God's work in those who trust Him (vss. 5-7).
5. Our troubles can seem overwhelming, but Christ gives us grace to endure them all (vss. 8-9).
6. Christians help one another endure tough times through steadfast prayer (vss. 10-11).

—Cheryl Y. Powell.

RESEARCH AND DISCUSSION

1. Why does Paul use the word "saints" in his introduction?
2. Who is the Comforter (cf. John 14:16)? How has God comforted you in your troubles? Discuss.
3. How does God use affliction and trials to make His people more effective? Discuss.
4. Why is it so important to display Christ's mercy and compassion?
5. How did Paul personally experience the mercy and comfort of God in his life?
6. Why is intercessory prayer so essential?

—Cheryl Y. Powell.

ILLUSTRATED HIGH POINTS

The sufferings of Christ abound in us (II Cor. 1:5)

Researchers have studied a social practice called "do-gooder derogation." This is when those who cannot or choose not to do good themselves try to stop the actual person doing good from looking that way to others.

In the study being referred to, the control group was given money that they could either keep or give to causes. All went smoothly. In the second group, the participants were told they would be giving an award to the most generous person. This group began to show hostility and to try to sabotage people in the group that were doing good things.

It is not just Jesus and His gospel message that the world hates; it is also you as you become more and more like Him!

Afflicted . . . for your consolation (vs. 6)

The boy saw a hand-written sign, "Puppies for sale."

"Sir," implored the boy, I have thirty-seven cents."

"That's just fine," replied the old softie as he called his dog and her brood.

Four furry pups leapt and scampered behind their mama, but the fifth hobbled weakly, far behind.

"I want that one," said the boy, and the farmer showed concern.

"That one is the runt, I'm afraid. Feel free to pick a stronger one."

The boy lifted his pant leg, revealing his heavily-braced leg. "Sir," he explained, "I don't run too well either. I understand."

We need someone who understands the difficulties of life. That someone is Jesus!

—Therese Greenberg.

Golden Text Illuminated

"[God] comforteth us in all our tribulation, that we may be able to comfort them which are in any trouble, by the comfort wherewith we ourselves are comforted of God" (II Corinthians 1:4).

If Paul's first letter to the Corinthians is mostly a rebuke, his second letter takes a more conciliatory tone. This is evident in the seven opening verses, where ten times he uses the Greek word (or a form of it) rendered "comfort."

Paul cherishes the idea of comfort, or consolation, in Christ. Later in this chapter, he records the tribulations he suffered in Asia. These troubles were so extreme that they made him despair "even of life" (II Cor. 1:8). We do not know all the details that Paul refers to here, but based on his other epistles, it likely involved persecution.

Paul knew that he was not alone in his distress. In describing the comfort that he experienced from God, Paul used a Greek word that carries the idea of encouragement and exhortation, to reach down and provide help and strength to someone in need.

The Bible tells us that all three Persons of the Trinity have a comforting ministry. The Father is "the God of all comfort" (II Cor. 1:3), while Christ advocates for us when we sin (I John 2:1). In the Gospel of John, Jesus calls the Holy Spirit "the Comforter" four times (14:6; 14:26; 15:26; 16:7). In biblical times, this Greek word could refer to an advocate or a defense attorney. The Holy Spirit counsels us with truth and defends us against the accusations of Satan.

Why did Paul write this letter? After establishing the church at Corinth and moving on to other missionary endeavors, Paul learned that some in the church had begun to deride his authority, persuaded by the so-called "very chiefest apostles" (II Cor. 11:5). Paul is not referring here to any true apostles, such as Peter or John. He is referring rather to Judaizers who, because of their adherence to Jewish law and rabbinical teachings, considered themselves superior to Paul and the other true apostles. These false teachers had infiltrated the Corinthian congregation and begun to undermine Paul's authority.

Paul considered himself the spiritual father of the Corinthian believers. He was careful to note that all consolation comes from the "Father of mercies" (1:3), that is, God the Father. Compassion is not a trait that God only acquired after Jesus appeared on the scene. The Old Testament describes the mercy and compassion of Yahweh in many memorable passages (cf. Ex. 34:6-7; Ps. 103:8-14; Neh. 9:17-25). During his crushing trials, Paul had personally experienced God's compassion. Paul especially praised God for comforting him through the ministry of Titus, a Gentile missionary who had served the church at Corinth. Titus reported that the Corinthians felt deep sorrow for their sins and longed to see Paul again (cf. II Cor. 7:13-16).

God's comfort is not merely for our personal satisfaction; God comforts us so that we may also comfort others in their tribulations. All of this is connected to Christ, who suffered for our sake, and who also reaches out to comfort and encourage us in our troubles. We in turn should share the comfort we have received with others in need.

—Mark Winter.

Heart of the Lesson

Sometime between the writing of I and II Corinthians, Paul apparently made a "painful" visit to Corinth (cf. II Cor. 2:1). Paul had heard about serious matters that needed to be addressed. There were moral issues, and false teachers had invaded Corinth and questioned Paul's authority as one of Christ's apostles (cf. 11:4-6). He had written to them another letter, now lost, about these situations. Now, as Paul prepared to make another trip to Corinth, he wrote this letter, which is called Second Corinthians.

1. God's apostle (II Cor. 1:1-2). Paul began his letter by establishing his apostleship (Acts 9:15; 22:14). Paul also vouched for Timothy as his protege and co-laborer in ministry.

As an apostle appointed to share the gospel with the Gentiles, Paul had faced severe persecution not only from Gentiles but more painfully from his own people, the Jews. In his suffering for Jesus, Paul proved not only his sincerity as an apostle but fulfilled Jesus' prophecy that he would endure hardships as His apostle (cf. Acts 9:16).

2. God's comfort (II Cor. 1:3-7). The Corinthian church had suffered much from division, sin, judgment, and persecution. Suffering tests the strength of our faith and the authenticity of our hope. In the midst of trials, Paul and the Corinthians had come face-to-face with their complete dependence on God.

Without the support of God's grace and sovereignty, the weight of pain would crush us. Paul wanted to remind the Corinthians that through the strength of the indwelling Holy Spirit, they could trust God to bring good from their suffering.

Many people object to Christianity because they cannot reconcile the existence of an all-loving, all-powerful God with the existence of suffering and evil in the world. While we cannot understand all of God's purposes for allowing suffering, II Corinthians explains one reason: to share God's comfort with others.

When two people share the same type of pain, they are able to extend comfort to one another. There is no better example of a source of comfort than Jesus Christ, the Son of God, who took humanity upon Himself, endured the pain caused by living in a sin-cursed world, and then died in our place so that we could receive God's perfect, eternal comfort (cf. Phil 2:5-8). As our perfect, sinless High Priest, Jesus identifies with our struggles and sorrows (cf. Heb. 4:14-16), and He connects us with the God of all comfort.

3. God's plan (II Cor. 1:8-11). Paul's experience of suffering was proof of his apostleship and the fulfillment of Jesus' prophecy when He called Paul as an apostle. Paul's life also illustrated for the Corinthians how to suffer with hope.

Paul and his associates endured so much hardship in Asia that they had at times despaired of their very lives. They faced beatings, riots, and cruelty. Discouragement and depression had pushed Paul past the limits of his own strength into the loving arms of our all-powerful, death-defeating God.

When Jesus rose from the dead, He and the Father sent the Holy Spirit to empower Paul and all believers to live with resurrection power and hope. Paul trusted that God was in control of his sufferings and had fulfilled His sovereign purposes through the Corinthians' intercession on his behalf. As Christians comfort and pray for one another, they fulfill God's will in the world.

—Malia E. Rodriguez.

World Missions

Six months after my sister lost her son in a tragic accident, she and I attended church while visiting our mother. There we met a couple my sister had known from high school. This outgoing pair modeled friendliness and Christian joy, so I was surprised when, during lunch, they told us they had lost their son through sad circumstances only two years previously. They told us how they had been inconsolable for an entire year. Then they had cried out to God to relieve them of the dark grief that had settled in their chests like a rock. My teary sister nodded. She knew about that rock. When they finished their story, she told them hers. They assured her that God would help her just as He had helped them. We left their company knowing that God had providentially arranged our meeting. To share her pain with those who really understood her grief was a tremendous comfort to my sister.

One of the purposes of our sufferings is that we will, after God has comforted us, offer like comfort to others (II Cor. 1:4). When we speak from experience, as this couple did, our words sing with the anointing of the Holy Spirit, for the Spirit Himself is the Comforter. He empowers our weak human attempts at comforting others. The word "comfort" comes from the Latin *confortare*, which means "to strengthen greatly."

After a surgery I underwent, while I was coming out of anesthesia, I felt not only physical pain but a dark mental fog. The room was busy with strangers. Then my husband entered the room, sat by my bed, and held my hand. I shall never forget the comfort that flowed into me from him. Without words, his touch had grounded me and eased me back into reality. Comforters are hand-holders. It is amazing how much comfort one can give simply by being present with one who needs comfort.

Prayer is an important component of being a comforter. When comforters pray, people feel the support of their prayers. How many have testified that in a time of suffering, when they could not pray for themselves, the prayers of others carried them through? How often has God alerted people, even awakened them from deep sleep, to pray for someone they had not even thought of for a long time? Stories of Spirit-empowered prayer could fill libraries.

I once had a dream in which I saw a friend wringing her hands and saying, "I'm falling apart!" I awoke and prayed for her. The next day, I contacted her. She said that the words I heard in my dream were the exact ones she had shared with her pastor the day before. That God had alerted me to pray for her meant to her that He was with her and she would not fall apart after all. She did not. Today, she herself is a comforter and an encourager to many.

A comforter is someone who not only encourages us but also sympathizes with us. In times when there is no human comfort, and we cannot confide in anyone, The Holy Spirit, the true Comforter, holds our hand and walks with us. He is the One who offers us supernatural comfort. If God shielded us from all pain, what stories of His goodness would we have to tell? How could we feel another's grief as that couple I told about felt my sister's grief?

Missionaries hold out the prospect of the comfort of the Holy Spirit to those who are in spiritual darkness without Christ. They offer them the grace and comfort that no false deity could ever offer. Comforting is a holy work.

—*Rose McCormick Brandon.*

The Jewish Aspect

As the Hebrew Scriptures record, when sin entered the world through the disobedience of Adam and Eve (Gen. 3:6-24), suffering began to plague mankind. The results of what would happen if the Israelites sinned against God were spelled out clearly to the Israelites when God gave Moses the Law on Mount Sinai. God told Moses that He would reward the Israelites if they followed His ways and that He would punish them if they did not (Deut. 11:8-32).

Throughout the Hebrew Scriptures, God appealed to the Israelites to live uprightly before Him. Their disobedience led to suffering and death. The prophet Jeremiah, in the book of Lamentations, wept and grieved bitterly over the destruction of Jerusalem and the temple as a result of the Israelites' continued rebellion against God.

Suffering, even by the righteous, was seen in the life of Job, who was tested by God and endured great suffering while he attempted to remain faithful to God. "Yet man is born unto trouble, as the sparks fly upward" (Job 5:7). But Job also acknowledged that God provided hope, healing, deliverance, and redemption for his people (vss. 15-27). "For he maketh sore, and bindeth up: he woundeth, and his hands make whole" (vs. 18).

Although the Lord used Assyria to punish Israel for its sinful ways, He then also punished Assyria for its sin and cruelty. The prophet Nahum predicted the downfall of Assyria. "The Hebrew name 'Nahum' means 'comfort' or 'consolation.' . . . Nahum's announcement was a 'comfort' or 'consolation' to the inhabitants of Judah, as it predicted the downfall of Assyria, a savage and cruel enemy of Israel and Judah" (lifehopeandtruth.com).

Isaiah admonished God's people for their sins and said that if they did not repent, God would purify them through suffering. However, Isaiah also said that God would forgive them if they returned to Him and that He would comfort them (Isa. 51:3-12). "The gospel is given in Isaiah 40:1, where he exhorts, 'Comfort, comfort my people, says your God.' The final twenty-six chapters of Isaiah are often called 'the volume of comfort' with its promise of present comfort and the future promise of the suffering servant who comes to give hope, help, and release—'to comfort all who mourn'" (61:3) (www.biblestudytools.com). Isaiah said that God was like a mother who comforts her children (cf. Isa. 66:13), and he also often referred to God as merciful and compassionate (cf. 30:18, 49:13, 54:10, 63:7).

When Paul spoke to the believers at Corinth, he expanded upon the synagogue prayer that described God as "The Father of Mercies" and included the phrase "God of all comfort"—words that were meant to strengthen and encourage. He communicated that one of God's purposes for suffering was to enable us to comfort others with the comfort we have received from God. "How did Paul comfort others with the comfort with which he had been comforted by God? Overall by his example—as they observed his attitude and deportment in and through and after his sufferings" (www.biblestudytools.com).

—*Deborah Markowitz Solan.*

Guiding the Superintendent

There is indeed such a thing as "good grief!" Our society tells us to avoid as much suffering as possible and that joy is found only in pleasure and ease. But Paul's approach to suffering is radically counter-cultural. Sufferings and trials, if understood biblically, help believers keep their focus on God as the God of all comfort.

DEVOTIONAL OUTLINE

1. Gracious greetings (II Cor. 1:1-2). In contrast to the confrontational tone of I Corinthians, the whole tenor of II Corinthians is much more directed toward conciliation and comfort. It seems that Paul intended to use this letter to supply balance to his relationship with the church at Corinth after all the rebukes and admonishments that characterized his earlier letter.

Paul identifies himself as an apostle by the will of God. He also identifies Timothy as the one who is helping him write this letter. He sends greetings not only to Corinth, but also to all believers in the region of Achaia. He commends God's grace and peace to them, as was his custom.

2. The God of all comfort (II Cor. 1:3-7). Paul begins by blessing God the Father for being merciful and comforting. The image is of a Father who is concerned, involved, and loving toward His children. This sets the tone for the entire epistle. Paul is coming to them as the emissary of God's mercy and comfort rather than to admonish them as he did in his first epistle.

There is a cyclical pattern to the comfort we receive from God. He comforts us so that we in turn can comfort others. Suffering, then, is intended by God to cause believers to reach beyond themselves.

"Comfort" is the Greek word that is often used to refer to the Holy Spirit, and it means to sympathize with, strengthen, and encourage someone in need. God enables us to comfort others by reassuring them that they are not alone in their troubles and that we ourselves can identify with them because we have experienced the same troubles that they are undergoing.

3. Paul's afflictions (II Cor. 1:8-11). The apostle was not offering trite clichés. His advice came from his own suffering and comfort. The Corinthians were well acquainted with Paul's sufferings (cf. II Cor. 6:4-10). Paul saw his own abundant sufferings as sharing in the sufferings of Christ. Along with his suffering, Paul could also testify to God's abundant comfort. The reason for his afflictions was for their comfort.

The hardships Paul had suffered in Asia had taken a great physical and emotional toll on him. There had been times when he had despaired of living and felt like someone who had been sentenced to death. But that had been God's purpose—to bring Paul to the end of himself so that he might trust totally in the God who raises the dead.

There was one more reason why Paul suffered so much. There is a special community that believers will experience in suffering. As believers go through great suffering, the body of Christ is drawn together to unite in prayer. Suffering drives the church to its knees.

CHILDREN'S CORNER

Children typically try to just make suffering go away. This lesson should direct their attention to the divine purpose behind suffering—to enable them to comfort others who are suffering.

—*Martin R. Dahlquist.*

SCRIPTURE LESSON TEXT

II COR. 3:7 But if the ministration of death, written *and* engraven in stones, was glorious, so that the children of Israel could not stedfastly behold the face of Moses for the glory of his countenance; which *glory* was to be done away:

8 How shall not the ministration of the spirit be rather glorious?

9 For if the ministration of condemnation *be* glory, much more doth the ministration of righteousness exceed in glory.

10 For even that which was made glorious had no glory in this respect, by reason of the glory that excelleth.

11 For if that which is done away *was* glorious, much more that which remaineth *is* glorious.

12 Seeing then that we have such hope, we use great plainness of speech:

13 And not as Moses, *which* put a vail over his face, that the children of Israel could not stedfastly look to the end of that which is abolished:

14 But their minds were blinded: for until this day remaineth the same vail untaken away in the reading of the old testament; which *vail* is done away in Christ.

15 But even unto this day, when Moses is read, the vail is upon their heart.

16 Nevertheless when it shall turn to the Lord, the vail shall be taken away.

17 Now the Lord is that Spirit: and where the Spirit of the Lord *is,* there *is* liberty.

18 But we all, with open face beholding as in a glass the glory of the Lord, are changed into the same image from glory to glory, *even* as by the Spirit of the Lord.

NOTES

Glory of the New Covenant

Lesson Text: II Corinthians 3:7-18

Related Scriptures: Exodus 34:29-35; II Corinthians 4:13-18

TIME: probably A.D. 56   PLACE: from Macedonia

GOLDEN TEXT—"Now the Lord is that Spirit: and where the Spirit of the Lord is, there is liberty" (II Corinthians 3:17).

Introduction

The old covenant that Israel was under was built around the Mosaic Law that God gave to the Israelites in the wilderness after their Exodus from Egypt. This law was binding until Christ came and ushered in the new covenant, which we are under today. The Jews were devoted to the law and cherished it (cf. Ps. 119:43-48). Under the new covenant, the law is still important in that it expounds on holiness, but we are not bound by it.

There was a stark problem with the law. It demanded absolute adherence and obedience to its provisions. The law thus showed the people their sin, but it provided for atonement and forgiveness in only a limited way. It pointed ahead to God's ultimate solution for sin but did not provide that solution itself.

The new covenant, however, set aside the old and revealed the fullness of God's grace and mercy. Since we could not satisfy the demands of the old covenant, Jesus fulfilled it for us and gave us a new covenant that reconciles us with God by grace through faith. The new covenant is not about keeping a set of rules, but about trusting and loving the Lord Jesus Christ.

LESSON OUTLINE

I. GLORY HIDDEN—II COR. 3:7-11

II. GLORY REVEALED—
    II Cor. 3:12-18

Exposition: Verse by Verse

GLORY HIDDEN

II COR. 3:7 But if the ministration of death, written and engraven in stones, was glorious, so that the children of Israel could not stedfastly behold the face of Moses for the glory of his countenance; which glory was to be done away:

8 How shall not the ministration of the spirit be rather glorious?

9 For if the ministration of condemnation be glory, much more

doth the ministration of righteousness exceed in glory.

10 For even that which was made glorious had no glory in this respect, by reason of the glory that excelleth.

11 For if that which is done away was glorious, much more that which remaineth is glorious.

Death in the law (II Cor. 3:7-8). In order to explain the difference between the old and new covenants, Paul makes a comparison that shows the superiority of the new over the old. {He refers to the old covenant as the ministry of death that was carved in stone (vs. 7).}[Q1] {The new covenant, on the other hand, is the ministry of the Spirit and gives life (vs. 6).}[Q2]

The problem with the old covenant is not that it was bad or evil in and of itself (cf. Rom. 7:12). {On the contrary, the law fulfilled God's intention for it by showing people their inability to please Him on their own; it revealed personal sin and pointed to their need for a Saviour (cf. Gal. 2:16; cf. Rom. 7:7).}[Q3] Paul calls the old covenant the ministry of death because the law can only condemn and has no saving power. Trying to be obedient to the law is futile because no one is able to keep all of the commandments in the law.

But what if you keep most of the law? The law is not divided up into different compartments or categories that we all need to work on to get better. It is a reflection of God's complete holiness and the righteousness He requires from us. {Therefore, in terms of obedience, the law should be seen as one unit; violating even one of its commandments constitutes violating the whole law (cf. Jas. 2:10).}[Q4]

This unity of the law is why John states that one who hates his brother is considered a murderer (I John 3:15). The same law that condemns murder (Ex. 20:13) also condemns hatred (Lev. 19:17). There is no mercy within the law itself. It condemns all who violate it, and everyone is guilty of violating God's perfect standard (cf. Rom. 3:23).

The law was not without glory, however. Since it came from God, it certainly was glorious not only in its effect but even in its presentation. Moses received the law on Mount Sinai from God Himself. It was not given to him in a vision or a dream. God gave it to him directly, in His very presence.

{Moses' face shone so brightly from the glory of God when he received the law that the Israelites were afraid and unable to look at him (cf. Ex. 34:29-31).}[Q5] The glory of the law was temporary, however, as Jesus would fulfill it in order to bring in the new covenant that all believers would be saved under.

Paul argues that if the "ministry of death" came with glory although it was coming to an end, how much greater would the "ministry of the Spirit" be? Because the ministry of the Spirit, or the new covenant, is eternal and far more powerful than the old covenant, it stands to reason that it far surpasses the old covenant in glory.

Glory in the covenants (II Cor. 3:9-10). It is a mistake to think that the old covenant, which Paul calls the ministry of condemnation (vs. 9), was of little consequence or impact. It should not be seen as unnecessary. It simply was incomplete.

Likewise, the new covenant, now referred to by Paul as the ministry of righteousness, should not be viewed as some sort of divine backup plan. The new covenant was prophesied centuries before it was actually inaugurated (cf. Jer. 31:31-34); it was not God's hasty reaction to an unforeseen failure of His first covenant. The old covenant accomplished God's purpose in His overall plan of redemption. Salvation was never to be found in the law, but in Christ.

{Christ is the reason the glory of the new covenant far exceeds the glory of the old covenant. Righteousness is much greater than condemnation, and life is preferred over death.}[Q6] The new covenant in Christ brings freedom and liberty, while the old covenant of the law brings bondage and oppression.

In comparison with the new covenant, the old covenant has no glory at all. That is quite a statement to make, because Paul has already said in his commentary on Exodus 34 that the old covenant had a glory so bright that Moses' face shone from it.

{Paul is not asserting that the old covenant was not glorious at all, but rather that it had no glory in comparison to the new covenant.}[Q7] It was far surpassed in glory by the new covenant to the point that its glory that was once extremely bright is completely overwhelmed by the glory of the new covenant.

The old covenant, while glorious at one time, is no longer glorious because it has been replaced with something new and far greater in scope and power. Its replacement did not come because God saw that it did not work and decided to try something else. Instead, Jesus came and fulfilled the old covenant (cf. Matt. 5:17), meaning that He satisfied all of its demands. In establishing the new covenant, Jesus did not simply add new teachings or provisions to the existing law; He completely fulfilled it on our behalf, thereby instituting a covenant that is eternal.

Glory in the new covenant (II Cor. 3:11). The old covenant has been brought to an end because of the realization of the new covenant. God knew that it was only a temporary covenant; it was never intended to be permanent. Even though the old covenant was very limited in what it could accomplish and how long it would last, it still contained great glory while it was in effect.

Paul's point is not to diminish the glory of the old covenant at all, but rather to show the greatness of the glory of the new covenant, which is perfect and permanent. The new covenant brings forgiveness of sin, redemption from bondage to sin, freedom in Christ, and liberty in the Holy Spirit. The old covenant brought none of these things.

The new covenant is an everlasting testament that will never be replaced. There is nothing that can possibly be greater than this covenant that brings righteousness and life. Because of Christ, the Mediator of the new covenant, the glory of the new covenant far exceeds the glory of the old.

GLORY REVEALED

12 Seeing then that we have such hope, we use great plainness of speech:

13 And not as Moses, which put a vail over his face, that the children of Israel could not stedfastly look to the end of that which is abolished:

14 But their minds were blinded: for until this day remaineth the same vail untaken away in the reading of the old testament; which vail is done away in Christ.

15 But even unto this day, when Moses is read, the vail is upon their heart.

16 Nevertheless when it shall turn to the Lord, the vail shall be taken away.

17 Now the Lord is that Spirit: and where the Spirit of the Lord is, there is liberty.

18 But we all, with open face beholding as in a glass the glory of the Lord, are changed into the same image from glory to glory, even as by the Spirit of the Lord.

The hope of faith in Christ (II Cor. 3:12-13). {The effects of the new covenant allow us to be bold in our faith because Jesus secured victory over sin for us on the cross. This is our hope in life and death.}[Q8]

The cross is where Jesus defeated the power of sin and darkness that once held us in its grip (cf. Col. 2:13-15). The cross is the place where the old covenant ended and the new covenant began. The cross is an offense to many today, but it is the power of God to those of us who are saved (cf. I Cor. 1:18).

Without the cross, there is no new covenant, no salvation, no forgiveness of sin. There is no victory over sin and death. An instrument of suffering, torture, and execution seems like a strange place to declare victory, but the cross is no usual place. It is the place where the love of God met the righteous demands of the wrath of God—and sin was destroyed.

{The victory that the new covenant gives us over sin causes us to be bold.}[Q9] Being bold should not be confused with being obnoxious, and being confident does not excuse being rude. We are bold in our proclamation of the gospel, but we are to be loving in our presentation (cf. I Pet. 3:15).

Moses was not able to be bold among the people under the old covenant because the glory shining from his face obliged him to put on a veil. The people were afraid when they saw him descend from the mountain after meeting with God. That glimpse of glory did not cause the people to rejoice. It caused them to run.

{The glory from the old covenant was fading even as it shone from Moses' face, showing its temporal effect. It had no eternal impact on the people.}[Q10] Moses veiled his face to protect the people from the radiant glory that shone from him. The people were terrified to come into the presence of God because they knew they had sinned, and the glory from the cove-nant mediated by Moses provided no lasting remedy for their sin problem.

The veil on Moses' face should be seen as a representation both of God's holiness and of His mercy. It showed that sinful man was not able to come into the presence of God and stand in His glory. It also served as a shield that protected man from God's glory and spared him from God's judgment. The fading glory of the old covenant shows us that it was incapable of providing us reconciliation with God. It could only bring division. But thankfully, it was coming to an end.

Veiled to faith in Christ (II Cor. 3:14-15). Tradition and old ways are very hard for many people to set aside, and this is especially true of the old covenant. Although good works cannot give us the righteousness we really need, it seems somehow more natural to us to work our way to salvation rather than accept mercy through faith. This is the major crux of the law. Works of obedience are necessary to adhere to it. But if it were possible to save ourselves through good works and by keeping the law, then Christ died for no reason (cf. Gal. 2:21).

Since their hearts remain veiled today just as in Moses' day, many people cannot see the glory of the new covenant. They fail to see and receive the message of the gospel and to realize all the wonderful blessings that God has for those who have faith in Christ.

The only way for the veil to be removed is if they turn to Christ. Jesus is the only one who can take the veil away. It is sad to realize that so many people are blinded by Satan and keep that veil in place, which prevents them from understanding the beautiful realities of the new covenant.

The problem facing the people of Israel in Moses' day was that their minds were hardened against God because of idolatry. They were rebels and insurgents. Christ is the only answer to our sin problem, and to reject Him is to keep the veil in place that prevents us from seeing His glory.

Obstacles to faith in Christ (II Cor. 3:16). There is hope for those who still have the veil over their hearts. The hope for these people is the same hope for those of us who have been saved: The hope is in Jesus Christ. Jesus—and only Jesus—can remove the veil and reveal the glory of God. Our best efforts will never dispose of the veil that separates us from God. When Jesus completed His sacrifice on the cross, the veil in the temple that separated everyone from the Holy of Holies was torn in half from top to bottom.

The significance of that event is that there is nothing that separates those who have faith in Christ from coming into the presence of God anymore. In Christ, we can now come boldly to the throne of grace (cf. Heb. 4:16).

Freedom in faith in Christ (II Cor. 3:17-18). Paul declares emphatically and without hesitation that the Spirit is the Lord. "That Spirit" refers to the Holy Spirit, and Paul states that the Holy Spirit is God.

Here we see the united work of the Trinity in action. God the Father gave the law to Moses, which put the people of Israel under the old covenant. He then sent His Son, Jesus Christ, to mediate the new covenant, redeem His people from sin, and reconcile them back to Himself. He now has given us the Holy Spirit to work in our hearts and continually point us to Christ as well as equip us to live the new life in Christ.

Where the Spirit is working, the people find freedom. There is no bondage in the Holy Spirit. He does not come to enslave people, but to set us free. Everywhere He goes, repentant sinners find the liberty that the law could never provide for them.

The Holy Spirit also works to transform us into people who can now behold the glory of God without having a veil to shield us. That is because of the changed hearts He has fashioned in us.

Instead of fading, the new life in the Spirit of God gets better all the time. We go from one degree of glory to another, and unlike the glory that shone from Moses' face, the glory that comes from life in the Spirit never fades or diminishes. This blessing only comes from the Holy Spirit and will never be produced by good works, no matter how devout we may be. Religion cannot produce the life that only the Holy Spirit can bring.

—*Robert Ferguson, Jr.*

QUESTIONS

1. What terms does Paul use to describe the old covenant?

2. What terms does Paul use to describe the new covenant?

3. How did the old covenant fulfill its purpose?

4. How should we view the law in terms of obedience?

5. Why were the children of Israel unable to look at Moses' face?

6. Why did the glory of the new covenant far exceed the glory of the old covenant?

7. What did Paul say about the old covenant in comparison to the new covenant?

8. What is the basis of the Christian's hope, according to Paul?

9. Why can we be bold in our proclamation of the gospel?

10. What does the fact that the glory faded from Moses' face tell us about the old covenant?

—*Robert Ferguson, Jr.*

Preparing to Teach the Lesson

The spiritual is more real than the material. Everything that is visible around us has been created by the invisible God, and all that happens around us is influenced and ultimately determined by the unseen spiritual forces beyond our perceptions. Think about that for a moment!

TODAY'S AIM

Facts: to realize how much more glorious the new covenant is than the old.

Principle: to understand how and why the new covenant is superior to the old covenant. The new fulfills the reality behind the mere types and shadows of the old.

Application: to live daily in the knowledge that the glory of our standing in Christ surpasses all other blessings of God.

INTRODUCING THE LESSON

Today's lesson draws a stark contrast between the temporary old covenant of law and condemnation and the eternal new covenant of grace, forgiveness, salvation, and eternal life.

DEVELOPING THE LESSON

1. Stone versus Spirit (II Cor. 3:7-11). Paul begins this section by contrasting what he calls the "ministration of death" (vs. 7) with the "ministration of the spirit" (vs. 8). Since he describes the first as "written and engraven in stones," we know he is referring to the old covenant of the law and comparing it to the new covenant of the Holy Spirit's ministry in regenerating sinners through the gospel and sanctifying them into saints.

Make no mistake: the old covenant was glorious—so glorious that the Israelites could not bear to look at the temporary glory of Moses' face after those times in which he had met with the Lord (cf. Ex. 33:23). Paul's point, however, is this: How much more glorious is the permanent and eternal new covenant of the Holy Spirit! The word translated "rather" in verse 8 can be (and more often is) rendered "more."

This is an essential idea in the doctrine of the new covenant that is often neglected and devalued: namely, that spiritual reality is more real and therefore more important than the physical and material reality of this present world. As those who are still bound to this earthly existence, however, we often have these priorities backwards. We value the literal and material of the present time as what is really important while holding what we think of as *merely spiritual* in lesser esteem. We can see this in the areas of answers to prayer and the interpretation of prophetic fulfillments.

Regarding answers to prayer, we often entirely overlook the spiritual benefits God bestows on us if we perceive that He has not answered our prayers materially. For example, if someone prays for relief from an illness, and God answers his prayer by giving him the spiritual blessings of patience, grace, and comfort in the midst of it instead of taking his sickness away, many are tempted to conclude that God has not answered his prayer and has abandoned him to his suffering.

In the area of prophetic fulfillment, if a Bible commentator sees a certain prophecy as being fulfilled in a spiritual sense, he can be roundly criticized for "spiritualizing" the text, often without receiving any consideration for the possible merits of his interpretation.

The modern church needs to be aware of this potentially dangerous blind spot. We can all too easily lose our proper high esteem for the spiritual realities that Jesus and the apostles held as paramount, while fixing our expectations almost exclusively on the material world. Granted, there is a long history of illegitimate spiritualizing by various cults and liberal scholars, but the vital truth remains: the writers of the New Testament all held the spiritual realities of the universe as more important than the visible and material realities of this present world.

We must resist the appeals of the enemy to remake our worldview into a primarily material one. We must tenaciously maintain our identity in a fallen world as a spiritual people, whose God, true riches, and citizenship are in what is now the invisible realms. As we are reminded elsewhere, "Through faith we understand that the worlds were framed by the word of God, so that things which are seen were not made of things which do appear" (Heb. 11:3; cf. II Cor. 4:18).

2. Veiled glory versus full glory (II Cor. 3:12-18). Having established the superior glory of the new covenant over the old on the basis of its spiritual and eternal nature, Paul presses on with the logical implications of this truth.

First, because his hope is based on the eternal realities of the new covenant, he does not need to speak in erudite riddles to veil the glory of his doctrine, as Moses veiled his temporarily shining face. Moses' face was veiled because the glory of the Mosaic covenant was a fading glory, destined to be abolished at the coming of the Messiah.

Paul explains that this is why many of the Jews are so blind to the glories of Christ: there is a veil over their understanding of the Scriptures. But even now, whenever a Jewish person's heart is turned to the Lord, that veil is lifted, and the full glory of Christ floods in!

The Holy Spirit uses the plain truth of the gospel to bring true liberty and eternal life to those who behold the eternal, unveiled glory of Christ.

ILLUSTRATING THE LESSON

The illustration contrasts the two covenants: the old and the new. Whereas the old was temporary, fearsome, condemning, and focused on Israel alone, the new is eternal, gracious, forgiving, and calls all the world to repent and believe in Christ for salvation!

THE GLORIES OF THE NEW COVENANT FAR SURPASS THE OLD

Temporary, law, stone, types, shadows, condemnation. For Israel alone.

Eternal, grace, Spirit, fulfillment, reality, forgiveness. For all people.

CONCLUDING THE LESSON

The spiritual reality of life in Christ is more real than the material world. This is an essential doctrine of the new covenant. If we are believers in Jesus, it should dominate our thinking and our worldview. Spiritual blessings should be far more highly esteemed among us than physical ones, for that which is spiritual is eternal, while that which is of this earth is temporary and fading away.

ANTICIPATING THE NEXT LESSON

Next week's lesson focuses on the blessings that await all believers in heaven. Our physical bodies will one day become obsolete; when that time comes, God will provide us with glorious, eternal bodies!

—John Lody.

PRACTICAL POINTS

1. In the Old Testament, God's glory made Moses' face shine, but the glory of the Holy Spirit dwelling in New Testament believers is far greater (II Cor. 3:7-8)!
2. In Christ through the Holy Spirit, believers have the power to glorify God before the whole world through their humble love and service (vss. 9-11).
3. Since we have the saving power of Christ in the gospel, we have no need of worldly sophistication (vs. 12).
4. Many cannot understand God's Word because of their worldly pride and traditions (vss. 13-15).
5. The gospel has power to soften the hardest of hearts and open the blindest of eyes (vs. 16).
6. Believers experience more and more freedom as we become more like Christ (vss. 17-18).

—Cheryl Y. Powell.

RESEARCH AND DISCUSSION

1. What are some major differences between the old covenant and the new covenant? Discuss.
2. Why was Moses veiled after encountering God? Discuss.
3. What are some examples of modern-day "veils" that hinder people from trusting Christ as Lord and Saviour?
5. Describe your own experience of having the veil lifted from your understanding of the gospel.

—Cheryl Y. Powell.

ILLUSTRATED HIGH POINTS

Engraven in stones, was glorious (II Cor. 3:7)

Magnificent Mount Tambora, in Indonesia, was the location of the most powerful volcanic eruption in recorded history. In 1815, this 14,100-foot mountain erupted with huge miles-high columns of smoke and ash. Volcanic ash was dispersed into the stratosphere, and 1816 was nicknamed "the year without a summer."

The law is magnificent; it is the expression of God's perfect righteousness. But it is deadly to fallen humans because we cannot hope to measure up to its righteous standard on our own.

The glory that excelleth (vs. 10)

The University of Michigan has been working on an itty-bitty, temperature-sensing computer that is only four hundredths of a cubic millimeter in size. This is about one tenth of the size of the computer that previously had been considered the smallest. To put this in perspective, this computer makes a grain of rice seem like Mount Tambora by comparison! But do not let its size fool you. It has a sensor that can measure the slightest change in temperature. Its tiny size can get right down to the cellular level of a human body and detect cancer cells that are slightly hotter than healthy ones. It could also provide treatment for glaucoma from inside the eye or monitor various other biochemical processes. The medical possibilities seem endless.

Jesus did not come with thunder and lightning as the law of Moses did. His entrance seemed small by comparison—like a proverbial grain of wheat—but oh, what power to save and heal the lost!

—Therese Greenberg.

Golden Text Illuminated

"Now the Lord is that Spirit; and where the Spirit of the Lord is, there is liberty" (II Corinthians 3:17).

The heart of this chapter contrasts the old covenant with the new covenant. The old covenant was engraved in stone, written by the very finger of God, but it could not save. No one—not even Moses or the high priest—had the power to perfectly fulfill the stringent moral codes established by the Lord in His holy Law.

Under the old covenant, Moses could not even sustain the glory of God in the presence of the people. Do you remember when the Israelites worshipped the golden calf? When Moses came down the mountain with the law, he witnessed this gross idolatry and furiously shattered the tablets. Later, when God inscribed a new set of tablets, Moses was unaware that his face was shining with the glory of Yahweh's presence. Yet it was a splendor that eventually faded. In fact, Moses hid his face with a veil so the people could not see the glory fading (Ex. 34:29-35; II Cor. 3:13).

God's law, though glorious, is unable to save anyone. The commandments are "holy and righteous and good" (Rom. 7:12), yet they can only reveal sin; they cannot solve the problem of sin. The law results only in condemnation, for no one can perfectly fulfill it—and the "wages of sin is death" (Rom. 6:23).

Using Exodus 34:29-35 as an illustration, Paul writes that those who strive to be right with God by following the letter of the law wear a veil over their hearts, a veil that blinds them to Christ, who has established the new covenant. When a person by God's grace trusts in Christ, the veil is taken away and the new covenant shines clearly, imparting freedom.

Spiritual freedom is a great theme in Paul's epistles (cf. Rom. 8:15-21; I Cor. 9:19; Gal. 5:1). However, Paul was not giving license to the Corinthians to do whatever they wanted. There was already too much of the wrong kind of freedom at Corinth, since some church members were sinning openly. Freedom to transgress is not genuine freedom, for Jesus Himself declared that whoever commits sin is a slave to sin (John 8:34).

What, then, is spiritual freedom as defined by the Bible? It means at least four things:

1. Freedom from adherence to the ceremonial laws under the old covenant, such as circumcision, sacrifices, and dietary laws. "For Christ is the end of the law for righteousness to every one that believeth" (Rom. 10:4).

2. Freedom from the power of sin. "For sin shall not have dominion over you: for ye are not under the law, but under grace" (Rom. 6:14).

3. Freedom from the fear of death. "There is therefore now no condemnation to them which are in Christ Jesus . . . For the law of the Spirit of life in Christ Jesus hath made me free from the law of sin and death" (Rom. 8:1-2; cf. Heb. 2:14).

4. Freedom to joyfully serve. "For, brethren, ye have been called unto liberty; only use not liberty for an occasion to the flesh, but by love serve one another" (Gal. 5:13).

Jesus made the startling announcement in Nazareth that He had come to set the captives free (cf. Luke 4:18). Now, through the power of the Holy Spirit, that freedom continues in all who believe.

—*Mark Winter*

Heart of the Lesson

After standing face-to-face with God, talking with Him as with a friend, Moses' face shone with a glorious, divine light. Just as the moon reflects the sun's rays, Moses' face reflected God's glory. When the Israelites saw Moses' radiance, they turned away in fear (cf. Ex. 34:30).

There are only two possible reactions to coming face-to-face with God's glory—guilty fear or adoring love—and often both at once!

1. The glory of the old covenant (II Cor. 3:7-11). Before addressing the differences between the old and new covenants, we note that at least one truth unites them: sinners have always received God's saving grace through faith, never by obeying the law.

The purpose of the old covenant was to shine a light on sin—not to lead people to despair but to point them toward dependence upon God. In a very personal confession, the apostle Paul wrote that if the law had not forbidden covetousness, he would not have recognized covetousness in his own heart (cf. Rom. 7:7).

No Israelite, including Moses, could perfectly keep the law. In this way, it ministered only death because it emphasized the knowledge of sin. And the chilling consequence of sin is death (cf. Rom. 6:23).

Even so, after receiving the sin-revealing law, Moses' face shone from his being in God's presence. Eventually, Moses' radiance faded, but the guilt of the law remained. Glorious as it was, the law was designed by God to prepare His people for Messiah. The old covenant came to an end when Jesus initiated the new covenant.

2. The glory of the New Covenant (II Cor. 3:12-16). The fading glory of the law cannot compare to the everlasting glory of the new covenant. When Jesus came, He inaugurated a new era in biblical history.

When Jesus died on the cross, the thick veil keeping people out of the holiest place in the temple ripped from top to bottom, showing that He had opened the way for believers to access God's holy presence (cf. Matt. 27:51).. After Christ rose from the dead and ascended to heaven, He and the Father sent the Holy Spirit so that God's glorious presence would dwell not in the temple but in Christians themselves. Jesus' death and resurrection initiated the new covenant (cf. Matt. 26:28).

Not all people in Paul's day believed in Jesus, of course, and this was the case especially among the Jews. Just as Moses veiled his face, a veil of unbelief spiritually blinds Jews and all others who do not believe in Jesus. The old covenant pointed to Christ, but only by faith can anyone truly see the glory of the new covenant.

3. The glory of freedom (II Cor. 3:17-18). Men and women have been created in God's image with a spirit that can commune with God. When a person believes in Jesus, the Holy Spirit fills him or her with the presence and mind of Christ. The presence of the Spirit serves as a constant reminder of God's grace.

While the reflection of God's glory in Moses' face faded, the glory of Christ shining in and through believers' lives increases over time. Ultimately, this will result in our glorification and sinless Christlikeness when, after we are raised from the dead, we will see God face-to-face (cf. Rev. 22:4).

—*Malia E. Rodriguez.*

World Missions

When Marshall and Helen Lawrence arrived in Papua, New Guinea, one of the first things they did was build a simple three-plank door for their primitive dwelling. They and their four sons made themselves at home among the Oksapmin people. Marshall's mission to translate the New Testament into a language that had never before been written down took many years.

During those years, the Lawrences opened their simple door to tribal friends, fellow missionaries, globetrotters, and hikers. People arrived from Germany, Israel, Canada, Australia, New Zealand, the U.S., Switzerland, and England. They all walked through that door, and each was welcomed. Marshall Lawrence wrote, "Our front door faced the small Oksapmin hamlet. We opened it in early morning and left it open until darkness settled" (*The World at My Door,* Guardian Books). Their open door showed them they were not at the end of the world after all.

An open door is a good symbol of the gospel. It reminds us of the holiest place of God's presence being opened at the moment of Christ's death, when the veil of the temple was torn in two from the top to the bottom.

Since Moses' day, the veil had existed as a reminder that sin separated the Israelites from their holy God. After the rending of the veil, animal sacrifices were no longer necessary because the once-and-for-all sacrifice had been made by God Himself in the person of Jesus Christ.

Everyone who trusts in Jesus knows the joy of boldly entering God's holy presence and finding welcome (Heb. 10:19-22). Under the law, there was limited access to God. The law did not offer the way of salvation, but rather showed the need for the true way. It was a closed door. For this reason, Paul condemned the work of false teachers who insisted on the necessity of keeping the old covenant law, thereby negating God's free gift of grace in Christ (cf. Gal. 5:1-12).

The closed door of the old covenant law separated us from God and led to death. The open door of the new covenant is Emmanuel, God with us. He leads us to eternal life (II Cor. 4:14).

There was some measure of glory in the old covenant; glory shone from Moses' face, but it was a fading glory. The glory of Christ's new covenant never fades (II Cor. 3:7-11).

The law demands that we keep God's commandments, whereas Christ's covenant brings us His indwelling Spirit. It is the Holy Spirit that makes it possible for us to please God and to follow His revealed will. Legalism, one aspect of which is that law-keeping is the way to salvation, undermines the gospel. It is a great temptation to reduce the gospel to a set of rules, but it is the Holy Spirit who gives us new life, and it is grace that secures our forgiveness and rewards us with eternal life in Christ. Ephesians 2:8-9 rings through the centuries, proclaiming that we are saved only by grace and not by any human effort.

Just as Marshall and Helen Lawrence opened their door and welcomed the world in, so Jesus, by rending the veil that separated man from God, opened the way for all peoples of the world.

You also have a door. When you open it, you never know whom He will send through it. You may live in an isolated rural area, in a teeming city, or on an island far from home like the Lawrences. But if you open the door of witness to the truth, you will find yourself living in the wide open spaces of God's grace and salvation for all peoples.

—*Rose McCormick Brandon.*

The Jewish Aspect

The Jewish concept of freedom is inextricably linked to Moses and the Exodus of the Israelites from Egypt, considered by many Jews to be the most important event of all time and commemorated annually by Jews throughout the world at the celebration of Passover. While modern Jews emphasize the story of the physical deliverance from slavery to Pharaoh, Jewish rabbis highlight a greater freedom—the freedom to serve God. "Despite what we teach our children through songs during Passover, God did not have Moses tell Pharaoh 'to let my people go.' Instead, God, through Moses, tells Pharaoh again and again to 'let my people go so they will serve me'" (www.myjewishlearning.com).

Following the Israelites' freedom from slavery in Egypt, God continued to use Moses as His divine messenger to receive His commandments on Mount Sinai. The Sinaitic covenant, also known as the Mosaic covenant, was a conditional agreement that required the Israelites' obedience to God. It was given for the good of the people (Deut. 5:29, 33) and to set them apart as a people unto God (28:9-10). God also wanted other nations to know Him better through the Israelites and their obedience to the law (4:6-8).

God established His covenant and provided divine promises to Israel on Mount Sinai, provided that they obeyed His voice and the commandments He had given them. After Moses received the commandments, as he descended from the mountain with the two tables of stone, his face shone because he had been in the presence of God (Ex. 34:29). This caused the Israelites to be afraid of Moses, and therefore he covered his face when he spoke to them (vss. 30-35).

Paul said that the commandments given to Moses on tablets of stone were merely a shadow of the glorious covenant that was established by Christ. This new covenant was not written with ink, but with the Spirit of the living God; He put His law in their inward parts and upon their hearts (cf. Jer. 31:33; II Cor. 3:3). Although the Mosaic covenant of the law was glorious, it was fading, as was the shining face of Moses. But the new covenant of the Spirit would not fade and was much more glorious.

The Mosaic covenant was a ministry of death, but the new covenant of the Spirit brought life. The old covenant was a ministry of condemnation, but the new covenant is a ministry of righteousness. The old covenant exposed sin, and atonement came through continuous blood offerings for sin; but the new covenant was established through the one perfect sacrifice of Christ, which brought complete atonement for all time for all who trust in Him.

The old covenant brought a yoke of bondage, but the new covenant brought liberty. This liberty represented freedom to access the very presence of God. "Freedom is presented as the supreme blessing of the new covenant of grace, which, in contrast with the old covenant of law, is represented as including independence from religious regulations and legal restrictions" (www.preceptaustin.org).

The Psalms speak often of the freedom and blessing of having access to God (cf. 65:4; 73:28; 145:18). When Jesus began His ministry, He said He was the fulfillment of the words spoken by the prophet Isaiah—to bring liberty to the captives and all who are oppressed (Luke 4:18-21).

—Deborah Markowitz Solan.

Guiding the Superintendent

From the beginnings of Christianity, believers have discussed and debated about the differences between the old and new covenants. The believers of first-century Corinth were no exception. False teachers had infiltrated the church, trying to persuade Christians to undergo circumcision and keep all the requirements of the law of Moses. In this week's lesson, Paul contrasts the glory of the two covenants. He extols the far greater glory of the new covenant. The old covenant indeed was glorious, but it was temporary. The glory of the new covenant is of much greater, everlasting glory.

DEVOTIONAL OUTLINE

1. Permanent glory (II Cor. 3:7-11). The focus of the new covenant is on life, not death. Here Paul argues from the lesser to the greater. He cites the fading glory that Moses experienced after he had been in God's direct presence on Mount Sinai (Exod. 34:34-35). Although the glory of Moses' shining visage was so alarming to the Israelites that he had to veil his face, it was but a fading glory. In contrast to the glory of the law engraved in stone, the glory of the new covenant is God's law written on believers' hearts by the Holy Spirit Himself. This glory is the reality of which the law of Moses was only a foreshadowing.

The new covenant focus is on righteousness rather than on condemnation. The law was meant to convict people of their hopeless sinfulness, while the new covenant provides not only atonement for all sins, but also the righteousness of Christ Himself for those who trust in Him as Lord and Saviour. The new covenant also offers believers the life-transforming power of the indwelling Holy Spirit.

Since the new covenant has come, that means the old covenant was never meant to last. There is no reason to go back to the law; its glory was always a fading glory, while the glory of the new covenant is permanent and eternal.

2. Bold hope (II Cor. 3:12-18). Since the glory of the new covenant is so superior to that of the old covenant, the believer in Christ has a boldness that those under the law could never even imagine. While the minds and hearts of those who are still under the law are veiled, hardened, and blinded to the glorious truth of the gospel, those who by grace have turned to Christ as Lord and Saviour have had this veil lifted from their perceptions by the power of the Holy Spirit. They have been freed from the bondage of the law to the glorious liberty of the Spirit.

Moreover, by being able to clearly see the glory of the new covenant in Jesus Christ, believers are being transformed to ever greater levels of glory as they are conformed to the likeness of Christ. This is the work of God the Holy Spirit, who indwells us.

Glory under the old covenant was measured by conformity to the perfect standard of the law. The glory of the new covenant is the perfect revelation of God Himself in Jesus Christ.

CHILDREN'S CORNER

Children today may be puzzled about the purpose of the old covenant. Paul compared the law to a school teacher (cf. Gal. 3:24). Until we learn enough, a teacher is necessary. Once we have learned enough, a teacher is no longer needed. Likewise, the old covenant teaches us that we need a Saviour. Once we know Jesus as Lord and Saviour, the law of Moses becomes obsolete.

—Martin R. Dahlquist.

Scripture Lesson Text

II COR. 5:1 For we know that if our earthly house of *this* tabernacle were dissolved, we have a building of God, an house not made with hands, eternal in the heavens.

2 For in this we groan, earnestly desiring to be clothed upon with our house which is from heaven:

3 If so be that being clothed we shall not be found naked.

4 For we that are in *this* tabernacle do groan, being burdened: not for that we would be unclothed, but clothed upon, that mortality might be swallowed up of life.

5 Now he that hath wrought us for the selfsame thing *is* God, who also hath given unto us the earnest of the Spirit.

6 Therefore *we are* always confident, knowing that, whilst we are at home in the body, we are absent from the Lord:

7 (For we walk by faith, not by sight:)

8 We are confident, *I say,* and willing rather to be absent from the body, and to be present with the Lord.

9 Wherefore we labour, that, whether present or absent, we may be accepted of him.

10 For we must all appear before the judgment seat of Christ; that every one may receive the things *done* in *his* body, according to that he hath done, whether *it be* good or bad.

NOTES

Our Heavenly Dwelling

Lesson Text: II Corinthians 5:1-10

Related Scriptures: I Corinthians 15:3-54; II Corinthians 4:1-12

TIME: probably A.D. 56   PLACE: from Macedonia

GOLDEN TEXT—"For we know that if our earthly house of this tabernacle were dissolved, we have a building of God, an house not made with hands, eternal in the heavens" (II Corinthians 5:1).

Introduction

The suffering we go through in life can cause discouragement and frustration. Even for the most spiritual person among us, the pain is real. Paul was a man familiar with suffering, and his suffering caused him to think about the hope of the resurrection and God's promise of eternal life (cf. II Cor. 4:14).

Remembering the promises of God was the key to Paul's endurance, even though he admits that his body was wasting away (vs. 16). For Paul, it was a matter of perspective. The outer self was wasting away, but the inner self was being renewed day by day. Satan tries to use suffering to destroy us, but we need not fear his malice.

Paul referred to the sufferings of this life as light and momentary (4:17), for they do not compare to the glory that lies ahead of us. If we suffer for Christ, then we will be glorified with Christ (cf. Rom. 8:17-18).

This caused Paul to look ahead and focus on the eternal instead of the temporal.

LESSON OUTLINE

I. LONGING FOR IMMORTALITY—II COR. 5:1-4

II. WALKING BY FAITH—II Cor. 5:5-8

III. PLEASING THE LORD—II Cor. 5:9-10

Exposition: Verse by Verse

LONGING FOR IMMORTALITY

II COR. 5:1 For we know that if our earthly house of this tabernacle were dissolved, we have a building of God, an house not made with hands, eternal in the heavens.

2 For in this we groan, earnestly desiring to be clothed upon with our house which is from heaven:

3 If so be that being clothed we shall not be found naked.

4 For we that are in this taber-

nacle do groan, being burdened: not for that we would be unclothed, but clothed upon, that mortality might be swallowed up of life.

Hope in the face of death (II Cor. 5:1). When dealing with the struggles of this life, Paul turns his attention to the glory that awaits the believer in Christ. Though God has compassion on our struggles, He does not want us to accept defeat. We know that we are going to have hard times, but during these hard times, we have been given great hope (cf. I Pet. 4:12-13).

{Paul references the "earthly house of this tabernacle." A "tabernacle" is a tent and refers to our earthly body.}^{Q1} Just as a tent is a temporary dwelling place, so are the bodies we live in here on earth. {One day, our bodies will be "dissolved," that is, die.}^{Q2} They were not made to last forever. Day by day, we all get closer to death. That may sound morbid to many, but it is actually a good and necessary thing to remember. We cannot enjoy the hope of eternal things by hanging on tightly to the temporary things of this world.

At the moment of death, God is not taking anything away from us but is giving us something new and better. {Paul was so sure of this promise from God that he speaks about it in the present tense.}^{Q3} He states that we *have* a building of God, not that we *will have* a building of God. Eternal life does not begin when we get to heaven. Eternal life begins at the moment of conversion.

The "building of God" and the "house not made with hands" both speak of our new glorified bodies that we will have in heaven. Paul expresses no sorrow in setting aside the "tent" that he currently lived in for the permanent house God had prepared for him. He also rejoices in the fact that the same promise is given to every person who trusts in Jesus.

Hope amid groaning (II Cor. 5:2-3). {Paul moves from the promise of eternity to acknowledge that presently we groan. What is he referring to? Certainly we groan as we feel the effects of sin in our bodies as we age and when we are in pain. But the groaning here likely extends even further, to a groaning and grieving over sin in the world.}^{Q4} We see the effects of sin when we lose a loved one, when there is injustice, or in broken relationships. We cry out to God that He would purify the world of sin and redeem not only our bodies, but the world in its entirety.

As long as it does not turn into complaining, groaning can be good for the believer. It reminds us to focus on our future rather than our present—on the great hope God has given us in His eternal promises. We can look forward to the time when God completely redeems us in body and soul, freeing us from the presence of sin (vs. 2).

This clearly looks forward to the resurrection of the believer. Just as Christ was raised from the dead, we too will be raised from the dead. Death has no lasting power over the believer (cf. John 14:19). We will not be found naked but will instead have glorified bodies in heaven. That is God's promise to all who believe in His Son, Jesus Christ.

Hope in new life (II Cor. 5:4). Paul does not run from the fact that the struggles of life are hard. He felt them too. While we are in these earthly bodies, we will experience painful and tragic situations. We are burdened sometimes beyond what we think we can bear. Paul said earlier in this book that at one point, he even despaired of life itself (1:8-9).

Paul states again that while we are in this earthly body ("tabernacle"), we groan and are burdened. {We long to be freed, but not merely to die and escape our present body. We long to be "clothed upon," to be given the eternal resurrected body that has been promised to us in Christ.}^Q5

The mortality we all face does not have the final say in our lives if we have trusted in Christ. When the time comes for our earthly bodies to pass away, God will give us new life—life that is far greater than anything we now know. Our physical body will give way to a new body, and mortality will be swallowed up by life (cf. Isa. 25:8; I Cor. 15:54). Death is not a cessation of existence. It is an entrance into eternity, where God will give us a brand-new, glorified body.

WALKING BY FAITH

5 Now he that hath wrought us for the selfsame thing is God, who also hath given unto us the earnest of the Spirit.

6 Therefore we are always confident, knowing that, whilst we are at home in the body, we are absent from the Lord:

7 (For we walk by faith, not by sight:)

8 We are confident, I say, and willing rather to be absent from the body, and to be present with the Lord.

Guarantee from God (II Cor. 5:5). The hope of future glory is not wishful thinking on Paul's part. It is based on God's Word. Since God cannot lie or fail, any promise He makes is guaranteed to come to fruition. We may not know the exact timing or details, but we can rest assured that God will fulfill His promises.

The Word of God is a sufficient guarantee of our hope in heaven, but to take it even further, {God has also given us the Holy Spirit as a guarantee of His promise.}^Q6 God does not require us to live in this earthly body without divine assistance, so He gives us the Holy Spirit to help us.

{An "earnest" is a pledge, usually money, that guarantees the terms of a contract.}^Q7 When making a large financial purchase, the buyer will often make an earnest payment, often called a down payment. It guarantees the transaction and is also a good-faith measure. The earnest payment is the buyer's guarantee that he will satisfy his end of the deal.

Of course, our very faith is based on the fact that we cannot complete our end of the deal, so Jesus had to come to earth to live in righteousness for us. It is a great sign of God's generosity, therefore, that He (who does not owe us anything) gives us the Holy Spirit as assurance that His promises will come true. The Holy Spirit assures us that God will complete the work of salvation that He began in our lives (cf. Eph. 1:13-14).

Joy in God (II Cor. 5:6-7). Although Paul was familiar with suffering and persecution, he remains quite joyful in his tone. The reason for this joyful spirit is that his hope rested in the Lord. {Because his hope was found in the Lord, he was always able to be confident.}^Q8

Paul was not relying on the word or wisdom of man, but rather on the divinely inspired Word that God had revealed to him. There was never a reason to doubt God, no matter how grim his circumstances may have seemed at any given time. If we do have doubts because of our circumstances, we should bring them to God in prayer and read His Word to remind us of His steadfast love for us.

Being a Christian does not mean that our heads are so far up in the clouds that we should ignore earthly reality and just tough it out till we get to heaven. Until then, however, we do exist apart from God in a certain sense. We long for the day when we will be reunited with Him in the full sense that is promised to us.

{Our present sense of apartness, of course, does not mean that God is not with us right now.}[Q9] Jesus Christ is Emmanuel, which means "God with us" (cf. Matt. 1:23). When Christ ascended to heaven, He did not leave us alone. The indwelling presence of the Holy Spirit means that God lives in us. We are never apart from God in the sense of being separated from His presence or deprived of His provision or protection.

Yet until we get to heaven and actually enjoy all of the blessings of eternity that God has for us, we will experience struggles, hardships, and bad times. Our lives will always feel somewhat incomplete because we long to be with Christ in our eternal home. As Augustine said long ago, "You have made us for Yourself, and our hearts are restless until they find their rest in You" (*Confessions*).

Until we finally enter into heaven and enjoy the Lord's rest from our suffering and struggles, we move forward in this life in faith. Sometimes this is difficult, and we do ourselves and one another a disservice when we pretend that life does not hurt at times. Paul reminds us, though, that the believer is guided by faith in God, not by what he sees with his eyes.

Our senses are often deceptive, and our perception is often faulty. God's Word, however, never fails and is always right. We are wise to trust in God's Word instead of relying on what we see.

Being with God (II Cor. 5:8). The deepest desire of the child of God is to be with Him. There is nothing that can satisfy us like being in His presence.

That is why we are able to be confident now as we go through personal tragedies and the hard times of life. We know that there is something much better that lies ahead if we persevere in faith.

Being a Christian does not mean we put on a phony smile, act spiritual around others, and pretend that we never hurt or cry. There is no comparison to being with the Lord. But because of His promises, we look forward to the day when we can shed this old tent we are living in and enter the eternal dwelling God has prepared for us.

PLEASING THE LORD

9 Wherefore we labour, that, whether present or absent, we may be accepted of him.

10 For we must all appear before the judgment seat of Christ; that every one may receive the things done in his body, according to that he hath done, whether it be good or bad.

Aiming to please (II Cor. 5:9). No matter where we are, whether we are here on earth or living in heaven, our ambition remains the same: we want to please the Lord. We no longer seek to satisfy ourselves with whatever appeals to us; we would rather please the Lord. We do not do these things in order to get saved or to stay saved, but because of the fact that we are saved.

Good works will never result in salvation, but they are the fruits of salvation. We seek to please the Lord out of gratitude and love, not out of duty and obligation. We do not have to earn God's love. We already have it. We do not have to earn God's favor. We already have it. We do good works because we are so happy in our relationship with Christ that we want to serve and please Him simply because we love Him. He died for us, so we are forever grateful to Him.

To be accepted by God is to be well-pleasing to Him. The way we live is important, and God will reward those who serve Him. No matter where we are, we should always want to please the Lord.

The judgment seat of Christ (II Cor. 5:10). {Paul reminds us that believers will appear before the judgment seat of Christ, which means we will be judged for the way we have lived.}[Q10] The way we live our lives is important.

Our appearance before the judgment seat of Christ will not be to determine whether we go to heaven or hell. Heaven was already determined for us when we put our faith in Christ. At that moment, God justified us, and our salvation was secured. God has already judged our sins at the Cross, so there is no reason to fear that He is going to judge them again. Your sins are forgiven if you have repented, and you can take comfort in knowing that God will not bring them up again.

What will be open for judgment, however, is our conduct as Christians. Did we represent Christ well? Were we stingy with our money and time? Were we hospitable in our homes? Did we obey God's Word? All of these things and more will be open for evaluation when we stand before Christ. The meaningless actions in our lives will burn away by fire, but we will be rewarded for works that glorify Christ (I Cor. 3:14-15). We will be rewarded in heaven based on our works on earth. We will give account for how we served Christ.

How can we serve Him? By serving others. Jesus said that when we serve "the least of these," we are also serving Him (Matt. 25:40). Likewise, if we fail to serve others, we fail to serve Him (vs. 45).

We dare not think that we can please the Lord and ignore people in the process. If you want to satisfy your Heavenly Father, then serve your earthly brother and sister. There is never a reason to be stingy or selfish. Those who are will answer for it at the judgment seat of Christ, where the works of man will be exposed for what they are. Gold, silver, and precious stones—works that glorified Christ—will be rewarded, but wood, hay, and straw—works that were meaningless—will be burned up (I Cor. 3:12-13).

Paul's focus was on the unseen realities of God's eternal promises. God has great things in store for us!

—Robert Ferguson, Jr.

QUESTIONS

1. What does Paul mean by our earthly "tabernacle" (II Cor. 5:1)?

2. What does it mean that our bodies will be "dissolved"?

3. How does Paul show that he was sure of God's promises?

4. What is Paul likely referring to when he talks about groaning (vs. 2)?

5. What longing does our groaning express?

6. Who does God give as a guarantee of our future hope?

7. What is an earnest payment?

8. What was the basis of Paul's confidence?

9. Does being in our bodies mean that the Lord is not with us?

10. What is the judgment seat of Christ, and who will appear before it?

—Robert Ferguson, Jr.

Preparing to Teach the Lesson

The apostle Paul has been trying to direct the focus of those in the church at Corinth away from earthly, material priorities and toward the blessings of the spiritual realm. One of the most precious hopes for the Christian is the truth that our sin-cursed physical bodies will one day be redeemed and replaced by eternally healthy, glorified bodies.

A famous song written by Mary Reeves Davis captures the frame of mind that Paul is advocating for all believers to cultivate and strive to maintain:

> This world is not my home, I'm just a passing through.
> My treasures are laid up somewhere beyond the blue.
> The angels beckon me from heaven's open door.
> And I can't feel at home in this world anymore.

TODAY'S AIM

Facts: to know that our present, earthly bodies will one day be replaced by glorified, heavenly ones.

Principle: to understand the implications of one day receiving glorified, eternal bodies.

Application: to live in the confidence of God's promise that if our physical body dies, we will one day stand before Him in an eternally perfect, glorified body.

INTRODUCING THE LESSON

In this week's lesson, Paul instructs the Corinthian church about the future Christian blessing of a glorified body to replace our present bodies that are subject to pain, sickness, and eventual death.

DEVELOPING THE LESSON

1. Death swallowed up in life (II Cor. 5:1-4). Paul has just established the idea that the invisible realm of the spirit is more important to us than the visible material realm around us. This leads him to speak about the future eternal existence Christians will enjoy after Christ's return.

If our physical bodies die before Christ's return (or for that matter, even if we are still alive at His return), our spirits will exchange their sin-cursed flesh for an eternally healthy, sin-free, glorified body!

Paul is careful to make clear that what awaits us is not an ephemeral existence as disembodied spirits (vss. 3-4). God always intended our lives to be lived in a tangible body like the ones He originally fashioned for Adam and Eve. But our future bodies will be far more glorious than even theirs! Paul refers to them as "our house which is from heaven" (vs. 2).

Though in our earthly bodies we groan because of their burden of sinful flesh, we do not long to be naked spirits; rather, we groan in anticipation of *a new wardrobe*! We look forward to the promise of a real, tangible, glorious, functioning body, given to us "that mortality might be swallowed up of life" (vs. 4).

2. Walking by faith, not sight (II Cor. 5:5-9). Having established the future Christian hope of the glorified body, Paul leverages this hope into an additional reason for Christian confidence. "The earnest of the Spirit" is the blessing every true believer has from the indwelling Holy Spirit.

Since God has given all believers these blessings and hopes for the eternal future, Paul reasons that this present earthly life is essentially a time of waiting while we endure being absent from the full revelation of the blessed, direct presence of Jesus Himself. Rather than be afraid of physical death, the true believer will be continually confident, looking forward to seeing Jesus face to face.

Verses 5 through 9 actually form a literary chiasm, with verse 7 as the crucial focus of Paul's reasoning. The following diagrams its structure:

> Vs. 5: Earnest of the Spirit.
> Vs. 6: Confidence.
> Vs. 7: Faith, not sight.
> Vs. 8: Confidence.
> Vs. 9: Service to God.

In summary, because we have the indwelling Spirit, we are confident that while we are in our bodies, we are merely absent from the Lord. This is all dependent on our walking by faith, not by sight. That, in turn, gives us confidence that if our bodies die, we will instantly be in the Lord's presence. And it is why we labor in kingdom service to please the Lord.

3. Appearing before Christ (II Cor. 5:10). Paul ends his discourse with a solemn warning: if we wish to stand before Christ approved and without shame, we must be diligent to labor earnestly for His kingdom while we are in this earthly body.

"Judgment seat" is the Greek word *bema*, which is a raised platform or dais designed for a throne or other judicial seat of authority. The implication here is not one of condemnation or eternal punishment, but rather of evaluation for greater or lesser rewards. That also implies, however, the receiving of either praise or a degree of shame.

As Paul reminds us in Romans 8:1, "There is therefore now no condemnation to them which are in Christ Jesus." Once we have trusted Jesus as our Lord and Saviour, death and hell no longer hold any threats for us. We now are free to dedicate ourselves wholly to gratefully serving the Lord Jesus Christ.

ILLUSTRATING THE LESSON

The illustration shows the difference between our present, earthly bodies and our future, glorified bodies.

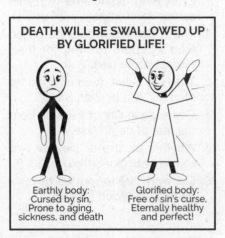

DEATH WILL BE SWALLOWED UP BY GLORIFIED LIFE!

Earthly body:
Cursed by sin,
Prone to aging,
sickness, and death

Glorified body:
Free of sin's curse,
Eternally healthy
and perfect!

CONCLUDING THE LESSON

In summary, because the invisible realm of the spirit is surpassingly more real and important than this present material one, our primary attention should be focused on that realm.

One day we will exchange our earthly existence for an eternal, glorified existence in a new, sin-free eternal body. We will then stand in the direct presence of the Lord Jesus Christ forever.

This reality should fill us with confidence toward whatever troubles this earthly life may bring. It should also motivate us to be diligent and faithful in laboring for the gospel!

But there is also a caution in this hope. When we stand before Jesus, He will judge our faithfulness and praiseworthiness in this life and will rightly determine our fitting reward.

ANTICIPATING THE NEXT LESSON

Next week's lesson discusses the implications of our call to be ambassadors for Christ to a lost world of sinners at enmity with God.

—*John Lody.*

PRACTICAL POINTS

1. Everything associated with this earthly life is temporary (II Cor. 5:1).
2. The sufferings of this life cause God's people to long for their eternal home (vss. 2-4).
3. The Holy Spirit gives us hope for eternal life in heaven (vs. 5).
4. Our hope in Christ frees us from the fear of death (vss. 6-8)
5. Whether we live or die, our aim should be to glorify the Lord (vs. 9).
6. Our work for the Lord will be tested and rewarded (vs. 10).

—Cheryl Y. Powell.

RESEARCH AND DISCUSSION

1. Contrast the outlook of a person who has trusted in Christ with the outlook of one who rejects Him. What are some of the significant differences?
2. What challenges do believers face in witnessing to the current generation of young people?
3. How did the sufferings that Paul endured throughout his ministry serve to advance the gospel (cf. II Cor. 4:8-12; 5:9)?
4. How do Christians experience the presence of God in this life? How will this experience be different when we are in heaven?
5. Is the judgment described in II Corinthians 5:10 the same one as described in Revelation 20:11-14 (cf. Rom. 8:1)? Why or why not?

—Cheryl Y. Powell.

ILLUSTRATED HIGH POINTS

Our earthly house . . . dissolved (II Cor. 5:1)

Remarkably preserved remains of ancient beasts are occasionally unearthed. Such was the case with a large tooth found in a creek near Yorktown, Virginia. It was a mastodon molar with a craterous cavity. This mastodon had clearly been an elderly animal, yet the tooth was quite intact.

Normally, the acid in rain water slowly erodes remains until they dissolve into dust. However, this animal fell upon a bed of sea shells, which leached alkaline into the water and neutralized the acid.

Despite alkaline, healthy foods, vitamins, fitness bands, or other efforts to preserve our temporary encasements, we will all eventually dissolve.

House not made with hands (vs. 1)

These days, 3D printers can print just about anything, including bones, rockets, or even human hearts. Larry Haines, founder of Austin-based Sunconomy, together with San Francisco's residential building company, Forge New, is developing a system called "We Print Houses." They have recently been licensed to print the first inhabitable model home!

The 3D printer moves about on a mobile platform, printing the building right on location. It will take two months to build the first model home.

As amazing as all this sounds, believers in Christ will one day have new bodies that God has designed—our new houses, free from sin's effects. Can we even imagine what will replace our current, fragile, earthly vessels? Indeed, a new residence has been programmed to a heavenly code by Christ our Creator, "Who shall change our vile body, that it may be fashioned like unto his glorious body" (Phil. 3:21).

—Therese Greenberg.

Golden Text Illuminated

"For we know that if our earthly house of this tabernacle were dissolved, we have a building of God, an house not made with hands, eternal in the heavens" (II Corinthians 5:1).

For ages, the concept of life beyond death has occupied the human imagination. The ancient Egyptians believed that the immortal soul was composed of several parts. After death, two of these parts, body and spirit, made a perilous journey to the kingdom of the god Osiris. The passage to the afterlife was aided by amulets, funerary spells, and mummification. The Greeks believed that Hermes, messenger of the gods, escorted departed souls to the River Styx, where a ferryman carried them to the land of the dead. Most people, who had lived average lives of little consequence, would exist without a personality, while the virtuous would live forever in the Elysian Fields, an idyllic garden. The very wicked would be condemned to the pit of Tartarus, a dark abyss of never-ending punishments.

Various views of the afterlife persist today. Hindus believe that life is a wheel of death and rebirth, and only by attaining enlightenment may one escape this earthly cycle and enter into a blissful state called nirvana. A Muslim teaching holds that the souls of the departed are tested. If the Muslim's faith passes muster, his grave is transformed into comfortable accommodations until the final resurrection; if the Muslim is found deficient in his beliefs, the grave becomes a place of discomfort, or even suffering.

In contrast to these fanciful views, the apostle Paul described an afterlife of beautiful simplicity. In II Corinthians 4:7-18, Paul recounted the hardships he had endured in the preaching of the gospel. But far from complaining, he considered his troubles to be light and temporary compared to the immortal glory that is to come for those in Christ.

Paul continued this theme of hope in the fifth chapter. He opens by contrasting the earthly and the eternal. First, he compares the mortal body to a tabernacle. Paul may have had in mind the wilderness tabernacle of the Israelites, a large, portable tent. This was the tent of meeting, where God would commune with Moses and dwell in the Holy of Holies, the inner room that contained the ark of the covenant. The glory of God, taking the form of a pillar of cloud, hovered over the tabernacle for all the Israelites to see. When the cloud moved, the Levites disassembled the tent and all the people followed God wherever He led them.

The human body is like the tabernacle—wonderfully made but transitory. Someday, we will break camp on this earth and move to an eternal destiny. Those who are in Christ will receive a new, everlasting place in which to dwell—a building of God. What was Paul's meaning here? He may have been referring to heaven itself, a place in which, as Jesus told His disciples, there are many mansions that He personally has prepared for them (John 14:2). More likely, Paul is writing about our resurrection bodies. Paul covered this extensively in I Corinthians 15:50-57, declaring that our perishable flesh must be exchanged for an imperishable body in order to dwell with God forever.

The word "building" can either mean a process of construction or a structure itself. It is all God's doing: the building that believers receive will be built and maintained by Him throughout eternity.

—Mark Winter.

Heart of the Lesson

We were born to live forever, but sin and death has raised a barrier. Adam and Eve's disobedience in Eden yielded spiritual and physical death.

The punishment for sin is death. Thankfully, Jesus endured death and rose from the grave in victory. We now anticipate His return, when He will throw death into the abyss (cf. Rev 20:14). In the meantime, we mourn the deaths of believers, but we do so with a sure hope, knowing that Jesus will one day give His followers victory over death.

1. Earthly frustration (II Cor. 5:1-4). Paul had suffered and nearly died while in Asia (cf. II Cor. 1:8). With his mortality at the forefront of his mind, he addressed the false teaching circulating at Corinth that there was no resurrection (cf. I Cor. 15:12).

Paul had taught the Corinthians to put their hope in God's promise that He would give them a permanent home—their resurrection bodies—in which they would live in God's presence forever. This hope enabled the Corinthian believers to face persecution and trials with hope.

As believers today, we have the same hope. Living in our weak, aging bodies can cause pain and frustration. But the answer is not to get rid of our bodies and liberate our souls into a purely spiritual existence. The view that our bodies are inherently bad and our souls are inherently good was part of a false system of belief called *Gnosticism.* This is not a Christian belief. Though Gnosticism did not come on the scene until somewhat later than Paul's day, some of the Gnostic ideas were already spreading around the Roman Empire.

After believers die and their bodies are buried, their souls continue to live in Jesus' presence. Paul referred to this time between death and resurrection as being "unclothed." But the final answer to our frustration with living in a sin-cursed body is not to get rid of our bodies but to experience resurrection and glorification.

2. Heavenly hope (II Cor. 5:5-8). One reason that God the Father and God the Son sent God the Holy Spirit to live in believers is to be a sign of the divine promise to raise us from the dead. Just as new homeowners put a down payment on their house, the Holy Spirit is like a down payment God has made on our heavenly dwelling—our resurrection bodies. In the meantime, the Spirit imparts resurrection life to believers as they await Jesus' return.

Our ultimate hope is not to be unclothed (without our body), but to be further clothed with our resurrection body. If we die before Jesus returns, however, we know that we will immediately pass into Christ's presence.

3. The judgment seat of Christ (II Cor. 5:9-10). Armed with the hope of resurrection and the power of the indwelling Spirit, Christians can live each day with the goal to please God. When Jesus returns, it will be for judgment, but for believers it will not be to determine salvation but to determine rewards. Jesus' death and resurrection have already paid for our sins and secured eternal life for us. By serving Christ, we can also store up eternal treasure (cf. I Tim. 6:18-19).

When Jesus returns, He will reward believers based on their faithful service. Service with merely earthly aims (wood, hay, and straw) will burn in His judgment. Service with eternal aims (gold, silver, and precious stones) will endure the fire of judgment and result in eternal rewards (cf. I Cor. 3:12-15).

—*Malia E. Rodriguez.*

World Missions

We may never have identified it as what it truly is, but it has been there, always nagging at our souls—this nameless pining. When it is finally identified, we find it to be a yearning for Christ and our heavenly home. We are apt to sense this longing most when the body we live in shows signs of failing us (II Cor. 5:1-4).

Carolyn, my roommate from college, never married. She moved west, away from me, thirty years ago. We kept in contact by phone and emails. After many months of sickness, she called to say that she had been diagnosed with Parkinson's. The disease proceeded to eat away at her life, forcing her into retirement and isolating her. Frequent trips to the hospital, dependence on others for daily needs, and a strict medication regimen stole her freedom. A frantic worry about the future tinged the edges of her voice. I continually sensed the thought, *What will become of me?* between the lines of all our conversations.

As months passed, she began to reflect on the past and shared memories of her happy childhood. She said she still enjoyed reading and studying the Scriptures (for many years, she had taught an adult Bible class). Instead of worries about the future, her focus began to shift toward thoughts of heaven. One day, through tears, she quoted the refrain from Don Wyrtzen's hymn, *Finally Home*: "Just think of stepping on shore, and finding it heaven/Of touching a hand and finding it God's/Of breathing new air, and finding it celestial/Of waking up in Glory, and finding it 'Home.'"

At the end of one conversation, Carolyn said, "I want you to know that in spite of my sufferings, I always feel the presence of God." Those words eased my concern for her. Although I imagined her with one foot in a nursing home and the other in the grave, God was there with her, beside her, sharing her suffering. Not long after this conversation, Carolyn stepped into heaven and found herself breathing the celestial air of God's forever home.

In John 14:1-3, knowing that He would soon face the cross, Jesus told His disciples not to be frightened by coming events, because He was going ahead of them to prepare a home for them. Jesus' message is meant for us too. Sin and madness appear to rule this present world. Unexpected events ruin our fondest plans. Anarchy shrieks in the streets, and lawlessness threatens our way of life. In all this, we need to be reminded that we are citizens of heaven (Phil. 3:20-21).

Exiled and alone on a remote island, the apostle John was visited by Jesus, who revealed heavenly things to him. As a door to heaven was opened, glorious and holy visions appeared, things that drove away his gloom and shined the light of God's ultimate victory on him.

The image of Christ as Shepherd—in Scripture, paintings, poems, and hymns—has, probably more than any other image, imprinted itself on the minds of believers. It reminds us that Jesus, who laid down His life for us, now lives to sustain us and lead us safely to our heavenly home.

When the time is right—when our home in heaven is ready—He will come to release us from this fallen world and take us home. How the heart warms at the thought of that home!

The longing for heaven, the product of God's gracious work in souls, is the fertile soil all missionaries hope and pray for among the people they seek to reach with the gospel. Pray for and along with our missionaries that the gospel seed they scatter will find good soil.

—*Rose McCormick Brandon.*

The Jewish Aspect

When Adam and Eve disobeyed God in the Garden of Eden, they then recognized that they were naked (Gen. 3:10), and God made coats of animal skins to clothe them (vs. 21). "God had to kill (sacrifice) an animal in order to show Adam and Eve how to make atonement for sin. It was only after atonement was made that Adam and Eve could regain the covenant relationship with God that had been lost after the Fall and it is this reconciled status or standing that is pictured by their clothing" (www.christcovenantcolorado.com).

Clothing is a biblical metaphor for atonement throughout the Hebrew Scriptures and the New Testament. Jacob and his household needed clean clothing before they could make a covenant with God (Gen. 35:2). Aaron and the Israelite priests were given specific instructions regarding their clothing (Ex. 28:40-43; Lev. 16:4). The psalmist also wrote that the priests were clothed with righteousness (Ps. 132:9). Job said, "I put on righteousness, and it clothed me; my judgment was as a robe and a diadem" (Job 29:14). In his vision of Joshua the high priest, the prophet Zechariah saw the Lord take off Joshua's filthy garments and the sin they represented and clothe him with robes of righteousness (Zech. 3:1-4).

In a messianic prophecy, Isaiah said, "I will greatly rejoice in the Lord, my soul shall be joyful in my God; for he hath clothed me with the garments of salvation, he hath covered me with the robe of righteousness, as a bridegroom decketh himself with ornaments, and as a bride adorneth herself with her jewels" (Isa. 61:10). The Jews of ancient times also understood that to be covered meant to be forgiven of their sins.

When Paul spoke to the believers in the Corinthian church about being clothed (II Cor. 5:1-4), he used the Greek equivalent to the Hebrew word *labash,* which means "to be covered." Adam Clarke writes, "When the apostle says that they greatly desired to be clothed upon with our house which is from heaven, he certainly means that the great concern of all the genuine followers of God was to be fully prepared to enjoy the beatific vision of their Maker and Redeemer" (www.godtube.com).

Paul compared our earthly body to a tabernacle or tent, emphasizing that it is not a permanent dwelling. He made a sharp distinction between our earthly house and our heavenly one.

The Lord gave Moses detailed instructions about how to build the tabernacle, including its materials and its structure. (Ex. 25:31, 35-38). "The tabernacle (*mishkan*), first mentioned in the Torah in Exodus 25, was the portable sanctuary that the Israelites carried with them in the wilderness. Mishkan comes from the Hebrew root meaning 'to dwell'; the tabernacle was considered to be the earthly dwelling place of God" (www.myjewishlearning.com).

The tabernacle, and the temple which came after it, represented the possibility of human fellowship with God. It also pointed to a dwelling, not made with human hands, that was the heavenly reality behind the earthly building. "Then said he, Lo, I come to do thy will, O God. He taketh away the first, that he may establish the second. By the which will we are sanctified through the offering of the body of Jesus Christ once for all" (Heb. 10:9-10). Jesus dwelt (literally, "tabernacled") among us, so that we might behold God's incomparable glory, grace, and truth (John 1:14).

—*Deborah Markowitz Solan.*

Guiding the Superintendent

Most people live day to day as if life as we know it will go on forever. But when we encounter a funeral procession or experience the death of a loved one, we get jerked back to reality.

The apostle Paul faced life-and-death issues just about every day. His attitude should be an example to all Christians: whether we are on earth or in heaven, we should strive earnestly to please the Lord. Paul's daily focus was on the Lord, not his earthly life.

Paul loved his ministry in this life, but he also longed to be with the Lord. He expressed this to the Corinthian believers using a series of contrasts in which he compared earthly life with life in heaven.

DEVOTIONAL OUTLINE

1. Earthly and heavenly (II Cor. 5:1-5). The fifth chapter of II Corinthians begins on a confident note. Paul, whose trade was tentmaking, likened our present life to a tent. Tents are only temporary dwellings. They are cold in winter, hot in summer, and often leaky when it rains. Tents wear out with constant use; they age and fray. Paul contrasts this with our future heavenly home, fashioned for eternity by the almighty invisible hand of God Himself.

While we live in our tents, we groan for our eternal, heavenly homes. This groaning is not merely due to the aches and pains of a physical body; it is also due to our longing to be in the presence of our beloved Lord Jesus Christ (Rom. 8:22-26). The indwelling Holy Spirit is God's earnest, or down payment, that one day believers will be clothed with immortality.

2. At home or away (II Cor. 5:6-10). Knowing that the Holy Spirit is God's down payment on eternity, we can live courageously in our daily service to God. We know that eventually we will come face to face with Jesus. Because we live daily by faith and not by sight, we can claim for ourselves Christ's own victory over the temporary sufferings of this earthly life.

Paul had one goal in life—to please the Lord. His single aim was to honor and glorify Jesus with all that he did. "Labour" carries the idea of being ambitious, an ambition with God's glory as its sole focus. There were no limits on this ambition of his. Nothing in this life would dissuade or discourage him from pursuing it.

Like Paul, whether we are facing life or death, we should make it our overriding ambition to please God in all that we do. The glory and honor of the Lord Jesus Christ, who offered Himself up for our salvation from sin, should motivate us to gratefully offer ourselves as living sacrifices to His service (cf. Rom. 12:1).

Paul's godly ambition was driven by the expectation that he would one day stand before Christ's judgment seat. Along with all other believers, he there would receive the rightful rewards for his service to Christ and His kingdom.

This judgment seat of Christ will not be about condemnation for sins, which were all atoned for by Jesus at the cross (Rom. 8:1). Rather, this judgment is about rewards for ministry and service to the Lord. The word used in verse 10 for "bad" carries the meaning of unworthiness or worthlessness rather than sin or moral evil.

CHILDREN'S CORNER

Children should find comfort and hope in the prospect of God's provision of their heavenly dwelling places.

—Martin R. Dahlquist.

Scripture Lesson Text

II COR. 5:11 Knowing therefore the terror of the Lord, we persuade men; but we are made manifest unto God; and I trust also are made manifest in your consciences.

12 For we commend not ourselves again unto you, but give you occasion to glory on our behalf, that ye may have somewhat to *answer* them which glory in appearance, and not in heart.

13 For whether we be beside ourselves, *it is* to God: or whether we be sober, *it is* for your cause.

14 For the love of Christ constraineth us; because we thus judge, that if one died for all, then were all dead:

15 And *that* he died for all, that they which live should not henceforth live unto themselves, but unto him which died for them, and rose again.

16 Wherefore henceforth know we no man after the flesh: yea, though we have known Christ after the flesh, yet now henceforth know we *him* no more.

17 Therefore if any man *be* in Christ, *he is* a new creature: old things are passed away; behold, all things are become new.

18 And all things *are* of God, who hath reconciled us to himself by Jesus Christ, and hath given to us the ministry of reconciliation;

19 To wit, that God was in Christ, reconciling the world unto himself, not imputing their trespasses unto them; and hath committed unto us the word of reconciliation.

20 Now then we are ambassadors for Christ, as though God did beseech *you* by us: we pray *you* in Christ's stead, be ye reconciled to God.

21 For he hath made him *to be* sin for us, who knew no sin; that we might be made the righteousness of God in him.

NOTES

Ambassadors for Christ

Lesson Text: II Corinthians 5:11-21

Related Scriptures: Romans 10:5-15; I Corinthians 3:5-9;
Ephesians 2:11-22

TIME: probably A.D. 56   PLACE: from Macedonia

GOLDEN TEXT—"For he hath made him to be sin for us, who knew no sin; that we might be made the righteousness of God in him" (II Corinthians 5:21).

Introduction

One of the sad realities of human relationships is the fact that they often become strained, if not severed. One person offends or hurts another, and the two rarely, if ever, speak to each other again.

God has never been faithless to man, but since the Fall, man has constantly and continually been unfaithful to Him. Sin created a barrier between God and humans that no human being could get past. Without a way to remove that barrier, man would be forever separated from God.

But then Jesus Christ entered the picture. In Christ, God took on human form

and became a man. Jesus stepped into history as the one and only God-man, fully human and fully divine. No one else is like Him, nor will anyone ever be.

The mission of Jesus Christ was to reconcile two estranged parties: God and man.

LESSON OUTLINE

I. MINISTRY OF PERSUASION—
II COR. 5:11-13

II. MINISTRY OF LOVE—
II Cor. 5:14-16

III. MINISTRY OF
RECONCILIATION—II Cor. 5:17-21

Exposition: Verse by Verse

MINISTRY OF PERSUASION

II COR. 5:11 Knowing therefore the terror of the Lord, we persuade men; but we are made manifest unto God; and I trust also are made manifest in your consciences.

12 For we commend not ourselves again unto you, but give you occasion to glory on our behalf, that ye may have somewhat to answer them which glory in appearance, and not in heart.

13 For whether we be beside ourselves, it is to God: or whether we be sober, it is for your cause.

Respect for the Lord (II Cor. 5:11).
One of the most neglected topics of current Christian teaching is the fear of the Lord. So many fail to recognize that we serve a God of holiness and power. He is not to be approached in a half-hearted way as though He were just any other person. We are not to take our relationship with the Lord lightly; we should maintain a healthy fear of Him.

God is not trying to scare us into loving Him. {To fear the Lord means to respect Him and to come to Him with a sense of awe and wonder at His power and beauty.}[Q1] It is that proper fear of the Lord that spurs us to go out and try to persuade other people to come to Christ. When we share our faith with others, we should do so in a way that seeks to win their hearts, not just give them a list of facts or a bundle of information.

The fear of the Lord is what leads people to obedience (cf. II Cor. 7:1). Without an awareness of who God is, it is natural to try to control our own lives. A healthy fear of the Lord will prevent us from trying to be our own lord. Knowing that we are "made manifest unto God" (5:11), that He sees every motivation of our heart, should motivate us to live in a way that honors the faith we share with others.

Respect for the gospel (II Cor. 5:12-13). Paul did everything in ministry with a clear conscience and could therefore defend his integrity. Unfortunately, he had many detractors in the Corinthian church. He did extensive work in Corinth, more than in almost any other city. It seems he had correspondence with the Corinthians beyond the two letters contained in the Bible—at least two other letters, not to mention personal visits.

No matter how vigorously he proclaimed and explained the gospel, Paul was always defending his apostolic authority to the Corinthians. Why? {Because in order for people to listen to our gospel message, we need their respect.}[Q2] Paul was not trying to gain their blessing or approval for his own self-esteem. He had all the confidence he needed from the Lord. However, he wanted the Corinthians to understand that his authority came from Christ.

Paul was under steady attack by several opponents, so he worked hard to protect the Corinthians' respect for him. Unlike his detractors, Paul does not ask for respect based on anything superficial but rests his claim on his integrity—the alignment of his actions with his inner conscience, or heart.

Many Corinthians were impressed with outward appearances and gave little credence to the inner working of the Holy Spirit. To them, Paul lacked the credentials of a gifted orator or philosopher. His message centered around the cross of Jesus, and they thought that to be foolish. Paul wanted them to know, accept, and live by the true gospel of Christ and not be swayed by outward appearances.

Paul's love for this church cannot be questioned. He knew that some people, especially in Corinth, thought he was a fool and out of his mind. He was content to let people think this way, but he did not want outside opinions of him to undermine the faith of the Corinthian church.

Paul might be called a fool by outsiders, but he wanted the church to know that if he was a fool, it was for the Lord. If they could see that he was in his right mind, then it would be to their great benefit. Either way, he was not trying to convince them because he feared man's opinions but because he wanted people to listen seriously to the gospel message.

MINISTRY OF LOVE

14 For the love of Christ constraineth us; because we thus judge, that if one died for all, then were all dead:

15 And that he died for all, that they which live should not henceforth live unto themselves, but unto him which died for them, and rose again.

16 Wherefore henceforth know we no man after the flesh: yea, though we have known Christ after the flesh, yet now henceforth know we him no more.

The love of Christ (II Cor. 5:14-15). With all the strife that existed between Paul and some of the Corinthians, we might think he was a glutton for punishment. Why would he continue to seek fellowship with people who insulted him, often to the point of rejection?

The answer to this question is important as we think of those who may have rejected us for proclaiming the gospel. Paul said that the love of Christ constrained him to persevere in these relationships. {To be constrained means to be inwardly compelled to press on in the face of adversity.}[Q3] {It was the love of Christ for the Corinthians that compelled Paul to be relentless in his proclamation of the gospel in Corinth.}[Q4]

Christians are to be controlled by Jesus' love for us, not by our feeble emotions. The difference is that His love is inexhaustible and perfect while our love has limitations and is imperfect. We are motivated by the love that Jesus has for us and others.

Paul and his companions never wavered on this truth: Jesus Christ died for mankind. Jesus paid the penalty for sin on behalf of sinners, and everyone who puts their faith in Christ is saved (cf. Rom. 3:21-26).

{Since Jesus died for all, then all who trust in Him have died with Him. All who believe are now dead to sin.}[Q5] What a remarkable change from being dead in our sins as enemies of God (cf. Eph. 2:1-4)! Because of Adam, we were dead *in* sin, but thanks to Jesus, we are now dead *to* sin (cf. Rom. 5:15). As a result of Christ's resurrection,

we are now alive in Him. We died with Him and were raised with Him to new life (Rom. 6:4). Since we are alive in Christ, we no longer live for ourselves. Our lives are no longer controlled by selfishness and greed, but rather by the Holy Spirit. We now live for Jesus, the One who gave us life.

Jesus died and rose again for our sake, not for His own. He did not have to die, because He had never committed any sin of any kind (cf. Heb. 4:15; I Pet. 2:22). He died willingly as an act of mercy toward us. Therefore, we do not live for Him simply because of our love for Him, but because of His love for us.

A change in perspective (II Cor. 5:16). Once Paul gained this knowledge, it changed the way he looked at people, even those who vehemently opposed him. The words "wherefore henceforth" mean "so from now on" and indicate that a definite change had taken place in Paul's thinking. He no longer saw people the way he once did when he was persecuting the church. He now saw people through the eyes of Jesus, as it was Jesus' love that controlled him.

{Paul had determined that he would no longer see people through the eyes of the flesh, but would see them as human souls in need of redemption.}[Q6] It is important for us to do the same. Since we are motivated by Christ's love for us, we no longer look at people according to the world's standards of success. We see that their need for Jesus is just as great as ours, and we view them with mercy and compassion.

MINISTRY OF RECONCILIATION

17 Therefore if any man be in Christ, he is a new creature: old things are passed away; behold, all things are become new.

18 And all things are of God, who hath reconciled us to himself by Jesus

Christ, and hath given to us the ministry of reconciliation;

19 To wit, that God was in Christ, reconciling the world unto himself, not imputing their trespasses unto them; and hath committed unto us the word of reconciliation.

20 Now then we are ambassadors for Christ, as though God did beseech you by us: we pray you in Christ's stead, be ye reconciled to God.

21 For he hath made him to be sin for us, who knew no sin; that we might be made the righteousness of God in him.

New creations (II Cor. 5:17).

{The great news for the believer is that once we come to Christ, our past sins are erased, and we are made new.}[Q7] Trusting Christ means our trespasses are forgotten. God removes the sin from the sinner and sets the sinner free. His sin has been removed from him as far as the east is from the west (cf. Ps. 103:12).

The blood of Jesus is the ultimate and infinitely powerful stain remover. When Christ took our sins away, He left no trace of them behind. God no longer sees us as sinners but as His children. There is no way we can continue in our old lives, for we have been made new. Our old self has passed away, and the new has come.

The newness of life we have in Christ far surpasses in greatness and glory anything we ever did for ourselves. {The power of sin has no dominion over us any longer because Jesus has set us free. Knowing this, it does not make sense that we would feel free to keep on sinning.}[Q8] Why would Jesus set us free from sin just to have us run back to it? Sin kept us in bondage, and Jesus broke the chains and let us go. We are not free *to* sin, but instead we are free *from* sin. We do not live in bondage anymore.

Reconciliation (II Cor. 5:18-19).

The work of salvation belongs to God and God alone. We did not do anything to contribute to our salvation whatsoever. Salvation is the gift of God that was purchased on the cross by Jesus Christ (cf. Eph. 2:8-9).

Because of the barrier between man and God that was caused by our sin, there was no way for us to get back to God. No amount of pleading or working would do anything to make us right with the Lord. The only way for the barrier to be removed is if God came and removed it Himself, and that is precisely what Jesus came and did.

God reconciled the world back to Himself through Jesus Christ, His Son. The barrier between God and man was uniquely signified by the thick curtain that hung in the Holy of Holies in the temple. This curtain prevented man from coming into the presence of God. Through what Jesus did on the cross, however, the curtain was torn in half. Through the work of Jesus, we have been reconciled with God and can now freely enter into His presence.

Once we repent and place our faith in Jesus, our sins are never held against us again (cf. Jer. 31:34; Heb. 10:17). But there is a responsibility for those who have experienced reconciliation with God. We are now charged, by the same Spirit who charged Paul, to take the message of reconciliation to the world so that others can have the same forgiveness we now enjoy.

We do not have the right to keep this message to ourselves. To keep the gospel to ourselves while people enter eternity in hell is the embodiment of selfishness. Sharing this message is not a condition of being saved, but those who are saved should see it not only as an obligation but as a privilege.

Ambassadors for Christ (II Cor. 5:20).

All Christians are called into the ministry. We may have specific callings within ministry, but we are all called and appointed to share the gospel of Jesus and tell people that God has reconciled the world back to Himself through Jesus Christ. Not through Muhammad or Buddha or the Dalai Lama or any of the false gods of the world's polytheistic religions, but through Jesus Christ alone.

Being proclaimers of the message of reconciliation makes us ambassadors for Christ. An ambassador is an official representative of a government to a foreign nation. He does not represent his own interests, but the interests of the one who sent him. {As ambassadors of Christ, we represent the interests of God and proclaim His message, which is for the salvation of man.}[Q9] God has not called us to be motivational speakers, but ambassadors.

God has declared a peace treaty because of the finished work of Christ on the cross, and it is up to His ambassadors to go out and make known the terms of this treaty. People need to know that their sins will be forgiven if they repent and trust in Christ. It is the church's assignment to go out and share this wonderful message.

The great exchange (II Cor. 5:21). The chapter closes with Paul's explanation of exactly how God reconciled man through Jesus Christ. {This is the ministry of reconciliation: Jesus Christ, who never committed any sin (cf. I Pet. 2:22), was made by God to be sin for our sake so we might be reconciled with our Heavenly Father.}[Q10] It was not for His own sake that Jesus died, but for ours.

God took the sins of the world and put them on Christ, and in turn took the righteousness of Christ and gave it to us. It was the most one-sided deal in all of history. Jesus Christ took our sins, and we received His righteousness.

When two people or two companies work out a deal, both sides are looking to receive something of equal or greater value than their concessions. God, however, did not work along these lines at all. Jesus did not receive anything of value from us, yet we received the most precious thing imaginable.

There is no point in trying to be self-righteous. Self-righteousness is, in fact, an oxymoron because there is no righteousness in us. We all need the righteous of Christ in order to go to heaven, and that is exactly what God gave us. Without it, we cannot come into His presence at all. But with it, we are reconciled to the Father, and our relationship and fellowship with Him is restored.

—Robert Ferguson, Jr.

QUESTIONS

1. What does it mean to fear the Lord?
2. What do we need from people if we expect them to listen to the gospel message?
3. What does it mean to be constrained (II Cor. 5:14)?
4. What was it that constrained Paul to preach the gospel?
5. What does it mean that "if one died for all, then were all dead"?
6. How did Paul see people from a different perspective after his conversion?
7. According to verse 17, what is erased when we become new creations in Christ?
8. Why is it nonsensical to continue living in sin after we have been set free by Christ?
9. What does it mean to be an ambassador for Christ?
10. What is the ministry of reconciliation, and how did God secure it?

—Robert Ferguson, Jr.

Preparing to Teach the Lesson

Last week we saw that our future holds the promise of standing in the direct presence of the glorified Christ. Accordingly, we should work diligently in service to Christ and His gospel to show ourselves worthy of praise and reward. Now Paul shows us what it means to own the responsibility of being Christ's ambassadors.

TODAY'S AIM

Facts: to grasp the truth that we have been commissioned to be ambassadors for Christ to the world.

Principle: to understand what it means to be ambassadors for Christ.

Application: to live daily in the realization that in everything we do and say, we represent Christ and His gospel to the world.

INTRODUCING THE LESSON

In this week's lesson, Paul explores our motivation for becoming good ambassadors for Jesus Christ, showing His saving love to a world of lost sinners whom Jesus died to save.

DEVELOPING THE LESSON

1. The fear of Lord (II Cor. 5:11). The Greek word translated "terror" here is actually the word commonly translated "fear," and there seems no contextual warrant to see it as implying any particular condemnation or dire punishment.

Thus, Paul is referring in general to the concept of "fearing the Lord," that is, of being rightfully awed, reverent, and therefore obedient toward the Lord and His authority as the sovereign Creator of the universe. This appropriate fear of God should motivate us to work diligently to persuade people to trust in Jesus Christ as their Lord and Saviour.

To be "made manifest" means to be fully known in terms of personal character. In other words, Paul is claiming to be known thoroughly by God as a reliable servant. He also expresses trust that the believers at Corinth likewise know him as a trustworthy mentor and spiritual example to emulate.

2. The love of Christ (II Cor. 5:12-15). There seems to have remained a few at Corinth who were still seeking to stir up division over which human leader should be followed. Paul was not concerned so much about commending himself to those who had obediently taken to heart the admonishments of his first letter. Rather, he desired to give them some assurance to counter any negative opinions about him that still stubbornly persisted. He wanted them to know that they could rely on his word and his teaching.

"Beside ourselves" (vs. 13) means to be unstable in heart or mind, and Paul may be referring to the way his enemies were characterizing him. Apparently, the trial that Paul had endured in Asia had been very intense, and word of it had gotten back to the remaining dissenters at Corinth. So Paul was concerned to assure his loyal readers that it did not matter how he was portrayed. Whether he was seen as mentally unstable or perfectly sane, they could be confident that he had been guided by God for His glory and their good.

The Corinthians could be confident of this because the love of Jesus Christ had sovereign control of Paul's motives and actions. And he asserted that God applied this power to the lives of all His true followers. Paul knew that Christ gave His life for all believers; he therefore was also certain that all believers died with Him spiritually. The purpose for which Christ died was that His people should no longer live for themselves but for the risen Christ.

3. Ambassadors for Christ (II Cor. 5:16-21). "Henceforth know we no man after the flesh" may sound strange and puzzling to our modern ears. But it simply means that since his conversion to Christ, Paul no longer evaluated any person by his family ancestry or his social reputation. Now all that mattered about a person to Paul was his spiritual condition in Christ.

"Yea, though we have known Christ after the flesh" must be understood in the historical context. Some of the Judaizers had been promoting themselves among the believers at Corinth, majoring on their special position of having been around to see and hear Jesus prior to His crucifixion. They were using this presumption to ingratiate themselves to the Corinthians, as if this circumstance alone (that is, without actually having faith) gave them genuine status as teachers with authority.

Such pretentions held no consequence with either God or with Paul. Indeed, he himself had seen Christ in the flesh, but that no longer mattered. What mattered now is that Paul knew Christ by genuine, saving faith!

Verse 17 is, of course, the famous creed of those who have been born again by the Holy Spirit through faith in Christ. Paul revels in the assertion that he and all true believers are new creations. All those old, worldly pretentions that used to matter so much to us have passed away, along with our old lives as unbelievers. Surprise! Both we and all that really matters to us have become brand-new!

Since Christ has already reconciled us to God, all that old baggage from our previous life has also been taken care of; it can no longer weigh us down or drag us away from our relationship with God.

Therefore, Paul announces, we are official ambassadors for Christ; we plead God's own case to a lost world: "Be ye reconciled to God" (vs. 20). And verse 21 sums up that reconciling message, namely, that the sinless Christ was made sin for us on the cross. How amazing that He would do this for the sake of us sinners! Why did He do it? So that we might be made the very righteousness of God in Him!

ILLUSTRATING THE LESSON

The illustration shows that Christians have been made ambassadors for Christ to a lost world of sinners for whom Christ died.

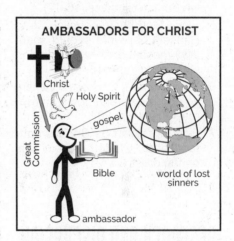

CONCLUDING THE LESSON

Being ambassadors for Christ is both a high honor and an awesome responsibility. We hold the precious message of eternal life in our fallible hands. But whom God has commissioned, He also guides and strengthens for His work!

ANTICIPATING THE NEXT LESSON

Next week's lesson will focus on our spiritual weapons and how we should make use of them to defeat our spiritual enemies to gain victory for Christ.

—*John Lody.*

PRACTICAL POINTS

1. Awareness of the coming judgment should motivate believers to share the gospel (II Cor. 5:11).
2. People may choose to deride and harass you for your faith, but only God's approval matters (vss. 12-13).
3. Jesus died for us, so believers should now live for Him out of gratitude for His love (vss. 14-15).
4. Jesus does not fix up our old lives; He gives us new lives when we trust in Him (vss. 16-17).
5. Since God has reconciled us to Himself, believers should share that message of reconciliation with others (vss. 18-19).
6. You represent Christ everywhere you go; be careful how you represent Him (vs. 20)!
7. God has given us Christ's righteousness; Christ bore our sins on the cross (vs. 21).

—Cheryl Y. Powell.

RESEARCH AND DISCUSSION

1. Why do our motives for witnessing and Christian service matter? Discuss.
2. Why might the Corinthians have been under the impression that Paul was not of sound mind?
3. What does it mean to be a new creature in Christ?
4. How would you describe the Christian's ministry of reconciliation?
5. Why is verse 21 significant?

—Cheryl Y. Powell.

ILLUSTRATED HIGH POINTS

Made manifest in your consciences (II Cor. 5:11)

There was a time when tens of thousands in America wore rose-colored glasses—thousands of chickens that is. It seems that chickens have a keen eye for the flaws and wounds of their fellow fowls. Once blood is spotted, a chicken is likely to peck his henhouse neighbor to death. The glasses apparently changed the offensive color into a pink hue, which successfully camouflaged each feathered fowl's flaws.

Sadly, when it comes to our own personal sins, most of us chickens put on our own rose-colored glasses—making us unable to see them. Only the preaching of the Word has the power to uncover our spiritual eyes to see the truth.

Glory in appearance, and not in heart (vs. 12)

Three billion people are currently involved in social media. Posted photos are often carefully posed, well-lit, and filtered for optimum glamour and appeal.

Sadly, this unending exhibition of seemingly flawless people living impeccable lives is producing insecurity and depression in many. Half of all social media users feel less attractive than their online friends. A study of Swedish Facebook users reported feelings of lessened confidence among users as they compared their own lives with those who seemingly had successful careers and happier homes.

We live in a time when glorying in appearance has become a worldwide pastime. Paul recommends instead that we turn to God and take an honest "selfie" of the internal condition of our own hearts!

—Therese Greenberg.

Golden Text Illuminated

"For he hath made him to be sin for us, who knew no sin; that we might be made the righteousness of God in him" (II Corinthians 5:21).

This is one of the most decisive verses in the New Testament on the substitutionary atonement of Christ. It tells us that Christ's death was much more than merely exemplary; Christ's death was a blood sacrifice that paid the penalty for the sins of all who would believe on Him as Lord and Saviour. But even more than that, Christ's perfect righteousness is also imputed to those same believers to secure an eternal standing before God.

The Bible teaches that Jesus Christ was "a lamb without blemish and without spot" (I Pet. 1:19), a High Priest who was tempted in every way, "yet without sin" (Heb. 4:15). At no time did Jesus allow ungodliness to enter His mind or body, even as His executioners tormented Him. Sin was never a part of His nature, even in death; it could not have been if He were to be the perfect sacrifice. Rather, Christ bore our sins. As Isaiah prophetically declared, "He was wounded for our transgressions, he was bruised for our iniquities" (Isa. 53:5).

What does this mean for us? Paul was writing about reconciliation in this section. Reconciliation is the act of restoring peace to parties who previously had been in conflict. There is no doubt that the relationship between God and humanity had been broken. It began in the Garden of Eden, when Adam and Eve disobeyed the Creator by succumbing to the temptations of the serpent. In Genesis 4, one chapter after the Fall, Cain murdered his brother, Abel, and Lamech boasted about killing a man merely for wounding him. Chapter 6 tells us that the wickedness on earth had become so pervasive that God actually regretted creating humanity. From cover to cover, the Bible testifies that we have all sinned, and sin separates us from God.

Paul uses the word for reconciliation in only four verses in all of his letters (cf. II Cor. 5:18-19; Eph. 2:16; Col. 1:20), but this does not diminish its significance. The Greek word means to exchange one thing for another. In a transactional sense, Jesus took our sins away and gave us His righteous standing with God; our enmity with God was exchanged for friendship with Him.

This great exchange is not only transactional, but relational—and even familial! Reconciled believers have been adopted into the household of God and made heirs of His redemptive glory with Christ. Because of this, we can rightfully call God "Abba" (Father).

This exchange also transforms us. In fact, the Greek word for reconciliation derives from a word meaning "to change," and was often used in Greek literature to denote a change in appearance, shape, or color. As Paul writes, in Christ "old things are passed away; behold, all things are become new" (II Cor. 5:17). When we embrace God through faith in Christ, we begin the process of inner transformation to holiness.

However, reconciliation is not just a private matter. Paul writes that we have been entrusted with the "word of reconciliation" (II Cor. 5:19). As God's ambassadors, we are to proclaim His priceless gospel to the world, as well as demonstrate it through our lives of Christian holiness.

—*Mark Winter.*

Heart of the Lesson

God has loved us, redeemed us, and welcomed us into His family. We should never, however, forget that God is holy and that in ourselves and our own power, we are not. The price for our redemption was Jesus' death. Reverence for God and gratitude for His grace should motivate us to obey Him and share the hope of eternal life with others.

1. Love for Christ (II Cor. 5:11-15). Paul and his associates labored in Corinth to establish a church on the foundation of the pure gospel. Paul worked hard, not in order to receive human admiration or wealth, but to bring God glory. Unfortunately, some Corinthians, through gossip and lies, had slandered him. Even so, he was confident that God knew his heart was pure, even if some of the Corinthians did not.

Paul had integrity—purity in his motives and actions. He knew who he was as an apostle of Jesus. He was the same person behind closed doors as he was preaching in front of a crowd. Paul committed himself to embodying and sharing the gospel. Why? Because he knew that he would one day stand before the judgment seat of Christ to be evaluated and receive rewards for his ministry (cf. vs. 10).

Those like Paul's opponents in Corinth, who do not have integrity and who boast and lie to make others think they are important, will also stand before Christ and be held accountable for their hypocrisy.

Paul's ministry was motivated by the love that Jesus showed in saving him. As a result, Paul lived to share Christ's love with others. He had died to his old life of pride and self-righteousness, and he wanted the Corinthians to trust him.

2. Reconciliation in Christ (II Cor. 5:16-19). Paul reminded the Corinthians that they were personally accountable to God for their actions, not as to a vindictive dictator, but as to a loving Father who had redeemed them and made them new in Christ. After Paul was saved, his perspective changed. He saw people as Jesus saw them, as dearly loved and with inherent worth.

Paul dedicated his post-conversion life to sharing the gospel, nurturing believers' spiritual growth, and helping those believers rest in their salvation. Once a person is in Christ, he or she becomes a new creation. As the Holy Spirit hovered over the deep waters of the original creation and sparked life in Adam and Eve (cf. Gen. 1:2; 2:7), so He sparks eternal life in those who trust in Christ, making them completely new creations.

3. Ambassadors for Christ (II Cor. 5:20-21). As redeemed people, reconciled to God through Christ, and as new creations, we now see life from a heavenly vantage point. Paul's calling was to reconcile people to God. God has called us to join Paul in this work by representing Christ as ambassadors of heaven, sharing the gospel with the people God has placed in our lives.

On the cross, when Jesus said, "It is finished" (John 19:30), He used a word that often means "paid in full." God the Father placed onto Jesus' account the sins of the world and poured His righteous wrath on Jesus. But Jesus remained the sinless Son of God so that He could be the holy Substitute for those who believe in Him. Those who put their faith in Christ receive Christ's perfect righteousness placed onto their account, as well as the promise of resurrection

—*Malia E. Rodriguez.*

World Missions

After many years of faithful service, the ambassador was fired. His offense? He became so entrenched in the politics and culture of his assigned country that he forgot whom he represented. It all came to light when a dispute arose between his home country and the one to which he was assigned as an ambassador. When he was called to speak on behalf of his homeland and confirm its stance as justified—a reasonable requirement for a diplomat—he instead used a press conference to take a brazen stand against his home country. The man's loyalties had turned. His career as a valued emissary swiftly ended in disgrace.

Missionaries are actually ambassadors for Christ to the foreign country of this fallen world. Paul himself used this analogy. All followers of Jesus are commissioned to live in this world and speak to this world on Christ's behalf like ambassadors (II Cor. 5:20). In addition to speaking for Him, our mission is to live before this fallen world as Jesus Himself did, striving to loyally represent His holiness and love to them. We can only do this by following His humble example of service to others, relying on the power of the Holy Spirit (Phil. 2:5-11).

The primary requirement of an ambassador is faithfulness (I Cor. 4:2). Can God trust you? Are you an ambassador who pays only lip service, or are you an active follower who remains steadfast in loyalty to his King?

Christians often struggle against forces that entice us to become overly comfortable in the land of our ambassadorship. Like the failed diplomat who sided with his assigned country instead of his homeland, we become unfaithful to Christ when we embrace the world's ungodly opinions. Turning away from the clear teaching of the Scriptures, we can get caught up in the prevailing ideas of the culture that surrounds us, causing us to forget who we are and who we are here to represent.

The world is adept at making its viewpoints appealing, peddling them as more loving and kind than what God's Word teaches us. The pressure to conform can be very strong. But love for Christ constrains us to make a decided commitment to remain faithful ambassadors for Jesus, regardless of the consequences.

Mordecai is an example of a true ambassador for God. An Israelite, he lived in exile in a foreign country, but he never forgot where he came from and whom he ultimately served. The Persian king unwisely promoted the evil Haman to the highest position in his cabinet, decreeing that all his subjects bow before Haman as he passed by them. All the king's subjects obeyed except one: Mordecai. Mordecai's colleagues questioned why he would not conform, but he remained resolute in his stance. Faithfulness can be dangerous! The prideful Haman went into a rage, vowing to destroy all the Jews because of Mordecai's refusal to honor him. This hateful spirit did not die with Haman—it still exists today!

Mordecai called on his niece, Queen Esther, to take a stand on behalf of her people. He warned her not to think that she would escape Haman's holocaust because of her position in the palace. He reminded Esther that God may have put her in her present position of power for just such a time as this (cf. Esth. 4:14). Without Mordecai, Esther might have forgotten who she was and her rightful responsibility to her people.

Mordecai's words are a guiding light to all ambassadors.

—*Rose McCormick Brandon.*

The Jewish Aspect

According to the Hebrew Scriptures, sin is present in a man's heart from his youth (Gen. 8:21). Judaism teaches that sin is a part of life and that there are consequences for sins committed willfully. There are, however, different levels of sin or transgression, the most serious of which is *Pesha* (crime) or *Mered* (rebellion), which is an action committed in deliberate defiance of God. "The word most commonly translated as 'sin,' *hata,* literally means 'to go astray.' Just as Jewish law, *halakha,* provides the proper 'way' (or path) to live, sin involves straying from that path" (en.wikipedia.org). The word "upright" in Hebrew means "straight," as in "to walk a straight path" (www.ancient hebrew.org). The Israelites were called to live righteously according to all of God's commandments, and they all accepted the terms of the covenant with God (Ex. 24:3).

The Israelites were called to do what was just and righteous in all relationships. "Blessed are they that keep judgment, and he that doeth righteousness at all times" (Ps. 106:3). The Lord commanded the Israelites to uphold all of the statutes that He had given to them. "And it shall be our righteousness, if we observe to do all these commandments before the Lord our God, as he hath commanded us" (Deut. 6:25). The Jewish people also recognized that it was impossible for any man to live a perfectly righteous life. "For there is not a just man upon earth, that doeth good, and sinneth not" (Eccl. 7:20).

When Moses instituted the Lord's covenant with the Israelites, blood offerings ratified the covenant (Ex. 24:5-8). Because of the sin of the Israelites, animal sacrifices of blood offerings were made for the atonement. "For the life of the flesh is in the blood: and I have given it to you upon the altar to make atonement for your souls: for it is the blood that maketh an atonement for the soul" (Lev. 17:11). "Another important concept is the element of substitution. The idea is that the thing being offered is a substitute for the person making the offering, and the things that are done to the offering are things that should have been done to the person making the offering. The offering is in some sense 'punished' in place of the offerer" (www.jewishvirtuallibrary.org). However, when the second temple in Jerusalem was destroyed by the Roman army in A.D. 70, blood sacrifices stopped. As a result, Jewish scholars since then have taught that repentance is also a means of atonement. Substitutionary blood atonement, however, was the norm in ancient Israel.

Jewish Christians in the first-century church believed correctly that the death of the Messiah fulfilled the substitutionary atonement required by God.

Paul exhorted the believers to be God's ambassadors for the Messiah and the atonement His death provided. Ambassadors in ancient Israel involved three things: being commissioned for a specific assignment, representing the sender, and exercising the authority of the sender. "It was universally expected that an ambassador, whatever his message and however delicate or risky his mission, would be treated with respect and dignity, accorded appropriate hospitality, and guaranteed a safe exit" (www.preceptaustin.org). Jesus was not often accorded any of these honors during His earthly life and ministry, and we, as His ambassadors, should not rely upon better treatment from the world than Jesus Himself received (John 15:18; I John 3:13).

—Deborah Markowitz Solan.

Guiding the Superintendent

When Christians make a commitment to get serious about living for Jesus Christ, they often become objects of suspicion to people who are close to them. Some may suspect their motives or the seriousness of their commitment, and some may just think they are crazy.

This is exactly what happened to the apostle Paul. In fact, soon after his conversion, many were very afraid of Paul, and later, some even thought he was crazy (cf. Acts 9:26; 26:24). Apparently some at Corinth had adopted this opinion about him.

DEVOTIONAL OUTLINE

1. Controlled by the love of Christ (II Cor. 5:11-15). It was obvious to many around him that Paul was a driven person. He was driven by "terror," that is, by great awe and reverence for God. It was not a fear that God would condemn or abandon him, but that he might somehow disappoint his beloved Saviour.

Paul was not engaging in a self-promotion campaign. He wanted the Corinthians to know the truth about him so that they would have a good answer for his critics. He wanted them to be able to boast about what was truly in his heart to those who were all about mere outward appearances.

Paul declared that even if he were not in his right mind, as some were alleging, his actions were still for God's glory. And if he was sane, it was for their sakes. It was the love of Christ that compelled him to act as he did because of one all-important, overriding conclusion: Christ died for them all, and therefore they had all died in Christ. The reason Christ died for them was so that they might no longer live selfish lives, but that they might live for Him who had secured their salvation.

2. The ministry of reconciliation (II Cor. 5:16-21). Paul no longer perceived anyone by mere outward appearances. Before his conversion, Paul had indeed judged even Christ by such shallow perceptions, but no more. Now that he was saved, he no longer operated by this standard.

The reason Paul no longer relied on mere appearances is because those who are in Christ have become entirely new people. Their old natures have died with Christ on the cross, and everything about them has become new. This is the work of God inside them: even though they look the same outwardly, they are no longer the same inwardly. This is because God through Christ has reconciled them to Himself; they have been sanctified by His cleansing blood.

Paul understood that reconciliation was the whole purpose of his ministry. Since God is in the business of reconciling the whole world to Himself in Christ, that was also Paul's business. God is not desiring to hold people's sins against them, but rather to cleanse them from sin, making them holy, and adopting them into His family through Christ. Because of this truth, Paul had become an ambassador for Christ to the whole world, appealing to everyone to be reconciled with God.

The whole basis for this reconciliation is the truth that God, for our sakes, has made His own perfectly sinless Son the sacrifice for our sins so that in Him we might become the very expressions to the world of God's own righteousness.

CHILDREN'S CORNER

The idea of being an ambassador is probably a new idea for most children. Help children understand what a Christian ambassador should do and say.

—Martin R. Dahlquist.

SCRIPTURE LESSON TEXT

II COR. 10:1 Now I Paul myself beseech you by the meekness and gentleness of Christ, who in presence *am* base among you, but being absent am bold toward you:

2 But I beseech *you,* that I may not be bold when I am present with that confidence, wherewith I think to be bold against some, which think of us as if we walked according to the flesh.

3 For though we walk in the flesh, we do not war after the flesh:

4 (For the weapons of our warfare *are* not carnal, but mighty through God to the pulling down of strong holds;)

5 Casting down imaginations, and every high thing that exalteth itself against the knowledge of God, and bringing into captivity every thought to the obedience of Christ;

6 And having in a readiness to revenge all disobedience, when your obedience is fulfilled.

7 Do ye look on things after the outward appearance? If any man trust to himself that he is Christ's, let him of himself think this again,

that, as he *is* Christ's, even so *are* we Christ's.

8 For though I should boast somewhat more of our authority, which the Lord hath given us for edification, and not for your destruction, I should not be ashamed:

9 That I may not seem as if I would terrify you by letters.

10 For *his* letters, say they, *are* weighty and powerful; but *his* bodily presence *is* weak, and *his* speech contemptible.

11 Let such an one think this, that, such as we are in word by letters when we are absent, such *will we be* also in deed when we are present.

12 For we dare not make ourselves of the number, or compare ourselves with some that commend themselves: but they measuring themselves by themselves, and comparing themselves among themselves, are not wise.

17 But he that glorieth, let him glory in the Lord.

18 For not he that commendeth himself is approved, but whom the Lord commendeth.

NOTES

Spiritual Weapons

Lesson Text: II Corinthians 10:1-12, 17-18

Related Scriptures: I Corinthians 2:1-16; Ephesians 6:10-18

TIME: probably A.D. 56   PLACE: from Macedonia

GOLDEN TEXT—"Casting down imaginations, and every high thing that exalteth itself against the knowledge of God, and bringing into captivity every thought to the obedience of Christ" (II Corinthians 10:5).

Introduction

Have you ever been in a position where you felt like you were constantly defending your qualifications? Sometimes no matter what you do, no matter your level of education, no matter how hard you have worked to show yourself approved, people still question you. That hurts on a personal level, but it can also damage your credibility.

If you have been through this, or are presently going through something similar, then you can relate to how Paul endured criticism from the Corinthians. His qualifications as an apostle or leader were called into question since he was not an impressive orator or philosopher like the ones who captured the Corinthians' admiration. In this week's lesson, he continues his defense of his ministry, further establishing his divinely appointed right to exercise authority in the church. Trusting in Christ, he continues to lead them.

LESSON OUTLINE

I. GENTLE AND BOLD IN CHRIST—II COR. 10:1-6

II. CONFIDENT IN CHRIST—II Cor. 10:7-12

III. BOASTING IN CHRIST—II Cor. 10:17-18

Exposition: Verse by Verse

GENTLE AND BOLD IN CHRIST

II COR. 10:1 Now I Paul myself beseech you by the meekness and gentleness of Christ, who in presence am base among you, but being absent am bold toward you:

2 But I beseech you, that I may not be bold when I am present with that confidence, wherewith I think to be bold against some, which think of us as if we walked according to the flesh.

3 For though we walk in the flesh, we do not war after the flesh:

4 (For the weapons of our warfare are not carnal, but mighty through God to the pulling down of strong holds;)

5 Casting down imaginations, and every high thing that exalteth itself against the knowledge of God, and bringing into captivity every thought to the obedience of Christ;

6 And having in a readiness to revenge all disobedience, when your obedience is fulfilled.

Paul's entreaty (II Cor. 10:1). Once again, as he did in the opening verse of the epistle, Paul identifies himself as the writer of this letter. For the topic being discussed here, it was especially important that the Corinthians knew it was coming from Paul himself.

Paul beseeches, or begs, the Corinthians to continue to pay close attention to his letter, especially to what he is about to say. {There were certainly other things he would rather have discussed with them (cf. I Cor. 3:1-2), but he continually had to assert his apostolic authority in Christ as a basis for his entreaty.}Q1

If Paul felt frustration concerning this, he did not let it overwhelm him, nor did he take it out on the church. Instead, he appeals to them by the meekness and gentleness of Christ. It was the humble attitude displayed by Jesus that moved Paul to address the Corinthians. It was not with anger that he wrote, but with gentleness and meekness that came from Christ. In all that Paul did, everywhere he went, he endeavored to display a Christlike attitude.

{The Corinthians did not seem to take Paul's authority very seriously. They accused him of being tough in his letters but timid when he was with them.}Q2 In other words, they thought he was all talk and no action. Some claimed that when he was away from them, he was a big, bad tough guy, but when he was face to face with them, he backed down.

Paul's stand (II Cor. 10:2). The last thing Paul wanted was to have to dis-play a harsh boldness to the Corinthians when he arrived. He much preferred a peaceful approach, one in which they could work out their differences calmly. It would be much better if the church came to a proper understanding on their own of his role in their lives.

It had never been Paul's aim or ambition as an apostle to throw his weight around. In fact, he tried every way possible not to do that. But even after much correspondence, many Corinthians still doubted him. Just like Christ, Paul would be humble when the situation required it, but he would also be bold when the credibility of the gospel was at risk.

Paul's desire to keep the peace is not to be dismissed as weakness on his part. Taking a peaceful approach when you are being attacked requires much more strength than does lashing out in anger. Restraining yourself when you have been wronged is much more difficult than giving someone a piece of your mind. Paul was doing all he could to keep the door of communication open with the Corinthians so that the gospel work could still go forward in that city.

Paul was ready, though, to show his boldness when he reached Corinth, and he did not shy away from saying so. He would not tolerate anyone accusing him of walking according to the flesh when he was controlled by the Holy Spirit. Allegations that he was working for selfish ambition were an attack on the very foundation of his life and ministry. If he had been operating according to the flesh, he would have long since thrown his hands up in the air and walked away. Led by the Holy Spirit, however, he moved forward in love and boldness.

Paul's weapons (II Cor. 10:3-4). When we are verbally assaulted by others, the first thing we should do is search our hearts before the Lord to see if the criticism has validity that we can learn from. If it proves unfounded, however, we should be willing to consider the possibility that the attack is demonic in nature. Satan wants to destroy us, and one of his most effective tools is divisiveness. As it did for Paul, this can come in the form of baseless questioning of a person's ability to serve in his or her calling.

It is becoming less and less popular to talk about Satan in today's cultural climate, and the devil actually prefers it that way. Sneak attacks are much more effective and more easily conducted when people do not believe the enemy exists. Satan does exist, however, and it is imperative that we are aware of his methods and presence.

{Paul understood that his battle was not with the Corinthians, but with Satan. His enemy was not the Corinthian people, but the devil.}Q3 The Corinthians were but a tool in the hands of Satan, and Paul recognized this. His battle was spiritual, not of the flesh.

Although Paul admitted that he lived in the flesh, he did not conduct himself as though the flesh controlled him. "The flesh" in this sense refers not to the physical body, but to the part of us that is opposed to God. He did not handle the Corinthian conflict in a way that reflected a worldly mindset. Paul saw the source of the conflict as Satan, and he was fighting him, not the people of Corinth. He was trying to reach them with the truth, which he was convinced was the only way to gain victory.

If Paul had been waging this war according to the flesh, he would have lobbed insults against his opponents and possibly tried to attack their character. He would have defended himself by trying to tear them down. Being led by the Holy Spirit, however, Paul did none of this.

The weapons Paul fought with were not carnal, or of this world. {The weapons we use as Christians include prayer, the Bible, faith in Christ, and the power of the Holy Spirit who resides in us.}Q4 Weapons of the flesh, whether they be guns, knives, or heavy artillery, will never be effective when fighting Satan. He is impervious to these things. In fact, when we resort to words of anger, attack, and division, it only bolsters his purposes.

Weapons with divine power such as Scripture, faith, the Holy Spirit, and prayer will secure victory. It may not come instantly, but victory will come to those who fight spiritual warfare with the proper weapons and in an appropriate way. The strongholds that Satan tries to impose on us will be destroyed when we fight in the Spirit and not by the flesh.

Paul's polemics (II Cor. 10:5-6). Paul spent a great deal of time going into uncharted territory for the Christian message. Many of the places he went were steeped in pagan worship practices and philosophies. There was very little common ground for him to stand on with these kinds of people when attempting to preach the gospel. For many of those Paul evangelized, it was the first time they had ever heard anything about the true God at all.

Paul always had to stand ready to give a defense of the gospel wherever he went and to whomever he met. He confronted a lot of bad ideology everywhere he went, so he had to be ready to tear down erroneous arguments in order to give a clear presentation of the gospel. {Two very important tools for Christians to use in personal evangelism are polemics and apologetics.}Q5 Polemics is the practice of exposing the error of false religions and ideas. Apologetics, on the other hand, is concerned with offering a vindication of the gospel and Christian doctrine. To use a sports analogy, polemics is offense and apologetics is defense.

When Paul talks about destroying arguments and opinions and punishing disobedience, he is talking about a polemical exposure of teachings that promote falsehood. Every thought is subject to Christ, and the idea behind such a polemical approach is to teach obedience to Christ, not just to win arguments.

CONFIDENT IN CHRIST

7 Do ye look on things after the outward appearance? If any man trust to himself that he is Christ's, let him of himself think this again, that, as he is Christ's, even so are we Christ's.

8 For though I should boast somewhat more of our authority, which the Lord hath given us for edification, and not for your destruction, I should not be ashamed:

9 That I may not seem as if I would terrify you by letters.

10 For his letters, say they, are weighty and powerful; but his bodily presence is weak, and his speech contemptible.

11 Let such an one think this, that, such as we are in word by letters when we are absent, such will we be also in deed when we are present.

12 For we dare not make ourselves of the number, or compare ourselves with some that commend themselves: but they measuring themselves by themselves, and comparing themselves among themselves, are not wise.

Power in the gospel (II Cor. 10:7-8). Paul asks the Corinthians why they were so concerned with outward appearance. In defending his apostolic ministry, he challenges them to consider that he is a brother in Christ, which should hold more weight than any earthly talents others might possess.

The truth of Paul's message as well as the validity of his ministry was not something that was hidden from the Corinthians. He was not secretive in his message or his motives. {He was there to share the gospel of Jesus Christ and was sent by Jesus as an apostle.}[Q6]

Paul notes that his apostleship and his message have greatly benefited the Corinthian church—for their edification and salvation. Paul was not sent there to destroy, but to build up. He was there to preach the gospel, not to build his own personal empire. Therefore, he was not ashamed to boast about his authority, because it aligned with the purpose of spreading the gospel.

Power unexpected (II Cor. 10:9-10). The intent of Paul's written correspondence was not to frighten or intimidate the Corinthians. While at times giving sharp correction for inappropriate or sinful behavior, Paul's purpose in writing was not to be overly critical or abusive in any way.

As he hinted at the beginning of the letter, some Corinthians sarcastically derided Paul, claiming that he was much braver when he was away than when he was with them. They said that he would never say to their faces what he wrote in his letters. They criticized Paul for being courageous only when he was several hundred miles away.

Based on the quote in verse 10, the Corinthian critics had little respect for Paul, saying that he was weak in physical stature and an inferior speaker. They wondered why God would choose such an inferior person instead of a strong, physical specimen or a philosopher who could speak with great eloquence (I Cor. 1:27).

Power in integrity (II Cor. 10:11-12). Paul had news for those who charged that he was different when he was with them than he was when he was on the road. There was no difference in his conduct either way. While he was away, the only way he could communicate with the Corinthians was through letters, but when he was with them, he could communicate both through words and actions, which are more potent. {He wanted the Corinthians to perceive his integrity so they would know that he was trustworthy.}[Q7]

In making this statement, Paul is not attempting to compare himself with any of the Greek philosophers that were so popular in Corinth. Instead, he actually sounds like he pitied them, claiming that they had no understanding. The people who considered themselves to be the wisest of the wise were really lacking in wisdom and true knowledge.

BOASTING IN CHRIST

17 But he that glorieth, let him glory in the Lord.

18 For not he that commendeth himself is approved, but whom the Lord commendeth.

Boasting in vain (II Cor. 10:17). The Corinthians were notorious for boasting in themselves. They loved knowledge, wisdom, and philosophy and felt a certain air of superiority over those who were uneducated or foreign. {Paul thought it wrong and misguided for a person to boast in himself, because we have nothing good in us apart from God.}[Q8] Even those who are highly intelligent among unbelievers receive their abilities from God. Of course, since they do not acknowledge the Lord as their Creator and Sustainer, they do not use these abilities for God's glory. They turn the gifts He has given them into a source of pride.

As far as Paul was concerned, there is nothing about human knowledge, ability, or skill that is worth bragging about. If someone must boast, he should reserve such boasting for the Lord (cf. Jer. 9:23-24).

Boasting in Christ (II Cor. 10:18). {The only thing any of us have to boast about is what Christ has done, is doing, and will do in our lives.}[Q9] We can do nothing of eternal value without Him (cf. John 15:5).

When a carpenter builds a beautiful house, does his hammer get the glory? Of course not. That would be downright absurd. The carpenter is the one who gets the praise and attention. The tool was just something that he used. While tools are important, it is the maker's hands that did the work. Without the carpenter, the tools would never leave the toolbox.

The same is true for us. We are tools in the hands of God to be used at His pleasure and discretion. Thankfully, He also looks on us lovingly as sons and daughters, but we still have no reason to boast in ourselves as if we could do anything apart from Him.

{The Lord will commend those who trust in Him.}[Q10] God is satisfied with those who love Him, and they will know His pleasure for all eternity.

—Robert Ferguson, Jr.

QUESTIONS

1. What was the basis of Paul's entreaty to the Corinthians?

2. Why did the Corinthians fail to take Paul's authority seriously?

3. What key truth did Paul understand about the conflict between him and the Corinthians?

4. What are some of the weapons we need to use in battling against Satan?

5. What are two important tools in personal evangelism?

6. What was Paul's motivation in going to Corinth?

7. What did Paul want the Corinthians to perceive about him?

8. Why did Paul think it was wrong for anyone to boast in themselves?

9. What is the only thing for us to boast about?

10. Who will receive commendation from the Lord?

—Robert Ferguson, Jr.

Preparing to Teach the Lesson

This week's lesson looks in on a showdown of sorts between Paul and those at Corinth who still stubbornly resisted his authority. They thought that he was hiding behind the boldness of his letters and considered him weak and contemptible in person.

But Paul assured them that his own weapons were spiritual and mighty in the Lord, and he was ready to visit them in person with the same boldness and authority that they found in his letters.

TODAY'S AIM

Facts: to realize that the weapons of our spiritual warfare must be the spiritual weapons ordained by God.

Principle: to understand that since our warfare is spiritual, our weapons in that conflict must also be spiritual if they are to accomplish God's spiritual victory.

Application: to resist the temptation to see other people as our enemies in our spiritual conflict, since even those who seem to side with Satan are actually his victims (as we once were) who need to be saved through faith in Christ.

INTRODUCING THE LESSON

In this week's lesson, Paul contrasts himself with those who oppose him at Corinth. His focus is on spiritual warfare and the spiritual weapons in such a conflict.

DEVELOPING THE LESSON

1. Mighty through God (II Cor. 10:1-6). Paul had a reputation among some at Corinth for being forceful and bold in his letters but humble and meek when he visited them personally (cf. vss. 9-11). He alludes to this reputation here in order to make a point: he wants those who have heeded his previous admonitions to distance themselves from those who have stubbornly chosen to remain divisive and selfish by their opposition to him.

Paul wants them to do this so that when he arrives in Corinth, there will be a clear distinction between them and those who oppose him. He intends to bring discipline upon the disobedient but to remain gentle and meek toward those who have obeyed.

Those who remained opposed to Paul's instruction were claiming that because he appeared small and weak in person and was not eloquent in his speech, he was not worthy of respect or admiration. As if his physical appearance were an accurate measure of his spiritual authority!

Paul wanted his readers to know that his authority had nothing to do with the physical impression he made. His power and authority were derived solely from the commission he had been given by Christ and the Holy Spirit, and his weapons were spiritual in nature.

Paul declares in no uncertain terms that in the might of Christ's spiritual power he was more than capable of utterly demolishing even the most formidable spiritual strongholds. God had sent him on a mission to throw down even the most arrogant and seemingly imposing human philosophies and the vain imaginings of worldly wisdom that stood in the way of the gospel. He was fully equipped to deal decisively with all rebellions, wherever he encountered them, subduing them into obedience to Christ.

When the faithful at Corinth had fully distanced themselves from the troublemakers in their midst, Paul would be ready to bring spiritual vengeance upon the rebellious. But he had no desire to punish the innocent along with the guilty; therefore, he warns the faithful ones to take a clear stand for righteousness.

2. Edification, not destruction (II Cor. 10:7-11). Paul challenges the Corinthians to disregard all outward appearances and evaluate their position spiritually. They need to realize that if they are Christ's, then Paul too is Christ's.

Paul draws a distinction between his own ministry and that of the rebellious and divisive. His authority is for his readers' edification, while his opponents' is for their destruction. He wants the Corinthians to realize their unity in Christ; the others seek division, conflict, and strife. His purpose is not to terrify anyone through his letters, but to call them back to faithfulness in Christ.

Again, those who opposed him claimed that he sounded impressive in his letters but was weak and detestable in person. Yet Paul assures them that when he came to them he would arrive with the same power and authority he demonstrated in his letters. Strongly implied in this statement is that they would be sorry when he did!

3. Boasting only in the Lord (II Cor. 10:12, 17-18). Paul would not stoop to the level of his opponents; he would refrain from comparing himself with those who sought to promote themselves for their own benefit. He denounces all such posturing and jostling for position as ignorant nonsense.

Paul's final appraisal is that the only thing anyone can properly boast about is that he knows the Lord and that the Lord knows him. No one's approval matters except His. A person can promote himself to his last breath, but all it amounts to is a lot of hot air. At the end of the day, the only opinion that counts is God's.

ILLUSTRATING THE LESSON

The illustration shows our spiritual weapons juxtaposed to a list of our spiritual enemies.

SPIRITUAL WEAPONS FOR SPIRITUAL ENEMIES

Holy Spirit

gospel

Anti-Christian philosophies
False arguments
Obstacles to faith
Rebellious thoughts

Bible

CONCLUDING THE LESSON

Paul's previous letter to the church at Corinth had done its work for the most part in the lives of the believers there. Now there was a faithful contingent who forsook their former selfish and divisive ways and embraced humble service to one another while maintaining unity in the Spirit. But some still resisted Paul's admonishments and disparaged his authority as an apostle of Christ.

Paul wanted to assure all those at Corinth that his unimpressive physical appearance notwithstanding, Christ had invested him with the full might of His spiritual power. The warfare they were waging was spiritual in nature, and Paul was ready when he arrived there in person to exert the full spiritual power of Christ's authority to discipline those who were disobedient.

Our warfare today is at its roots much the same spiritual conflict that Paul faced. Our weapons in that warfare are likewise spiritual (cf. Eph. 6:10-18).

ANTICIPATING THE NEXT LESSON

Next week we consider our final lesson for this quarter. In it, Paul focuses on how weakness and infirmity actually make us stronger by magnifying God's glory in us!

—*John Lody.*

PRACTICAL POINTS

1. The Holy Spirit leads His people to be bold at times (II Cor. 10:1-2).
2. Believers invite failure when they attack spiritual problems with mere human wisdom (vss. 3-5).
3. Victory in Christ is won through obedient submission to Him (vs. 6).
4. God gives spiritual authority to people for building others up, not for intimidating them or oppressing them (vss. 7-9).
5. Be careful about criticizing other Christians; it displeases the Lord and invites Him to teach you humility (vss. 10-11).
6. People who blow their own horns cannot avoid playing a sour and discordant music (vs. 12).
7. We have nothing to boast about ourselves; all that we are is by the grace of God in Christ (vss. 17-18).

—Cheryl Y. Powell.

RESEARCH AND DISCUSSION

1. In what situations might a Christian need to take a more gentle approach?
2. Why must believers always be mindful of being involved in spiritual warfare?
3. What weapons are Christians to use in spiritual battles?
4. What happens when Christians lose sight of the true identity of their spiritual enemy?

—Cheryl Y. Powell.

ILLUSTRATED HIGH POINTS

Casting down imaginations (II Cor. 10:5)

History is replete with tales of men and women who have defied great obstacles and thereby accomplished seemingly impossible feats. One such man is United States D.E.A. Special Agent George Hood, who distinguished himself at age 54 as the only man who could hold his body up off the floor in the plank position for nearly an hour and a half!

Impressive, yes, but there is an obstacle which requires even greater ability to overcome. Only the most powerful can wrestle it and bring it into captivity. It is the unruliest force in the universe: the imaginations of people's hearts! Self-exalting thoughts cause people to oppose God, and only His spiritual resources and disciplines can conquer such brutes.

Measuring themselves by themselves (vs. 12)

As a girl, I spent some time watching an ant colony and noting to myself that the ants all looked the same. Then it occurred to me that somehow, on their level, they must be quite aware of their differences.

A well-known American magazine features an edition in which it determines the 100 most powerful persons of the current year. They ranked the general secretary of the Communist Party of China as number 1 and the Russian president (who had been number 1 for the four previous years) as merely number 2. The American president and the German chancellor fill the third and fourth positions. Number 6 is the pope.

Like the ants, small as we are, we measure ourselves against each other and fail to see the true majesty of God, our all-powerful Observer and King.

—Therese Greenberg.

Golden Text Illuminated

"Casting down imaginations, and every high thing that exalteth itself against the knowledge of God, and bringing into captivity every thought to the obedience of Christ" (II Corinthians 10:5).

Have you ever sent a confrontational email to someone because you did not want to deal with that person face to face?

If Paul were around today, he might be unfairly branded by some as a "keyboard warrior." His detractors in Corinth questioned why he was so bold in his epistles, but so timid when visiting the church in person. Since they believed Paul's bark was worse than his bite, they accused him of walking in the flesh. These opponents also criticized him for not presenting letters of recommendation to validate his ministry (II Cor. 3:1) and for being such an inelegant speaker (10:10).

Many people will return insult for insult. Paul does not. He takes another road, opening the chapter by appealing to the "meekness" of Christ (II Cor. 10:1). Aristotle defined meekness as the reasonable halfway point between losing one's temper and never getting angry at all. It includes the kind of anger that does not seek to destroy an opponent; it is the strong and sure restraint that Jesus himself modeled.

The other word that Paul employs in verse 1 of this chapter is "gentleness." When Paul rebukes, he strives to do so in the spirit of Christ, who never took personal offense or revenge for the slights directed against him. This gentleness does not seek retribution for wrongs, but answers wrongs with the righteous love of God.

Paul goes on to state that he would only use weapons that are spiritual; that is, he will not resort to the worldly methods of his opponents, such as clever arguments and underhanded insults.

Paul lays out his spiritual warfare strategy. First, the battle involves tearing down "imaginations," those proud thoughts that do not come from the Holy Spirit. Paul would attack criticisms with the Word of God, not his own human reasoning.

Next, his spiritual warfare is aimed at demolishing "every high thing": arrogant human wisdom and philosophies that set themselves against the revealed knowledge of God. Finally, believers are to take their thoughts "captive" to the obedience of Christ. The term alludes to the practice of ancient conquerors leading a procession of their prisoners of war in chains through the streets upon their return from a great victory. We are to give our every thought over to the control of the victorious Lord Jesus, who has disarmed the powers of Satan and publicly shamed them by the power of His cross (cf. Col. 2:15).

Though this language is all rather militant, Paul reminds his readers that Christians do not wage war as others do. We do not retaliate in kind against our attackers. We cannot control what others do to us, so our battle is within our own hearts. We are to be renewed inwardly, not submitting to the flesh and its lusts, but to the guidance of the Holy Spirit and the love of Christ.

Paul admitted that he was unimpressive in person, but his fruitful work at Corinth proved that God worked through him. He refused to commend himself—he would boast only in the Lord!

—*Mark Winter.*

Heart of the Lesson

Much of reality is invisible. We often see our lives only as the product of natural circumstances and completely ignore the unseen spiritual world. But a spiritual war rages all around us. Even if we do not perceive this battle, we are involved in it and experience its effects. There are two armies in this battle: God's heavenly armies, headed by Jesus and His followers, and Satan's demonic forces.

1. Spiritual warfare (II Cor. 10:1-6). Paul framed many of his arguments in terms of the contrast between the flesh and the spirit, the natural and the supernatural. As Paul battled attacks against his apostolic authority, he appealed not to his worldly pedigree but to Christ's calling on his life through the Holy Spirit.

Even though Paul had received cruel treatment from some of the Corinthians, he showed meekness and gentleness in return. A meek person does not react to mistreatment with cruelty and vindictiveness, but with patience and kindness. How? By remembering that God sees everything and will hold all people accountable according to His perfect justice.

Paul knew that if we pull back the curtains on persecutions, we will see the spiritual reality behind them all—Satan's minions waging war on Christ's disciples and the truth of His Word by spreading false doctrines and influences (cf. Eph. 6:12). Christ has already triumphed over Satan, sin, and death, so our role as believers is to stand firm in His victory (cf. vs. 13).

Paul reminded the Corinthians that the most crucial battle to win is the battle against our own sinful thoughts. Like a fortress that protects a city against its enemies, our minds must be fortified with truth. We must examine every thought to see if it aligns with God's Word or not. As believers meditate on biblical truth, the Holy Spirit reveals our sins to us so that we can repent and seek forgiveness for them.

2. Carnal warfare (II Cor. 10:7-12). Often, people who want to discredit Jesus will first discredit His followers. If they can hide behind a Christian's indiscretions, they feel that they will not have to deal with whether or not Christ really is the Son of God to whom they owe their allegiance. That is what Paul's opponents were doing. The false apostles who harassed the Corinthian church questioned Paul's authority and therefore cast doubt on all his teachings. Paul knew that behind these false accusations, evil spiritual forces were waging war against the souls of the believers at Corinth.

Paul encouraged the Corinthians to judge between him and his opponents by their works. Paul, an apostle appointed by Jesus Himself, had poured his heart and soul into the Corinthian church, founding it on the pure gospel of grace and nurturing it with true doctrine and loving discipline. The false apostles, on the other hand, had neither founded the Corinthian church, nor had they any authority from Christ. Paul appealed to the Corinthians to use the wisdom he had equipped them with to reject these false apostles and their corrupting doctrines. If they did not, Paul would have to take strong action when he came next to visit them.

3. Spiritual victory (II Cor. 10:17-18). As sinful people living in a fallen world, we often compare ourselves to others instead of fully recognizing our debt to God's grace.

—Malia E. Rodriguez.

World Missions

Merely believing that God exists is not the same thing as being a follower of Christ. Even the devils believe in the reality of God (Jas. 2:19). This thought on devils leads us to the subject of spiritual warfare. Corrie ten Boom wrote, "Before His return there will be a hard battle so it is good to prepare ourselves. Every Christian is called to take his place in the army of King Jesus and to wrestle as a fellow-conqueror with Him" (*Marching Orders for the End Battle,* Christian Literature Crusade).

When I was fourteen, my pastor's wife asked if I would like to receive Jesus as my Saviour. "Yes," I said, not understanding what she meant but knowing it was exactly what I needed. She did not ask if I wanted to enlist for battle. If she had told me what Paul told Timothy—that he was called to wage war (I Tim. 1:18)—I might have said, "No thanks, fighting's not my thing. I'm only interested in peace, love, and joy."

Spiritual warfare makes us uncomfortable. We want to put it in the spiritual gift category. Let those who are called and gifted for warfare take it on. But who are these called and gifted ones? Could it be that in truth every believer falls into this category?

Like it or not, when we signed on as Jesus-followers, we signed up for battle. Our celebrity-conscious way of being the church has made many of us act like spectators, but Christianity is not a spectator sport.

Jesus left us with the tools for warfare, and we must pick them up and use them. A.B. Simpson wrote, "Before we put on our clothes, let us put on our weapons, for we are stepping out into a land of enemies and a world of dangers; let us put on the helmet of salvation, the breastplate of faith and love, and the shield of faith, and stand armed and vigilant as the dangers of the last days gather around us" (*Days of Heaven Upon Earth,* Christian Alliance).

Peter reminds us to beware of our adversary, for he is wily and dangerous (I Pet. 5:8). A good intellect and a quick wit will not suffice in spiritual battle. Spiritual tactics are needed. Nor can we ignore the battle: "For God has appointed this whole life, as a state of labor, to be all, as a race or a battle; the state of rest wherein we shall be so out of danger, as to have no need of watching and fighting, is reserved for another world" (Jonathan Edwards, *Some Thoughts Concerning the Present Revival in New England,* Leavitt & Allen).

The tools of spiritual warfare are not complicated. First, we need to pray. Jesus taught His disciples to be on guard and constantly in prayer (Luke 21:36). Second, Jesus confirmed the value of fasting (Matt. 17:21). The early church continued this practice, and so should we (Acts 14:23). Third, Jesus encouraged His followers to use His name. When they did, they rejoiced because even demons obeyed them (Luke 10:17). Paul used Jesus' name to cast out a demonic spirit (Acts 16:18). Crowning all of these tools is the power of the written Word. Jesus quoted Scripture during His temptation by the devil (Matt. 4:1-11). The Word is alive, effective, and powerful (Heb. 4:12).

These tools are especially indispensable for spiritual battle on the mission field, where false gods and evil spirits have long claimed territory and souls for themselves that they are loathe to relinquish. Only through the power of Christ and His Word can these evil forces be rendered powerless and the souls of the lost be freed from their captivity in spiritual darkness.

—Rose McCormick Brandon.

The Jewish Aspect

The Hebrew Scriptures provide detailed accounts of enemies coming against Israel and Judah to destroy them. In most cases, these enemies were cruel, oppressive, cunning, more numerous, better equipped, and determined to destroy them. However, as early as the Exodus from Egypt, God assured His people that He would fight for them (Ex. 13:14).

When the Amalekites came against Israel, the Israelites prevailed when Moses lifted up his staff as God had instructed him to do (Ex. 17:11). The staff signified the power of God. Following that victory, Moses built an altar and called it *Jehovah-nissi* (vs. 15), which means "the Lord is my banner." David called the Lord his refuge (Ps. 46:1, 7, 11; 91:2). A title for God that is used over 200 times in the Hebrew Scriptures is *"Yahweh Sabaoth,"* translated "the Lord of armies" or "the Lord of hosts."

When David faced Goliath, the Philistine giant, he said, "And all this assembly shall know that the Lord saveth not with sword and spear: for the battle is the Lord's, and he will give you into our hands" (I Sam. 17:47). Similarly, when Judah was attacked by Moab and Ammon, the Lord spoke through Jahaziel the Levite, "Hearken ye, all Judah, and ye inhabitants of Jerusalem, and thou king Jehoshaphat, Thus saith the Lord unto you, Be not afraid nor dismayed by reason of this great multitude; for the battle is not yours, but God's" (II Chr. 20:15).

The Lord also instructed Joshua to use unusual weapons (which would highlight God's power) to bring down the walls of Jericho (Josh. 6:1-27). And the Lord used the prophet Zechariah to encourage Zerubbabel, the leader of Judah, who had the responsibility of finishing the work of rebuilding the temple: "This is the word of the Lord unto Zerubbabel, saying, Not by might, nor by power, but by my spirit, saith the Lord of hosts" (Zech 4:6).

In the New Testament, the Lord gave specific instructions to believers not to rely upon natural means to defeat their spiritual enemies, but to rely on the power of the Lord. Paul told the believers at Ephesus that their fight was not against flesh and blood and that they would only triumph against the spiritual forces of evil by putting on the whole armor of God (Eph. 6:10-18). Old Testament prophets sometimes used the imagery of God or God's people wearing armor to fight on behalf of God's justice (cf. Isa. 11:5; 49:2; 59:17).

Paul told the believers at Corinth that they needed spiritual weapons to pull down strongholds (II Cor. 10:4). In the Hebrew Scriptures, strongholds meant fortresses or places with strong fortification. Even these material strongholds were to be conquered by Israel not primarily by reliance on military might, but by reliance on Yahweh, the Lord of armies. When Paul said that the Corinthian believers should pull down spiritual strongholds and take every thought captive to the obedience of Christ, here too he was using military imagery.

As more than conquerors, Christians are to use the spiritual weapons that God has provided in Christ to lay siege to the spiritual strongholds of wickedness. Indeed, Jesus has told us that not even the very gates of hell itself can stand against the spiritual might that God has bestowed upon the church (cf. Matt. 16:18)!

—*Deborah Markowitz Solan.*

Guiding the Superintendent

In both of his letters to the Corinthian church, Paul addressed how worldly priorities had crept into the church and had led to selfish discord. One of the main reasons the believers were so divided was that they were following false teachers who were trying to persuade them that the gospel alone was inadequate to save them. They advocated the necessity of keeping the law of Moses, including the practice of circumcision. They also accused Paul of being hypocritical, of overemphasizing his apostolic authority, and of being unimpressive in speaking ability and appearance.

How could Paul defend his integrity without appearing to be arrogant? He did not try to defend himself but only his divine calling and apostleship. He boasted only in what God had graciously done through him. If it was war these false teachers wanted, Paul was formidably equipped for it by the grace of God.

DEVOTIONAL OUTLINE

1. Divine warfare (II Cor. 10:1-6). Paul saw his ministry as spiritual warfare, but he would use only the spiritual weapons that God had given him. He would address the Corinthians in the meekness and gentleness of Jesus Himself. The false teachers had accused Paul of being all bark and no bite. They said he was bold in his letters but weak in person. Paul advised them to avoid making it necessary for him to be as bold toward them as he intended to be toward those who had accused him.

Although Paul freely admitted that he was as merely human as anyone else, he warned that the weapons of his warfare originated from a divine source, possessing more than enough power to demolish the charges leveled against his divine commission. Paul's commission was to destroy all such high-sounding pretentions raised against the truth of God and to compel all such rebellious thinking into obedience to the gospel of the Lord Jesus Christ. Moreover, once this was accomplished, he was prepared to suitably punish the rebels themselves, whoever they might be.

The false teachers had used their worldly skills and erudition in an effort to undermine and subvert his ministry. But he would meet and overcome them with only the spiritual powers that God had graciously given to him.

2. Apostolic authority (II Cor. 5:7-12). Paul challenged his readers to see what was obvious: if his accusers were confident about their standing in Christ, then they also must acknowledge his own standing in Christ. Paul refused to be ashamed of the apostolic authority God had given to him for the building up of His church, and not for its destruction, which was evidently the motive of his accusers.

3. Divine approval (II Cor. 5:17-18). In contrast to his detractors, Paul would only measure himself by God's own standards, not by comparing himself with other people. If he had anything to boast about, it would be the Lord Himself. Self-promotion is vain; the only approval that matters is God's own approval, and Paul was fully confident that God would back him up in any conflict with such people. Paul did not need to justify himself. He looked to God alone for his approval.

CHILDREN'S CORNER

Children are very sensitive to what others say about them. Children can often be cruel in their teasing and taunting of each other. Encourage them to look to God alone for approval.

—*Martin R. Dahlquist.*

SCRIPTURE LESSON TEXT

II COR. 12:1 It is not expedient for me doubtless to glory. I will come to visions and revelations of the Lord.

2 I knew a man in Christ above fourteen years ago, (whether in the body, I cannot tell; or whether out of the body, I cannot tell: God knoweth;) such an one caught up to the third heaven.

3 And I knew such a man, (whether in the body, or out of the body, I cannot tell: God knoweth;)

4 How that he was caught up into paradise, and heard unspeakable words, which it is not lawful for a man to utter.

5 Of such an one will I glory: yet of myself I will not glory, but in mine infirmities.

6 For though I would desire to glory, I shall not be a fool; for I will say the truth: but *now* **I forbear, lest any man should think of me above** that which he seeth me *to be,* or *that* he heareth of me.

7 And lest I should be exalted above measure through the abundance of the revelations, there was given to me a thorn in the flesh, the messenger of Satan to buffet me, lest I should be exalted above measure.

8 For this thing I besought the Lord thrice, that it might depart from me.

9 And he said unto me, My grace is sufficient for thee: for my strength is made perfect in weakness. Most gladly therefore will I rather glory in my infirmities, that the power of Christ may rest upon me.

10 Therefore I take pleasure in infirmities, in reproaches, in necessities, in persecutions, in distresses for Christ's sake: for when I am weak, then am I strong.

NOTES

Paul's Thorn in the Flesh

Lesson Text: II Corinthians 12:1-10

Related Scriptures: I Kings 19:9-13; Romans 5:1-5;
I Corinthians 2:1-10; II Corinthians 11:16-33

TIME: probably A.D. 56   PLACE: from Macedonia

GOLDEN TEXT—"Therefore I take pleasure in infirmities, in reproaches, in necessities, in persecutions, in distresses for Christ's sake: for when I am weak, then am I strong" (II Corinthians 12:10).

Introduction

The idea of "unanswered prayer" permeates Christian teaching. Unfortunately, this is the result of an inadequate understanding of Scripture.

The teaching that God does not answer us when we pray is without biblical merit. Just because God does not give us all our requests does not mean that He does not answer our prayers. I recall several times in my youth asking my parents for a particular thing only to be told to wait. That did not mean they failed to answer me. It just meant I had to be patient.

Sometimes, as we will see in this week's lesson, God even says "no" to our requests. Again, "no" is an answer just as "wait" is an answer.

God does not ignore you. If He is telling you to wait, then wait. If He tells you "no," then ask Him to bring your desire into line with His perfect will. God loves you and has your best interests in mind.

LESSON OUTLINE

I. PAUL'S VISION OF HEAVEN—
   II COR. 12:1-4

II. PAUL'S THORN IN THE FLESH—
   II Cor. 12:5-7

III. PAUL'S CRY FOR RELIEF—
   II Cor. 12:8-10

Exposition: Verse by Verse

PAUL'S VISION OF HEAVEN

II COR. 12:1 It is not expedient for me doubtless to glory. I will come to visions and revelations of the Lord.

2 I knew a man in Christ above fourteen years ago, (whether in the body, I cannot tell; or whether out of the body, I cannot tell: God knoweth;) such an one caught up to the third heaven.

3 And I knew such a man, (whether in the body, or out of the body, I cannot tell: God knoweth;)

4 How that he was caught up into paradise, and heard unspeakable words, which it is not lawful for a man to utter.

Vision from Christ (II Cor. 12:1).
{If the Corinthians wanted to boast of their accomplishments, Paul thought it better to boast in what the Lord accomplished in his weaknesses.}[Q1] Paul chooses throughout his letter not to dwell on his academic accomplishments, such as being the prized pupil of the renowned first-century rabbi, Gamaliel. He does not bring up the fact that he could speak multiple languages fluently. Instead, he gives a list of his many sufferings (cf. 11:23-33).

Paul acknowledges that nothing is ever to be gained by boasting in the flesh. The Corinthians were looking for someone who had impressive credentials, but Paul would not indulge them. {In both of his letters to the Corinthians, he makes it evident that if he boasted, he would boast only in the Lord.}[Q2]

To show that he was totally reliant upon the Lord while also furthering his apostolic authority, Paul states that he would move on to "visions and revelations." Why would he now focus on these? Because a claim to have a vision or revelation is a claim to a certain degree of conferred authority. The vision and revelation he would speak of came from the one true God. Paul did not make it up, nor could he have given it to himself.

The Lord spoke to Paul through revelation and revealed unspeakable glories to him in a vision. In the following verses, notice that Paul does not boast in the fact that God chose him to receive such a glorious vision. Instead, he simply focuses on God, who gave the vision.

"Caught up" by Christ (II Cor. 12:2).
Paul is somewhat hesitant to speak of this vision, possibly because it was very personal for him. Also, he surely did not want to discredit what he had just taught—that boasting in yourself is meaningless. Therefore, he is careful to give all glory to God.

To further drive home the point that he is not boasting in himself, he refers to himself in the third person as if it had possibly been someone else's vision. {But New Testament scholars agree from the context of the passage that Paul is most definitely referring to himself as the man that he knew. The details that he gives could only be provided by the one who actually saw the vision.}[Q3]

Fourteen years before he wrote II Corinthians, that is, back somewhere around A.D. 42–43, Paul had a vision from the Lord that is not recorded elsewhere in Scripture. He is mentioning it here only to validate his apostolic authority. Again, the Corinthians liked to boast about themselves, but Paul said that he would only boast in the Lord (cf. 10:17). This vision was about Christ, not Paul. Paul does not claim to have done anything to deserve to see the glories that he witnessed.

In this vision, Paul was "caught up" to the third heaven. Notice that he does not say that he went up, but that he was "caught up." This is reminiscent of his words in I Thessalonians 4:17, speaking of when believers will be "caught up" in the clouds to meet Jesus (see also John's experience in Revelation 4:1-2). No one can ascend to God on his own; he must be called by the power of God.

The Jews had been taught that the "third heaven" is the dwelling place of God. The first heaven is the earth's atmosphere, the second heaven is outer space, and the third heaven is the unseen domain where God lives. Paul did not know whether he was in his body or not, but he does not seem concerned with that detail. He is content to leave it with God, who knows all things perfectly.

Glory of Christ (II Cor. 12:3-4). Paul affirms once again his certainty that the vision was real. He was caught up into paradise, which is another reference to heaven, the blessed dwelling place of God. Again, he notes his ignorance as to whether he was in his body or not, probably to emphasize the mysterious glory of God—that it was beyond the grasp of our earthly knowledge.

Paul does not describe every detail of his vision, because it was not possible or permitted to repeat the things he heard. {The prohibition may have come directly from God, but there is also an aspect that human language simply lacked the words to describe the sounds and speech of heaven. Therefore, Paul is not able to provide specific details about the scene.}[Q4]

PAUL'S THORN IN THE FLESH

5 Of such an one will I glory: yet of myself I will not glory, but in mine infirmities.

6 For though I would desire to glory, I shall not be a fool; for I will say the truth: but now I forbear, lest any man should think of me above that which he seeth me to be, or that he heareth of me.

7 And lest I should be exalted above measure through the abundance of the revelations, there was given to me a thorn in the flesh, the messenger of Satan to buffet me, lest I should be exalted above measure.

Paul's boasting (II Cor. 12:5-6). Paul is not telling the Corinthians of this vision to impress them or to brag about how great he was. His entire argument on human boasting is that it is empty. Human achievement is nothing compared to the glory of God.

Paul's intention was never to draw attention to himself or to put himself on equal footing with Greek philosophers. So instead of touting any perceived strengths, he focuses on his weaknesses. He wanted the Corinthians to see Christ at work through his weaknesses, not his strengths at work for Christ.

Paul does clarify, however, that if he had wanted to boast in himself, he could have done so. The Corinthians' preferred speakers and leaders were in no way superior to him in intellect (cf. Phil. 3:4-5). If he had spoken of his personal accomplishments, he would have been telling the truth. But he had a higher purpose for writing to the church.

The goal here was not to brag about what he had done in his own life. That would have benefited no one. His stated goal all along was to preach Jesus Christ and Him crucified (I Cor. 2:2). He was not out on a personal glory campaign for himself, nor was he trying to gain a personal following. {Paul was perfectly content with exposing his weakness in order to emphasize God's power at work in him.}[Q5]

Paul's humility (II Cor. 12:7). The glorious vision Paul experienced did not come without a cost to him personally. It is easy for those who have intimate experiences with the Lord to become conceited and to look down on others as unspiritual, ironically letting their pride turn a precious gift into a snare and a hindrance to them.

But God graciously helped Paul to see that he was not immune to this tendency. He was not above acting in his flesh and becoming conceited because of this vision. If his ego was not kept in check, it very well could have destroyed his ministry by inducing him to treat others with contempt instead of love. To prevent Paul from using his experience to boast in himself, God gave him a "thorn in the flesh" that afflicted him for the rest of his life.

Much debate has been aired as to what exactly the thorn was, but Paul does not tell us. Therefore, it is absolutely futile to speculate. There simply is no way to know. {If we follow the intention of the text, it is much more important to understand the thorn's purpose than to determine exactly what it was.}Q6

Paul called the thorn a "messenger of Satan," so it was extremely unpleasant and at times torturous. Paul knew the thorn was sent by God, but he could also correctly call it a messenger of Satan, who may have been the one directly afflicting him and seeking to destroy him by it (cf. Job 2:3-7). God, however, had a useful purpose for the thorn that could not be overcome.

{Satan hoped the message of the thorn would bring evil to Paul, but God had a beneficial message in mind: Don't become arrogant and prideful.}Q7 God had blessed Paul in a very unique way, and He had placed a unique calling on his life, which was to take the gospel to the Gentiles (cf. Acts 9:15). Paul, like Abraham centuries before him, was blessed greatly by God to be a blessing to others (cf. Gen. 12:3).

Humility is important in the Christian life, but it is especially important for people in leadership. In addition to his amazing supernatural experience, Paul had successfully planted a number of churches. This made him a spiritual father to many people. On one occasion, he was even called a god (cf. Acts 14:11-18). Any or all of these things could have allowed pride to creep in and ruin his ministry. God used the thorn in the flesh to prevent this from happening. He was more interested in developing Paul's character than in making him comfortable.

PAUL'S CRY FOR RELIEF

8 For this thing I besought the Lord thrice, that it might depart from me.

9 And he said unto me, My grace is sufficient for thee: for my strength is made perfect in weakness. Most gladly therefore will I rather glory in my infirmities, that the power of Christ may rest upon me.

10 Therefore I take pleasure in infirmities, in reproaches, in necessities, in persecutions, in distresses for Christ's sake: for when I am weak, then am I strong.

Paul pleads for help (II Cor. 12:8). While we do not know—nor can we know—precisely what this thorn in the flesh was, we do know that it tormented Paul. It was some type of affliction that caused him great discomfort and possibly a lot of pain. Whether spiritual, emotional, mental, or physical, this messenger of Satan would not leave him alone.

Paul knew that he could not relieve himself from this problem. He could not simply pull the thorn out of his flesh and obtain relief. {When it would not go away, he pleaded with God three times to remove it from him.}Q8

God answers (II Cor. 12:9-10). {But God did not remove it. He responded to Paul's request by telling him that His grace was sufficient for him.}Q9 What did Paul need more than relief? Grace. Not grace to deliver him from his affliction, but grace to continue on in spite of it. God would get greater glory by using Paul in spite of the thorn than by removing it altogether.

The thorn in Paul's flesh should be seen as an instrument of grace rather than judgment. God loved Paul enough to give him something that prevented him from sliding into the sin of pride and arrogance. In a way, this thorn was actually God's protection. Paul was a tremendous missionary, preacher, theologian, and writer, but he was not above becoming arrogant. After all, he was still human.

The power of God is demonstrated through us when we accept His purpose to work through our weaknesses and suffering. It is easy and even understandable to resist any kind of suffering and pain. And it is not wrong to pray that He will heal us or bring an end to our trials. Until God removes the affliction, however, it is best to trust His work through us in spite of it. You never know how He will use it. He might be using you to minister to others who are hurting too (cf. II Cor. 1:3-5). If they see you persevere in faith and rely on God's grace, it may make a difference in their lives.

{Paul learned a great lesson in contentment from the thorn in his flesh.}Q10 He learned to boast in his weaknesses instead of his strength because it was his weakness that magnified the power of God in his life. Others could see that Christ was working through Paul even when he was weak.

Paul had said before that if he boasts, he boasts in the Lord. But Paul did more than just teach this scriptural truth (Jer. 9:23-24); he also showed this is true in his life. It is one thing to tell people that you boast in the Lord. It is another thing entirely to boast in the Lord while hurting. Paul could easily have delved into complaining and grumbling against God, but that would have only made him bitter against God. Instead, Paul was able to trust in God's goodness.

God taught Paul how to be satisfied with grace through the things that he suffered. Because of this lesson, he did not brag to the Corinthians about his greatness. Instead, he boasted about how God's strength overcame his weakness. God used Paul in spite of his ability, not because of it.

As a result of leaning upon God's grace, Paul learned to be content in weakness. He no longer resisted, nor did he strive in prayer, demanding deliverance. He was willing to be insulted, persecuted, and to endure personal troubles that could have caused him to give up. By the grace of God, he endured everything that Satan threw at him. He trusted that God would never leave him, and God came through on that promise.

You may be experiencing your own thorn in the flesh. Perhaps you have been pleading with God for relief. God is likely trying to teach you the same lesson He taught Paul. Learn to seek God's will and grace and not just His relief.

Jesus asked God to take the cup of His wrath away from Him, but He then acquiesced to God's will. God did not spare Jesus from the agony of the cross but sent an angel to help Him do the will of His Father (Luke 22:41-43). It is best for all of us to seek God's heart, and not just His help. God wants to work mightily in your life, especially when you are weak.

—Robert Ferguson, Jr.

QUESTIONS

1. What did Paul focus on instead of his accomplishments?
2. What did Paul choose to boast about in his letters?
3. Why can we be confident that Paul is speaking of himself in mentioning the heavenly vision?
4. What is a possible reason why Paul did not provide a lot of detail about the vision?
5. Why was Paul content to expose his weakness to the Corinthians?
6. Why are we not told what Paul's thorn in the flesh was?
7. What message did God bring to Paul through the thorn that Satan tried to use for evil?
8. How did Paul respond to the thorn at first?
9. How did God respond to Paul's plea for help?
10. What lesson did Paul learn from his suffering?

—Robert Ferguson, Jr.

Preparing to Teach the Lesson

Speculation among commentators about the specific health condition Paul is referring to in today's lesson text has been prolific, but of dubious value. The particular ailment Paul had in mind is of secondary importance, at best. It may have been a chronic eye condition left over from his blindness on the Damascus road (cf. Acts 9:1-9), or it may have been related to the nearly fatal affliction he mentions near the beginning of this epistle (cf. II Cor. 1:8-10), or it may have been something else entirely.

What is important about Paul's "thorn in the flesh" is why it was given to him. To prevent him from becoming arrogant and self-important because of the magnificence of heavenly revelations granted to him, God permitted an emissary of Satan to afflict him with a besetting physical condition.

TODAY'S AIM

Facts: to know that God can use our physical infirmities to glorify Himself in our lives.

Principle: to understand what it means to allow God to manifest His glory through our infirmities.

Application: to begin to see our perceived inadequacies as instruments God can use to glorify Himself in our lives.

INTRODUCING THE LESSON

In this week's lesson, Paul glories in the infirmities God has laid upon him because they are the means He uses to glorify His power through him.

DEVELOPING THE LESSON

1. A vision of paradise (II Cor. 12:1-4). This first portion of the chapter poses an interpretational question: in verses 2-4, is Paul really speaking about himself, using a time-honored literary device? Most commentators and interpreters hold that he most assuredly is. Others scrupulously deny this possibility, thinking it would make the apostle guilty of what amounts to a lie, even if only a harmless one.

However, the majority is almost certainly correct. If the literary device of "I knew a man" was well known, then he is not being deceitful. And the motive for using such a device is a godly one: it would be inappropriate for him to boast about this spiritual experience. By using the device of writing in the third person, he is being consistent with his whole point of God's working through our limitations so that He receives the glory, not us.

Paul speaks of a Christian who was taken up to the "third heaven." The meaning of this term is derived from Scripture itself. The first heaven corresponds to the expanse of the earthly sky (cf. Gen. 1:6-8). The second corresponds to the starry heavens (cf. vs. 17). The third heaven is the level of heaven beyond the stars, where the Lord's own throne and dwelling are located (cf. Ps. 11:4; Isa. 66:1; Rev. 4:2). In other words, Paul's vision involved the very highest heaven, where God Himself is eternally enthroned.

Paul declares that he does not know whether this event occurred physically or only spiritually. And he discourages further speculation about it by simply declaring that "God knoweth" (II Cor. 12:3).

In whatever manner this experience happened, Paul was "caught up into paradise, and heard unspeakable words, which it is not lawful for a man to utter" (vs. 4). Some commentators speculate that he heard an utterance of the true pronunciation of the Tetragrammaton, God's actual name as spoken to Moses from the burning bush (cf. Ex. 3:14).

Devout Jews assiduously avoid speaking this name or even thinking it while reading the Scriptures. Rather than speak or think it, the pious Jew will always replace it with the Hebrew terms *Adonai* ("Lord") or *Hashem* ("the Name"). In English we often see the transliterations "Jehovah" or "Yahweh."

As a former Pharisee, Paul might have likewise avoided any actual utterance or writing of what he heard. Yet it is just as possible that he was referring to the totality of what he heard in heaven; after all, his whole point is that we have not been let in on that secret!

2. Refraining from boasting (II Cor. 12:5-6). Paul concedes that if it had been someone else and not himself, he would readily boast of that person. With this admission, he puts the finishing touch on his use of the third-person device in deflecting attention from himself.

The only things Paul is willing to boast about regarding himself are his "infirmities." This translates the common Greek word for weakness, sickness, disease, or anything else that causes physical pain or disability.

3. Sufficient grace (II Cor. 12:7-10). Though Paul may have desired over the years to relate his experiences from that time, for fourteen years he had kept his silence on the matter. But now he realizes that it would be foolish to keep quiet under the present circumstances. So he breaks his silence for the sake of his readers.

But at this juncture, Paul believes he has disclosed enough; he will say no more on the subject. He does not want his reputation to become inflated in the minds of his readers. Although he refrains from further talk of his visions, he does go on to speak of one of their consequences: his "thorn in the flesh" (vs. 7).

Three times Paul pleaded with the Lord to take away this infirmity. But God declined his request, declaring that His grace would be sufficient and turn this weakness into strength. God would use Paul's disability to manifest His glory.

Because of this, Paul declared that he now took pleasure in all physical afflictions—and also in being insulted, in being needy, in being persecuted, and in being tormented for the sake of his service to Christ. Paul understood that when he was physically at his weakest, it was then that his spiritual strength in Christ was at its peak!

ILLUSTRATING THE LESSON

The illustration shows that our physical weaknesses and infirmities are actually opportunities for God to show His power through us and glorify Himself.

GOD USES OUR INFIRMITIES TO MANIFEST HIS POWER IN US

GOD

POWER

Spiritual Strength

Powerful Gospel Witness

CONCLUDING THE LESSON

Our weaknesses are a means for God to manifest His perfect power in our lives. The next time you are tempted to bemoan your physical shortcomings, instead pray that God would use them to glorify Himself in your life.

ANTICIPATING THE NEXT LESSON

Next week we will begin our lessons for summer quarter. Our first lesson will be on God's call to Samuel from I Samuel 3.

—*John Lody.*

PRACTICAL POINTS

1. When God leads believers to boast, it is for His glory and not their own (II Cor. 12:1)
2. God uses both the highs and lows in our lives in our ministry to others (vss. 2-4).
3. God's goodness speaks for itself without any need for us to boast (vss. 5-6).
4. Without trials, believers would forget to rely on God (vs. 7).
5. Persistent prayer demonstrates faith in the midst of trials (vs. 8).
6. God wants His people to minister in His power, not their own strength (vs. 9).
7. God's light shines brightest in a believer when his own light is most faint (vs. 10).

—Cheryl Y. Powell.

RESEARCH AND DISCUSSION

1. In what other New Testament passages does God use visions and revelations to communicate with one of His people?
2. What are some of the ways in which God has revealed Himself to His people?
3. What comes to mind when you think about heaven? What Scriptures teach us about heaven?
4. How is it possible for Paul to boast in his infirmities?
5. What Scriptures could you use to encourage a friend or family member who lives with chronic pain or illness?

—Cheryl Y. Powell.

ILLUSTRATED HIGH POINTS

Above that which he seeth me to be (II Cor. 12:6)

"Pay no attention to that man behind the curtain!" This is the familiar cry of the unimpressive, elderly gentleman at the controls in his booth of magical deceits. From this place of anonymity, the Wizard of Oz could create amazing though dishonest visual and audio effects. His greatest fear was that someone would pull back the concealing curtain and expose him for who he really was.

Paul's heart was quite the opposite. Although he could impressively boast of unspeakable visions, revelations, visits to paradise, and many other impressive experiences, he preferred that men see nothing but his weaknesses. He gloried in nothing but his infirmities.

Glory in my infirmities (vs. 9)

A crow happened upon a majestic swan and decided to challenge the beautiful creature to a flying contest. He said to the swan, "I shall fly displaying a hundred and one different kinds of motion!"

The swan, taking up his challenge, replied, I, however, fly only one kind of motion, for I do not know any other!"

The two took flight, and the crow seemed quite adept until their course found them over open seas. The overconfident crow began to panic, since there was no land where he might rest. He was finally forced by fatigue to fall into the sea. Now drowning, he cried out to the swan, "Caw! Caw!" And the swan lovingly came to his rescue.

As long as we think we are strong, we are weak. When we finally know how weak we truly are, hopefully then we will call upon the Lord, and He will by His grace save us!

—Therese Greenberg.

Golden Text Illuminated

"Therefore I take pleasure in infirmities, in reproaches, in necessities, in persecutions, in distresses for Christ's sake: for when I am weak, then am I strong" (II Corinthians 12:10).

In this chapter, Paul continues a defense of his ministry, but with an interesting turn—how God had once humbled him so he would not become arrogant.

He begins by talking about an amazing experience in which a man he knows received visions and revelations from God. Here Paul was referring to himself, but he writes in the third person to avoid boastfulness. Paul was caught away into "the third heaven," an expression referring to the dwelling place of God, where he heard inexpressible things. He emphasizes that he is not boasting about this, but simply relating the truth.

Paul knew all too well that he was a mere man, capable of falling into pride and vanity. Therefore, he reported that God gave him a "thorn in the flesh" to keep him from becoming conceited.

What was this thorn? To this day, no one knows for certain. Many believe it was some affliction of the eyes. In Galatians 4:13-15, Paul refers to an infirmity for which the church members would have plucked out their own eyes to help him. Also, Paul often used someone else to do the actual writing of his letters, sometimes signing his name at the end for verification that he was the real author (I Cor. 16:21; Gal. 6:11; II Thess. 3:17; Phm. 1:19).

Other theories include physical disfigurement, a speech impediment, epilepsy, or continual persecution from Paul's opponents. Whatever this thorn was, God refused to remove it; but to keep Paul from despair, the Lord reassured him that His grace would be sufficient to carry him through his ministry in spite of this affliction. Because of this grace, Paul proclaimed that he would gladly boast about this affliction and all his other frailties.

This may seem odd to us, especially in a world that so prizes comfort and success. Why would anyone boast about their weaknesses? Not only that, but Paul writes that he takes pleasure in insults, hunger, thirst, persecutions, and other distresses, including imprisonment, shipwreck, stoning, exposure to the elements, flogging, and even his anxiety about the churches (II Cor. 11:24-28). This indicated no perverse temperament on Paul's part. Rather, Paul knew that these troubles, properly yielded to God, demonstrated the power of Christ in his life.

Paul did not believe that his problems and predicaments were intrinsically good. Rather, he was content that God was working through them to produce something of eternal value in him. Paul shows a similar attitude in Romans 5:3-5 when he writes that he will exult in his tribulations, knowing that they produce a godly chain of results: troubles lead to perseverance, which leads to strong character, which in turn produces hope, finally culminating in the love of God flowing from his heart.

Paul concluded this chapter with his characteristic mixture of humility and sternness. He reminds the Corinthians that neither he nor any of his emissaries have ever been a burden to them. Indeed, he vowed to expend everything he had for them. But he also hopes that on his next visit they would not disappoint him.

—*Mark Winter.*

Heart of the Lesson

The false apostles had won over some members of the Corinthian church. How? By casting doubt on Paul's authority as Christ's apostle and by boasting in their own knowledge, experience, and authority. So, instead of spending chapters eleven and twelve encouraging the Corinthians or equipping them with sound theology, Paul had to defend himself against his critics. Even so, in His sovereignty, God used the struggles in Corinth to teach His church about foolishness and wisdom, pride and humility, and human weakness and divine power.

1. Paul's vision (II Cor. 12:1-4). To demonstrate his Christ-ordained apostolic authority, Paul reluctantly shared his vision of the third heaven, which is God's dwelling place. Paul had probably refrained from sharing this vision before to avoid exalting himself. But the false teachers at Corinth had given him no choice.

Just as the false apostles had foolishly boasted about themselves, Paul would have to play the same game. But Paul's motivation, unlike that of his detractors, was to reveal his frailty and God's glory. So it was in this spirit that Paul recounted some aspects of his divine vision of the third heaven.

We do not know exactly what Paul meant by referring to the third heaven, but Jewish tradition commonly held it to be the foundation of God's throne. The third heaven was purported to be inhabited by the spirits of Abraham, Isaac, Jacob, Moses, Aaron, and other illustrious persons of the Old Testament. This, of course, is pure speculation, but it may help us understand how Paul's words would be received.

Whether Paul's transport to the third heaven was physical or spiritual, he did not know. But while he was there, he heard and witnessed ineffable things. Paul was forbidden from sharing the substance of his vision with others.

2. Paul's thorn (II Cor. 12:5-8). In order to keep Paul humble after his extraordinary vision, God gave him a "thorn." Some scholars believe Paul's thorn was a physical ailment; others think it was a demonic adversary, sent to persecute him. Perhaps this messenger from Satan was even working through Paul's adversaries in Corinth to torment him by threatening to tear his beloved Corinthian church apart. Paul cared for the Corinthians, and all the members of the churches he started, like his own children. When they were attacked, it was a dagger in his heart.

Whatever the specific nature of this thorn, Paul begged God to remove it from his life. But instead of removing it, God graciously strengthened Paul to endure it.

3. Paul's confidence (II Cor. 12:9-10). In the midst of his pain and frustration, Paul was reassured that God's unending supply of strength and grace would equip him to fulfill his apostolic calling. Paul's recognition of his weakness was the key to unleashing God's power in his life.

What is your thorn? A strained close relationship, a physical limitation, a financial hardship, an antagonistic person? Though most of us probably have not experienced a demonic attack like Paul did, we all have at least one difficult situation that forces us to our knees each day. God uses these struggles to remind us of our frailty and of His grace and power at work in our lives.

—*Malia E. Rodriguez.*

World Missions

Paul was troubled with something he called a thorn in his flesh. The reader is left to speculate on the exact nature of Paul's affliction. Evidence indicates his eyesight was poor, and some have wondered if this was his affliction. But Paul's description of this thorn as a torment and a messenger from Satan leads us to wonder if it was not something more serious (II Cor. 12:7-9). His mention of Satan reminds us of Job's sufferings (Job 2:1-7).

Could Paul's thorn be related to his many harrowing experiences? These included floggings, shipwrecks, attacks from Gentiles and Jews, accusations from false teachers, hunger, cold, danger in the city and in the country, and the threat of thieves (II Cor. 11:22-29). Wherever Paul preached, emissaries of evil hindered him.

Whatever the thorn was, Paul prayed three times for the Lord to release him from it. Paul did not lack faith in God's ability to heal him or take care of him. Sickness and suffering are not evidence of a lack of faith. God answered Paul's prayer with a qualified no. The thorn must stay, but He promised Paul sufficient grace to live with it. The Lord taught Paul something astonishing—human weakness is the perfect platform to showcase His power (II Cor. 12:9)! And God had another purpose for the thorn—to keep Paul humble. Paul had many supernatural experiences, which could have led him to seek adulation from others. Instead, his wisdom and knowledge were undervalued by some churches, who preferred to listen to Judaizers who sought to enslave them to the old covenant law (11:19-21).

Since Paul wrote that everyone who strives to live a godly life will suffer (II Tim. 3:12), it is not surprising that all followers of Jesus possess some type of thorn in the flesh. Perhaps it is a learning disability, a fragile mental or physical condition, overly sensitive feelings, social awkwardness, or even extreme temptations—all these can cause distress and bring people to their knees. Other thorns may come into our lives in the form of difficult and exhausting people. Moses suffered from these, as do many of God's servants. For the protection of one's health, wisdom prescribes periodic rest from such energy-drainers.

A disciple's life is seldom soft. Jesus said that men like John the Baptist did not wear fine clothes and live in palaces (Matt. 11:8-9). More disciples are poor than rich; more are ordinary than remarkable in any worldly sense.

Paul's thorn was his cross. We are called to follow Christ's example by taking up our cross and trusting Him for the strength to carry it (Luke 9:23). The Cross is evidence that God understands our misery, for on it His Son suffered the pain of death for our sins. Like Jesus, Paul prayed for release from his cross. Then, like Jesus, Paul looked beyond his cross to the joy that awaited him on the other side (cf. Heb. 12:2).

As a young missionary, Amy Carmichael prayed that God would never let her become a bedridden burden to others. At age 64, she fell into a hole, breaking her leg and damaging her spine. For the next twenty years she rarely left her room. But there she wrote sixteen additional books, several poems, and continued to manage the mission at Dohnavur, India. Missionaries sought her wisdom. Like Paul, God had a purpose for Amy's affliction and supplied her with daily grace to persevere. She wrote: "It is a safe thing to trust Him to fulfill the desire that He creates."

—Rose McCormick Brandon.

The Jewish Aspect

One of the greatest prophets of the Old Testament, Elijah is remembered for both miraculous deeds and also for moments of abject weakness. His name in Hebrew, *"Eliyahu,"* means "My God is Yahweh," which aptly described his life as he defended the worship of the true and living God against the false prophets of the Canaanite deity Baal. His greatest victory came when he challenged these prophets to invoke their god to consume a sacrifice on Mount Carmel. Despite many hours of animated supplications and entreaties, there was no response when the prophets of Baal cried out to him. But the Lord demonstrated His great power by immediately answering Elijah's prayer with fire from heaven that consumed not only his sacrifice, but also the stones of its altar (I Kgs. 18:19-38). Elijah then had all the prophets of Baal killed.

But not long after this great victory, King Ahab's wife, Jezebel, threatened Elijah's life, and Elijah fled into the wilderness. Deep despair overwhelmed him there (I Kgs. 19:3-14), and he complained that he was the only person in Israel who remained zealous for the Lord.

Other great leaders in the Hebrew Scriptures also faltered in responding to the Lord's call upon their lives. This was the case with Moses (Ex. 4:10), Isaiah (Isa. 6:5), and Jeremiah (Jer. 1:6). "God does not choose people who speak with their own voice, telling the crowds what they want to hear. He chooses people who are fully aware of their inadequacies, who stammer literally or metaphorically, who speak not because they want to but because they have to, and who tell people what they do not want to hear, but what they must hear if they are to save themselves from catastrophe" (outorah.org/p/41129).

David continuously lamented his sins and cried out to God for mercy. He recognized his need for God and for humility when he said, "The sacrifices of God are a broken spirit: a broken and a contrite heart, O God, thou wilt not despise" (Ps. 51:17). David also thanked God for his afflictions because they brought him closer to God (cf. 119:67, 71, 75).

The apostle Paul also spoke frequently of his afflictions and said that in his weakness he became strong (II Cor. 12:10). Paul was given a thorn in the flesh, from which he sought deliverance, but God refused (vss. 7-8). The ancient Greek translation of the Old Testament, known as the Septuagint, at times used the word *skolops* (thorn) in a figurative sense to indicate some constant bodily ailment or infirmity. It also was sometimes used to refer to people who were sources of affliction (Num. 33:55, Josh. 23:13, Judg. 2:3).

Paul's thorn may have corresponded to his many persecutions. He had been beaten, stoned, and shipwrecked. He had suffered many perils on his journeys, including weariness, pain, hunger, thirst, and exposure to the elements (II Cor. 11:24-27). Paul confessed that he actually took pleasure in and even gloried in his infirmities, reproaches, and persecutions (11:30; 12:9-10; Rom. 5:3). By writing in this way, Paul affirmed his complete dependence upon God, as did the psalmists when they wrote, "Be of good courage, and he shall strengthen your heart, all you that hope in the Lord" (Ps. 31:24), and, "My flesh and my heart faileth: but God is the strength of my heart and my portion for ever" (73:26).

—*Deborah Markowitz Solan.*

Guiding the Superintendent

From time to time, Paul was compelled to defend his ministry. This was something he was always very reluctant to do, but his opponents at Corinth were forcing his hand. They were insinuating that their own authority and experience were far superior to Paul's.

In our Scripture text for this week, in order to show how wrong they really were about him, Paul related a heavenly vision of far greater significance than they could ever have imagined. He boasted only in his weakness and suffering for the cause of Christ's church. Paul insisted that what qualified him to minister as an apostle was the fact that he had received special revelation from the Lord Jesus Christ Himself.

DEVOTIONAL OUTLINE

1. Paul's vision (II Cor. 12:1-6). Although Paul hated it and considered it futile, he realized that he needed to continue to talk about his own qualifications to be an apostle.

It was often a custom of rabbis to use the third person when speaking of themselves. Paul here referred to himself merely as "a man in Christ." Fourteen years previous to his writing of this epistle, Paul had been caught up to paradise and shown things of which he was not permitted to speak. Exactly how this had happened, whether he had been transported physically or in spirit, he did not know. Although Paul was willing to speak of himself in the third person, he refused to boast directly about himself, although if he had been willing to do so, he would have been relating only what was true, not some foolish imagining. Nevertheless, he refrained from doing it so that no one would think more highly of him than what was warranted by who he really was.

2. Paul's thorn (II Cor. 12:7-10). To prevent Paul's extraordinary experience from causing him to become conceited and arrogant, God allowed Satan to afflict Paul with a particular disorder, the actual nature of which we do not know. Paul referred to it as a thorn in his flesh. He also called it a satanic messenger assigned to torment him and keep him humble.

Three times Paul earnestly entreated the Lord for deliverance from this tormentor. But the Lord declined, assuring Paul that He would graciously provide sufficient strength for him to endure it, because His power is perfected in weakness. Therefore, Paul was more than willing to boast about his infirmities and illnesses so that the power of God's grace in Christ might be more abundantly glorified through him.

God has the remarkable ability to disguise great opportunities as times of suffering. Pain, disease, and all other evils may be things that Satan seeks to employ, but God can sovereignly use the sufferings they cause in our lives to advance and accomplish His purposes. God also uses trials and tragedy for our spiritual benefit as well, driving us to become more humble and dependent upon Him. Paul's thorn was God's constant reminder to him to remain humble. Satan can only harass a believer by God's permission (cf. Job 1:12).

CHILDREN'S CORNER

Children can often be boastful. Use this week's lesson to help them understand that bragging about themselves does not help them make friends; rather, it drives people away from them. Encourage them to realize that the only thing that is worth bragging about is how loving and kind Jesus has been to them!

—*Martin R. Dahlquist.*

with his hands the thing which is good, that he may have to give to him that needeth. Let no corrupt communication proceed out of your mouth, but that which is good to the use of edifying, that it may minister grace to the hearers" (vss. 22-25, 28-29).

It is not always easy to be different, however. Because Christians are different, they sometimes find themselves in conflict with the world. In His Sermon on the Mount, Jesus warned His followers that they would be persecuted. He said, "Blessed are they which are persecuted for righteousness' sake: for theirs is the kingdom of heaven. Blessed are ye, when men shall revile you and persecute you, and shall say all manner of evil against you falsely, for my sake. Rejoice, and be exceeding glad: for great is your reward in heaven: for so persecuted they the prophets which were before you" (Matt. 5:10-12).

We may feel honored when Jesus refers to us as "the light of the world" (vs. 14). Yet we may be intimidated when He says, "For every one that doeth evil hateth the light, neither cometh to the light, lest his deeds should be reproved" (John 3:20). We do not like to be hated! But when it happens, we are in good company, for we are following Jesus.

At the Last Supper, Jesus told His disciples, "If the world hate you, ye know that it hated me before it hated you. If ye were of the world, the world would love his own: but because ye are not of the world, but I have chosen you out of the world, therefore the world hateth you. Remember the word that I said unto you, The servant is not greater than his lord. If they have persecuted me, they will also persecute you; if they have kept my saying, they will keep yours also" (John 15:18-20).

Christians are different. We are not of this world. We are called to challenge the world and to stand in contrast to the world.

The difference shows unbelievers that God has changed us. As Paul testified in II Corinthians 5:17, "Therefore if any man be in Christ, he is a new creature: old things are passed away; behold, all things are become new." What a difference that is!

Earthen Vessels

Arnold Studebaker

I have in my home a beautiful example of handmade Navajo pottery. Being handmade, the pot is unique. It was formed in the potter's hands, not turned on a wheel. It was pressed from special clay found on the Navajo homeland in Arizona. It was varnished and fired in primitive fashion.

The pot is not symmetrical. It leans to one side. The texture of the varnish varies from smooth and shiny to sandy and rough. The chestnut color is of inconsistent hue. Yet its imperfections combine in a work of exquisite elegance.

Clay pottery is relatively common and inexpensive, as it has been historically. It is useful now mainly for decor, but in past times, clay pots were used to hold water, store grain, and preserve seed for future planting.

It is also fragile.

Paul holds up the image of clay pottery as a metaphor for the human body. He says, "We have this treasure in earthen vessels" (II Cor. 4:7). God entrusted the ministry of making known the good news of the knowledge of God through Jesus Christ—including God's plan of salvation and promise of eternal life—to Paul, a man of mere flesh like the rest of us. He is unique, but imperfect. He is vulnerable. He is fragile. Yet his weakness calls attention to the power of God, who entrusts such treasure to an earthen vessel.

As the indigenous people of America once entrusted precious commodities to clay jars, even so God has entrusted the treasures of the gospel to us as Christians in our human bodies.

Paul's reference to the human body as an "earthen vessel" is astute, for physicians know the body is made up of the elements of the earth blended with water. Moses tells us, "The Lord God formed man of the dust of the ground, and breathed into his nostrils the breath of life; and man became a living soul" (Gen. 2:7). (Recognizing that human life is derived from the very breath of God, we realize that all human life is sacred!)

Our origin in dust is emphasized in the judgment God pronounced upon Adam for his disobedience, saying, "Dust thou art, and unto dust shalt thou return" (Gen. 3:19).

Abraham understood this. As he negotiated with the Lord for the safety of his nephew Lot, then living in Sodom, Abraham humbly referred to himself as "dust and ashes" (Gen. 18:27).

We may be flawed by sin and fragile creatures of mud, but we are nevertheless very special, for we are made in the image of God. "So God created man in his own image, in the image of God created he him; male and female created he them" (Gen. 1:27). This is the basis of human dignity and worth. This is the source of human equality and inalienable rights. Because every man bears the image of God, he should be treated with respect out of respect for God.

God first authorized capital punishment for murder after the Flood, when He told Noah, "Whoso sheddeth man's blood, by man shall his blood be shed: for in the image of God made he man" (Gen. 9:6). The rationale for capital punishment here is intriguing. It is not deterrence of the criminal, nor justice for the victim. Rather, it is respect for the image of God in man!

As Christians, we should treat our own bodies with respect for the same reason. We should seek to avoid abusing our bodies by intemperate living, and we should stay away from harmful substances. This is consistent with New Testament teaching that we should honor our bodies as the temple of God, since the Holy Spirit dwells within us (I Cor. 6:19-20).

Paul refers to our bodies as "corruptible" and "mortal" (I Cor. 15:53-54). We are "corruptible," being vulnerable to injury, illness, and advancing age. We also enjoy sensual pleasure, which may lure us into sinful activities. Being subject to dying, we are "mortal."

Being corruptible and mortal due to sin, our "earthen vessels" present a distortion of the image of God. But Jesus provides the remedy! He is the perfect "image of God" (II Cor. 4:4; cf., Col. 1:15). Although Jesus was tempted as we are, He did not commit sin (Heb. 4:15). Therefore, He presents an accurate image of the Creator.

Jesus took on a human body. Then He offered that earthen vessel as the perfect sacrifice for the sins of the world! While eating the Last Supper with His apostles, Jesus broke the unleavened bread and passed it to them, saying, "This is my body which is given for you" (Luke 22:19).

Peter says that Jesus "bare our sins in his own body on the tree, that we, being dead to sins, should live unto righteousness" (I Pet. 2:24).

Yes, we can "live unto righteousness" even in these earthen vessels. It is not always easy. Paul describes the inherent conflict between the desires of the flesh and the intent of the Spirit, noting that these often oppose each other (Gal. 5:17). Even so, he exhorts, "Let not sin therefore reign in your mortal body, . . . but yield yourselves . . . as instruments of righteousness unto God" (Rom. 6:12-13).

Our bodies are part of the creation that Jesus has redeemed. Paul assures us of "the redemption of our body" (Rom. 8:23). Jesus' resurrected body is the prototype (I Cor. 15:23). His resurrection is the guarantee of our redemption. "As we have borne the image of the earthy, we shall also bear the image of the heavenly" (vs. 49). That is God's plan for our earthen vessels.

TOPICS FOR NEXT QUARTER

PARAGRAPHS ON PLACES AND PEOPLE

ASIA

The Roman province of Asia, created in 133 B.C., was an area of land in westernmost Asia Minor (modern-day Turkey) that occupied approximately 25 percent of that landmass. It is mentioned in the New Testament twenty-one times. The familiar New Testament cities of Troas (Acts 16:8-11; 20:5-6; II Cor. 2:12; II Tim. 4:13) and Colosse (Col. 1:2) were located in this province. Some of the New Testament references to Asia may refer to the entire area of Asia Minor rather than the more narrowly defined Roman province.

A mix of ethnic groups comprising city-states and kingdoms occupied this area prior to it becoming a Roman province, including the famous Hittites, Lydians, and Galatians—a Celtic people.

The seven churches of Revelation were all located in the Roman province of Asia.

THE THIRD HEAVEN

In a cryptic comment in II Corinthians 12:2, Paul makes mention of a "third heaven." As Paul explains in these verses, he could not tell whether it was his physical body that had been transported to another region or only his spirit. Whatever the case, Paul's experience was real. In this realm, he heard things that were not expressible in human language.

It cannot be determined from the biblical text if Paul is referring to two different events in II Corinthians 12:2-4 or one event mentioned twice. The "third heaven" is generally believed by theologians to be the realm of God. In this view, the first heaven consists of the material atmosphere (the sky and clouds) in which humans and all other creatures on earth live. The second heaven refers to space—the abode of stars, planets, comets, asteroids, and all other celestial objects.

CHLOE

Chloe is a Greek name meaning "verdure," which refers to the greenness of new vegetation. Consequently, the name has been translated "green herb" or "young green shoot." Chloe was a Greek believer in Corinth mentioned in I Corinthians 1:11.

Paul was evidently a guest in her home during his stay in Corinth. It was from her household that he later heard about the strife in the church there.

SOSTHENES

There are two mentions of a Sosthenes in the New Testament—in Acts 18:17 and I Corinthians 1:1. Do these references point to the same person?

In discussing Paul's missionary endeavor in Corinth, Luke mentions that "Sosthenes, the chief ruler of the synagogue," was beaten in the aftermath of an effort to harm Paul (Acts 18:17). We should take note that earlier in the chapter (vs. 8), and at an earlier time, Crispus, who came to faith in Jesus, is named as the leader of the synagogue (vs. 8).

Paul was in Corinth for more than a year and a half, and during this time a new leader of the synagogue, Sosthenes, was chosen. If the Sosthenes of Acts 18:17 is the same person as the man mentioned in I Corinthians 1:1, then it is possible that Crispus passed on his faith in Jesus to Sosthenes, who may subsequently have become an associate of Paul.

—*James Parry.*

Daily Bible Readings for Home Study and Worship

(Readings are for the week previous to the lesson topics.)

1. March 6. Divisions in Corinth

M — Brothers Living in Unity. Ps. 133:1-3.
T — Neither Jew nor Greek. Gal. 3:26-29.
W — God's Chosen People. Col. 3:12-17.
T — One Spirit. I Cor. 12:1-11.
F — One Body. I Cor. 12:12-31.
S — All for God's Glory. I Cor. 10:31-33.
S — Is Christ Divided? I Cor. 1:1-16.

2. March 13. True Wisdom

M — Worthy to Receive Wisdom. Rev. 5:9-14.
T — Drink Wisdom Freely. John 7:37-39.
W — Foolish Hearts Darkened. Rom. 1:18-32.
T — To God Be Glory. Rom. 11:33-36.
F — Boast in the Lord. Jer. 9:23-24.
S — The Spirit's Power. I Cor. 2:1-16.
S — We Proclaim Christ Crucified.
        I Cor. 1:17-31.

3. March 20. Christ—Our Only Foundation

M — Be Like-Minded. Phil. 2:1-4.
T — Build Up Fellow Believers.
        Rom. 15:1-13.
W — Members Together. Eph. 3:1-13.
T — A Chosen People. I Pet. 2:1-10.
F — Christ the Chief Cornerstone.
        Eph. 2:19-22.
S — God Gives the Growth. I Cor. 3:1-9.
S — Building Carefully on the Foundation.
        I Cor. 3:10-23.

4. March 27. Members of Christ

M — Counted Dead to Sin. Rom. 6:1-14.
T — Hidden in Christ. Col. 3:1-11.
W — Called to Holiness. I Thess. 4:3-8.
T — Disunity Among Believers. I Cor. 6:1-11.
F — Expel the Wicked Person. I Cor. 5:1-6.
S — Marital Obligations. I Cor. 7:1-7.
S — Glorify God in Your Body. I Cor. 6:12-20.

5. April 3. Concern for a Weaker Brother

M — Be Kind to Everyone. II Tim. 2:24-26.
T — Love One Another. I John 4:7-21.
W — Give to the Needy. Matt. 25:31-46.
T — Weak and Strong. Rom. 14:1-23.
F — Love Your Neighbor. Gal. 5:1-15.
S — Seek the Good of Others. I Cor. 10:23-30.
S — Knowledge Puffs Up. I Cor. 8:1-13.

6. April 10. Thoughts on the Lord's Supper

M — Flee Idolatry. I Cor. 10:14-22.
T — Mediator of a New Covenant.
        Heb. 9:11-28.
W — Reconciled to God. Rom. 5:6-11.
T — Redemption Through Christ's Blood.
        Eph. 1:3-14.
F — In Remembrance of Me. Luke 22:17-20.
S — The Blood of the Covenant. Mark 14:22-24.
S — This Is My Body. I Cor. 11:20-34.

**7. April 17. Witnesses to Christ's Resurrection
        (Easter)**

M — Mary Magdalene Sees Jesus. John 20:1-18.
T — Two Women See Jesus. Matt. 28:1-9.
W — Mary and Others See Jesus. Mark 16:1-13.

T — Disciples See Jesus. Luke 24:13-49.
F — Jesus Appears to Many. Acts 1:1-4.
S — Christ Is Indeed Risen. I Cor. 15:12-28.
S — Risen on the Third Day. I Cor. 15:1-11.

8. April 24. God's Comfort in Trouble

M — Encouraging like a Father. I Thess. 2:10-12.
T — Encouragement from God Our Father.
        II Thess. 2:13-17.
W — The Comforting Shepherd. Ps. 23:1-4.
T — Comfort in God's Word. Ps. 119:76-82.
F — Year of the Lord's Favor. Isa. 61:1-7.
S — The Sufferings of Christ. I Pet. 4:12-19.
S — The God of All Comfort. II Cor. 1:1-11.

9. May 1. Glory of the New Covenant

M — Eyewitnesses of Jesus' Majesty.
        II Pet. 1:16-18.
T — Glory of the Preincarnate Christ.
        John 1:1-13.
W — The Transfiguration. Mark 9:2-12.
T — The Radiance of God's Glory.
        Heb. 1:1-14.
F — Eternal Glory. II Cor. 4:13-18.
S — Moses' Veiled Face. Exod. 34:29-35.
S — The Lord Is the Spirit. II Cor. 3:7-18.

10. May 8. Our Heavenly Dwelling

M — A Heavenly Home. Heb. 11:3-16.
T — The Dead in Christ Rise. I Thess. 4:13-18.
W — A Multitude in Heaven. Rev. 7:9-17.
T — Citizenship in Heaven. Phil. 3:15-21.
F — Treasures in Clay Jars. II Cor. 4:1-12.
S — The Resurrection Body. I Cor. 15:35-54.
S — An Eternal House in Heaven.
        II Cor. 5:1-10.

11. May 15. Ambassadors for Christ

M — Ambassadors Commissioned.
        Matt. 28:18-20.
T — Paul Made an Ambassador. Acts 22:1-21.
W — How Shall They Hear? Rom. 10:9-18.
T — Ambassadors Scorned. Matt. 22:2-10.
F — Peter as Ambassador. Acts 3:14-26.
S — A Better Covenant. Heb. 12:18-24.
S — Be Reconciled to God! II Cor. 5:11-21.

12. May 22. Spiritual Weapons

M — Fight a Good Fight. II Tim. 4:1-8.
T — The Christian's Strength. Gal. 2:17-21.
W — Strength in God. Ps. 84:1-12.
T — Weapons of Righteousness.
        II Cor. 6:3-10.
F — Paul's Desire. Rom. 1:8-15.
S — Spiritual Alertness. I Thess. 5:1-11.
S — Paul's Defense. II Cor. 10:1-12, 17-18.

13. May 29. Paul's Thorn in the Flesh

M — Worthy to Suffer for Him. Acts 5:17-41.
T — Suffering for the Gospel. II Tim. 1:8-12.
W — Blessed for Suffering. I Pet. 3:13-17.
T — God in a Still, Small Voice. I Kings 19:9-13.
F — Paul Boasts in Suffering. II Cor. 11:16-33.
S — Glory in Sufferings. Rom. 5:1-5.
S — God's Power Is Sufficient. II Cor. 12:1-10.

REVIEW

What have you learned this quarter?

Can you answer these questions?

Training

UNIT I: Instructions to a Troubled Church

March 6

Divisions in Corinth

1. What does it mean to be sanctified?
2. What is a saint?
3. What was the major issue in Corinth that Paul dealt with first in this letter?
4. What was the cause of division in the Corinthian church?
5. Why was Paul glad that he had not baptized many in Corinth?

March 13

True Wisdom

1. What was Paul's emphasis in his ministry?
2. How does the world perceive the message of the cross of Christ?
3. What were the Greeks most impressed by?
4. How did the Greeks receive Paul's message?
5. When is boasting a good thing for a Christian?

March 20

Christ—Our Only Foundation

1. According to Paul, on what foundation is everything is built?
2. What will be applied to each person's work?
3. What will happen to those whose works survive God's judgment?
4. What is the New Testament temple of God?

5. Why is it a terrible idea to boast in men before God?

March 27

Members of Christ

1. How did Paul respond to the claim that "all things are lawful"?
2. What did Paul mean when he said that we are members of Christ?
3. What picture did Paul use to demonstrate how reprehensible sexual sin was?
4. How did Paul say we are to deal with sexual temptation?
5. Why can we not say that our bodies belong to ourselves?

April 3

Concern for a Weaker Brother

1. What is the problem with having knowledge without love?
2. What is the greatest blessing of loving God?
3. What did Paul understand about idols that the pagans did not?
4. Why was eating food offered to idols such a stumbling block for some Christians in Corinth?
5. How do other people's weaknesses often show us our own weaknesses?

April 10

Thoughts on the Lord's Supper

1. Why does Paul tell the Corinthian church that they were not actually eating the Lord's Supper?
2. Where did Paul receive his instructions concerning the Lord's Supper?
3. What do we proclaim when we partake of the bread and the cup?
4. What does eating and drinking in an unworthy manner mean?
5. What is the purpose of God's discipline of a believer?

April 17
Witnesses to Christ's Resurrection (Easter)
1. What is the focal point of the gospel?
2. According to Paul (I Cor. 15:3-4), what three statements summarize the gospel?
3. What was significant about Jesus' appearance to over five hundred men at one time?
4. Why did Paul consider himself to be the least of the apostles?
5. What was the result of God's grace in Paul?

UNIT II: Encouragement from a Tested Servant

April 24
God's Comfort in Trouble
1. How did Paul end up in the apostolic ministry?
2. What assurance do we have about sharing in Christ's sufferings?
3. How can your suffering help another person?
4. What is one reason why suffering comes to all believers?
5. What is the key to perseverance?

May 1
Glory of the New Covenant
1. How did the old covenant fulfill its purpose?
2. Why did the glory of the new covenant far exceed the glory of the old covenant?
3. What is the basis of the Christian's hope, according to Paul?
4. Why can we be bold in our proclamation of the gospel?
5. What does the fact that the glory faded from Moses' face tell us about the old covenant?

May 8
Our Heavenly Dwelling
1. What does Paul mean by our earthly "tabernacle" (II Cor. 5:1)?
2. How does Paul show that he was sure of God's promises?
3. What is Paul likely referring to when he talks about groaning (vs. 2)?
4. Who does God give as a guarantee of our future hope?
5. What was the basis of Paul's confidence?

May 15
Ambassadors for Christ
1. What does it mean to fear the Lord?
2. What do we need from people if we expect them to listen to the gospel message?
3. What does it mean that "if one died for all, then were all dead"?
4. What does it mean to be an ambassador for Christ?

May 22
Spiritual Weapons
1. What was the basis of Paul's entreaty to the Corinthians?
2. Why did the Corinthians fail to take Paul's authority seriously?
3. What did Paul want the Corinthians to perceive about him?
4. Why did Paul think it was wrong for anyone to boast in themselves?

May 29
Paul's Thorn in the Flesh
1. What did Paul focus on instead of his accomplishments?
2. Why was Paul content to expose his weakness to the Corinthians?
3. Why are we not told what Paul's thorn in the flesh was?
4. How did Paul respond to the thorn at first?